THE NFER-NELSON ASSESSMENT LIBRARY

Educational Assessment of the Primary School Child

Edited by
Leonora Harding and John R. Beech

Published by The NFER-NELSON Publishing Company Ltd,
Darville House, 2 Oxford Road East,
Windsor, Berkshire SL4 1DF, UK.

First published 1991
© 1991, Leonora Harding and John R. Beech

Printed by Billing & Sons Ltd, Worcester.
Phototypeset by David John Services Ltd, Maidenhead, Berkshire.

Softback:
ISBN 0 7005 1260 8
Code 8506 02 4

Hardback:
ISBN 0 7005 1259 4
Code 8505 02 4

British Library Cataloguing in Publication Data
Educational assessment of the primary school child. – (NFER-NELSON
    assessment library).
  1. Primary schools. Students. Academic achievement.
  Assessment
  I. Harding, Leonora 1944– II. Beech, John R.
  372.1264

ISBN 0-7005-1259-4
ISBN 0-7005-1260-8 pbk

Contents

List of Boxes, Figures and Tables

List of Contributors

John Beech is Lecturer in Psychology, University of Leicester.

Alan Blyth is Honorary Senior Fellow, University of Liverpool.

Robert Cameron is Tutor for Continuing Professional Development in Educational Psychology, Southampton University.

Tricia David is Lecturer in Education, University of Warwick.

Lynda J. Eaton is Solicitor, Partner, Josiah Hincks Son and Bullough, Leicester.

Leonora Harding is Clinical Psychologist, Royal Aberdeen Children's Hospital and Research Fellow, University of Aberdeen.

Wynne Harlen is Professor of Science Education and Head of Department of Education, University of Liverpool.

Sheila Henderson is Research Lecturer, Institute of Education, University of London.

Geoff Lindsay is Educational Psychologist, Sheffield Local Authority and Associate Tutor and Honorary Lecturer, University of Sheffield.

Ann Lewis is Lecturer in Education, University of Warwick.

Roger Murphy is Professor of Education, University of Nottingham.

Jim Ridgway is Lecturer in Psychology, University of Lancaster.

Margaret Snowling is Lecturer in Psychology, The National Hospitals College of Speech Sciences.

Susan Spence is Lecturer in Psychology, University of Sydney, Australia.

Michael J. Tobin is Reader in Special Education and Director of the Research Centre for the Education of the Visually Handicapped, University of Birmingham.

Alec Webster is Research Fellow, Clwyd County Council.

Series Editors' Preface

The word 'assessment' conjures an adverse emotional reaction in many people. We have all, at some stage, undergone an assessment in some form — for instance when sitting an examination — and many of us have found it a distinctly unpleasant experience. Why should we make assessments on people, and even more to the point, why launch a series of volumes on the subject?

Assessment is usually to do with making a judgement on an individual in relation to a large group of people, based on the acquisition of a body of knowledge concerning that individual. In carrying out an assessment, the professional believes that it is necessary to make such an assessment as a basis for deciding a particular course of action. This activity is considered to be predominantly in the best interests of the person being assessed; at times, it will also protect the interests of society, or an organization, such as a company. Whether or not one agrees with the concept of making an assessment, the practice continues in our society, even if it waxes and wanes in some professional sectors. Our own view is that assessment is here to stay and in many cases is beneficial to the individual.

It is important that the best available means of assessment are taken by professional workers to provide an accurate body of knowledge on which to base decisions. Errors of diagnosis can sometimes have serious consequences in situations in which a diagnosis must be carried out. The national press seems to report almost every day on situations in which diagnosis has been problematic, such as releasing a violent prisoner prematurely, or making erroneous accusations of child abuse, and so on. Less dramatic situations would be ones in which a child is inaccurately assessed and is then put on a training programme which is not appropriate for his or her needs, or where an elderly person is inaccurately considered as unable to live in his or her own home and transferred to another environment. Given that many of these assessments are essential, improving the accuracy of assessment is a worthwhile goal. If this series of volumes is instrumental in improving accuracy to some degree, we shall be well pleased.

When planning the series we decided early on that we were not going to produce exhaustive manuals giving thorough reviews of all possible assessment techniques. There are many books of this nature already available. We thought that it would be a much better idea to produce fairly short books targeted at a particular category of person requiring assessment, such as the elderly, or those with speech and language difficulties. Our readership would be the professional workers involved with such groups, either directly or indirectly, students training for these professions and interested members of the public. Therefore, we set our writers a very difficult task. Each contribution had to be easy to read, but at the same time, provide information which the current professional worker would find useful for making assessments. The writer might point to a new test which has been developed, or highlight the inadequacies of one currently used. The chapters were not to be just orientated to describing the application of tests. There was a range of other useful information, dealing with, for instance, check-lists, case-studies, points to bear in mind with certain types of patient, and so on.

In most of the volumes we have a final section of reviews on the main test currently applied in that area. Making choices about what to include has been difficult; but it is based on consultations with practising professionals and researchers. The end result might seem a little idiosyncratic, however, the main tests used by the majority of workers have been included. The problem is that there is usually a large variety of more minor tests, each of which is probably used by only a few workers. Only a small proportion of these could be covered in the space available.

All of the test reviews are written within a pre-arranged structure. Information is given about the purpose of the test, how to use it and an evaluation is also made. Some technical information is provided, such as the number of people who were tested in order to develop the test. Where available, the reliability and validity is supplied. The *reliability* shows the extent to which applying the same test again will give the same result. A low reliability indicates that assessment could be inaccurate as the outcome changes on successive occasions. The *validity* of the test shows how well the test is associated with similar tests measuring the same properties. The reader does not necessarily need any prior knowledge in order to understand these text reviews. However, the interested reader is referred to the first volume in this series entitled *Testing People: A Practical Guide to Psychometrics* which goes into the statistical basis of testing in more depth. This is a corner-stone volume in the series, and is intended for professional people who wish to update their statistical knowledge in order to understand the basis of the tests. It does not assume any previous statistical knowledge.

Turning more specifically to the contents of this current book, this volume covers the assessment of children in primary schools. The scope of the book is very broad, covering traditional forms of assessment (norm-referenced tests) as well as developments in criterion-referenced assessment and other forms of assessment such as diagnostic assessment, informal evaluation and observation. It includes much lively debate on the usefulness of the various methods. Although norm-referenced tests are thought to have a place most authors tend to favour informal and criterion-referenced assessments, which can be of immediate benefit to the child.

The volume begins with a discussion of the purposes of assessment in the primary school and the relevance of intelligence testing with reference to a particular case. Following this there is a chapter on the assessment of the child coming into the infant class, which emphasizes the role of the teacher in assessment. The debate then turns to the assessment of cognitive abilities and intelligence, which remains a controversial area, but the chapter makes some very positive suggestions. The child within the school environment is seen as the focus for assessment in these areas.

Attention is then given to the curriculum areas, beginning with reading and writing and other language skills. Excellent examples of children's work are used to illustrate the various approaches recommended here. Assessment in mathematics, science and humanities follow with a shift in emphasis towards the assessment of thinking processes and concept development in these areas.

Although emotional problems are not covered in this volume, the chapter on social skills focuses on an area useful for teachers. In the main, the assessment of mild and moderate learning difficulties is covered by the various chapters. Diagnositic testing and criterion-referenced assessments are useful here. However, one chapter is devoted to the assessment of children with visual, hearing and physical problems. The latter is particularly pertinent as the assessment of motor skills is often a neglected area.

The volume draws to a close with a discussion on educational law and the proposed changes in school-based assessment, the National Curriculum and assessment at ages seven and 11. The final chapter draws our attention once more to the current issues involved in assessing children within schools and gives a composite view of criterion-referenced assessment.

As a whole this volume will form an introductory guide for teachers and other professionals to the vast range of approaches to, and materials available for, the assessment of primary school children, as well as providing much that is practical and useful.

Diana Hilton-Jones and Ian Florance of NFER-NELSON have given valuable help with this series. We thank them for their support and also the many contributors and advisers.

Leonora Harding and John Beech

Introduction to Educational Assessment

Leonora Harding and John R. Beech

Assessment has become increasingly important in primary schools. Precise and rigorous assessment procedures for children with special educational needs have become the norm since the Warnock report and the 1981 Education Act. Assessment was further extended by the 1988 Education Reform Act with the introduction of the National Curriculum. Within this framework pencil-and-paper tests together with assessment in the classroom at ages seven and 11 are seen by some commentators and practitioners as of paramount importance. Despite this, many teachers and educational psychologists have come to mistrust traditional forms of assessment, which are alleged to provide information which is useful neither to the teacher nor the child.

Purposes of Assessment

At the outset, we should recognize that assessment has different aims. Broadly speaking these fall into two categories, the interests of society or a wider group, and the interests of the child. Of course, assessments carried out to help the child may also be of value to society and vice versa. Children thought to have a learning or behavioural problem, who are not coping with the school environment may, as a result of a special needs statement, be placed in a special school or class. Assessment in this context not only benefits the child, but it may also benefit a wider group in that the teacher will be left with a class that is easier to manage. The increased integration of children with special needs into normal primary school resulted from a shifting of the balance from the needs of society towards the needs of the child, though it can be claimed that the policy benefits both child and society (Hegarty, Pocklington and Lucas, 1981).

Sumner (1987) outlines two broad purposes of assessment, which are assessment for purposes external to the school and assessment for purposes internal to the school. It is interesting that he does not mention assessment designed to benefit the child, which must surely be the central purpose of assessment.

ASSESSMENT FOR PURPOSES EXTERNAL TO THE SCHOOL

Local education authorities (LEAs) routinely require information on individual children in order to organize transfer from one school to another. Up until the late 1960s this occurred for all children taking the 11-plus examination. Today only 12 per cent of children in England and Wales take the examination, usually by an opting-in procedure. Though the examination has been maintained for all pupils in Northern Ireland, selectivity has been totally eradicated in Scotland.

Assessment procedures help identify the children who require special needs teaching in the primary school, be it help with reading or mathematics. In order to allocate resources effectively, LEAs will need information on different areas of educational attainment, for example, reading standards within the school, together with the identification of the numbers of children who are behind average in reading. As an adjunct to this, children in specific categories may be identified – for example, children who are generally behind in their work and require special class or group placement. Such children will usually have special needs statements prepared for them, which will inevitably require further detailed assessment. Sometimes LEAs request schools to carry out screening procedures in order to identify children who may be 'at risk' educationally or who may be in need of special education. Such screening will quite often be carried out in the infant class (see the chapter in this volume by Tricia David). Increasingly, schools will be required to give information on standards with the intention that this will make them more accountable to parents and the local community. Despite the difficulty of comparing one school with another without taking account of their different circumstances and catchment areas, monitoring of educational standards by LEAs, researchers and organizations like the Assessment of Performance Unit, occurs regularly. Whatever view is taken on the direction of current government policy, it is undeniable that assessment will figure large in relating the individual school to other parts of the educational system and to the wider society.

ASSESSMENT FOR PURPOSES INTERNAL TO THE SCHOOL

Assessment is useful within the school environment as it assists with the organization of the school and helps to monitor standards. The headteacher or class teacher will use such assessments to group pupils within the class or school curriculum. The use of assessment in the grouping or setting of pupils has been criticized as contributing to a process which produces less able pupils by making predictions which are self-fulfilling (Nash, 1976). Despite these often-expressed reservations, it is common practice to group children in primary schools for reading and mathematics even if the groups are called 'red' and 'yellow'.

Assessments can help the teacher with curriculum development. In particular, criterion-referenced assessments will identify the attainments of children and pinpoint next steps in the curriculum. Although such assessments may be carried out for the school's own purposes, they will also assist individual pupils by identifying problem areas and providing feedback on performance.

ASSESSMENT FOR THE PRIMARY PURPOSE OF BENEFITTING THE PUPIL

Assessment which has as its purpose the needs of the school or the wider group may also be of benefit to the individual pupil. However, such assessments often only indicate that a child may have a specific problem. Diagnostic assessment, of the type covered in the chapters by Margaret Snowling and Jim Ridgway, is desirable if the focus is to be on benefitting the child. The encouragement of different types of thinking and concept development (see the chapters by Wynne Harlen and Alan Blyth) or 'enabling a potential' (Alan Blyth) reflect pupil-focused assessment. Where information is needed regarding the next steps to be taken in teaching, criterion-referenced assessment comes into its own (see especially Robert Cameron's chapter). Emphasis on ongoing formative assessment (see the chapter by Tricia David) also enables the teacher to plan these next steps. Focusing on children's needs may highlight social and other problems, where the approaches covered in Sue Spence's chapter can be very useful. Children with specific impairments may need some of those procedures outlined in the chapters by Mike Tobin, Alec Webster and Sheila Henderson.

Types of Assessment

Two main types of assessment are common in the primary school. First, there are informal evaluations made by teachers and others. This may occur, for example, when a teacher notices a child with a special educational need. Such an evaluation is based on professional experience and is very valuable in that it is more likely to pinpoint individual needs, abilities and deficits which can be further investigated. Some of the procedures outlined by Margaret Snowling (for example, the examination of a written passage) would fall into this category. It would also include classroom observations of children at work or play, for example, in the infant classes (see Tricia David's and Ann Lewis's chapter) or later on in school (see Sue Spence's chapter).

The second type of assessment is norm-referenced assessment involving statistical tests. Here an individual's score is compared with a distribution of scores provided by a representative sample of the population. The results are interpreted in relation to the performance of others. Both types of assessment can be used for the purposes outlined above but the second form, involving statistical tests, are more likely to be used for purposes external to the school.

A third type of assessment increasingly used in schools is the criterion-referenced assessment discussed by Geoff Lindsay and Robert Cameron. These involve a precise analysis of the learning process and an attempt to identify the position of the individual pupils in that learning process. A result for an individual is given in terms of whether or not he or she can meet or surpass the standard of the criterion (for example, being able to list all the combinations of two numbers which add up to ten). The individual's result is not given in relation to performance of others, but provides information regarding his or her stage in the learning process, indicating the next steps to be taken in the hierarchy of learning a particular subject or skill. There is a dispute between the value of norm-referenced and criterion-referenced assessment, but the difference is, perhaps, more apparent than real. Criterion-referenced assessments implicitly make reference to norm-referenced procedures, because the criteria must be set against what could be expected for a child at a particular age or stage of development. The only way in which this can be achieved is with reference to the 'normal' population.

Although assessment may be divided into three different types – informal evaluations, norm-referenced and criterion-referenced – there is really no simple classification of test types. Sumner (1987) mentions 12 ways in which tests may be distinguished, ranging from pencil-and-paper tests versus performance tests to convergent versus divergent tests. One which he does not cover, but is of major importance in the area of humanities, mathematics and science, is the distinction between process (for example, the type of thinking involved) and product (or knowledge). As is mentioned above, a frequently used distinction is between norm-referenced and criterion-referenced tests.

This point is covered by the distinction that is made between summative and formative assessment (see Lloyd-Jones and Bray, 1986). Summative assessment, as the name suggests, is a final summing up which is usually made on the basis of examinations and tests. In order to make such an assessment an individual is frequently compared with his or her peers, and norm-referenced tests are often used. Public examinations would be a prime example of summative assessment and reflect the purposes of such an assessment, that is, for society. Formative assessment is a formulation of an individual's strengths, weaknesses and potential (which is a kind of working hypothesis). This is constantly changing throughout time, as it occurs throughout learning. The information is available to both teacher and learner, is immediately given and so helps to motivate the pupil. Criterion-referenced assessments would assist this kind of assessment, which is essentially made in order to help the individual child.

The Case for the Assessment of Intelligence

The assessment of intelligence is the prime example of norm-referenced assessment and has been the focus of much debate. In his chapter, Geoff Lindsay advances a strong argument about the value of the assessment of intelligence, and its relevance to school-age children. In this section we shall examine the main arguments for and against the value of intelligence testing. The following points can be briefly made concerning the decline of the role of the concept of intelligence.

1. There is bias in IQ tests in that they discriminate against certain groups. This particular point became a passionate issue, especially in the 1970s.
2. The IQ test is limited in its usefulness. The IQ test can give a general asessment of intellectual functioning which was useful in the days of deciding placements in the old, two-tier 11-plus system, but this function is no longer necessary, especially when there has been an integration of children with special educational needs in the mainstream classroom.
3. The IQ test has been justified as a means of finding out if a child is underachieving. But critics of IQ tests question the value of this information for teaching purposes. To elaborate, if one produces a regression equation between IQ and attainment one is supposedly able to see whether a child is underachieving. A regression equation is ob-

tained by collecting data on a large sample of children concerning their IQ score and, for instance, their reading performance. The resulting regression line means that for a new child who is tested one can predict reading performance on the basis of the child's intelligence score. The stronger the correlation between intelligence and reading the more confidence one can place on this procedure. Some might wonder what the difference would be in teaching if one child has learning difficulties (in other words, poor on intelligence on the regression line and poor in reading in our example, but at a level predicted by the regression equation) and if the other has a specific reading difficulty, perhaps at the same level of reading as the first child, but much brighter (and whose level of reading, consequently, one would expect to be higher).

Despite such arguments, the intelligence test will probably never disappear; it is far too useful an instrument for the professional. We take the point concerning the cultural, gender and other biases within the intelligence test. This is something to be very careful about especially as it could underestimate the potential of the child. Nevertheless, the criticism of bias is directed at the assumption of the intelligence test as a gross measure of intelligence which is subsequently used exclusively for determining the allocation of that child to a particular educational institution. But the professional worker uses profiles of subtests on an intelligence text in order identify areas of impaired intellectual functioning. This should then be allied to an appropriate programme of training. New intelligence tests now examine a broader range of abilities more closely linked to the cognitive development of the child and therefore provide a richer insight into problematic areas. They also seek to reduce bias as much as possible.

The most important use of the intelligence test is when it is coupled with a regression equation to predict future performance. Professionals have to assess the correlation in order to consider its predictive value and whether that population from which the regression is derived is representative. The intelligence test can then give an assessment of the child with respect to present intellectual functioning rather than merely to chronological age.

We shall now deal with the implication of making a distinction between the reader who has specific reading difficulties and the one who has learning difficulties. Yule et al. (1974) in an important study tested the entire population of nine- and ten-year-old children on the Isle of Wight using a test of non-verbal intelligence and a group reading test. They produced a reasonable correlation of 0.6. This enabled them to distinguish groups of readers with specific reading difficulties and learning difficulties. Rutter and Yule (1975) made a comparison between these groups and found some contrasts: three-quarters of the readers with specific reading difficulties were boys, but the sex ratio was about even for the readers with learning difficulties; signs of organic disorders were present in 11 per cent of the readers with learning difficulties, but these were infrequent in the readers with specific reading difficulties; the frequency of 'soft' signs of impairment (for example, clumsiness) was twice as prevalent among the readers with learning difficulties. As far as predicting future progress was concerned, the readers with specific reading difficulties made poorer progress than the

others over a four- to five-year period. Jorm *et al.* (1986) conducted a longitudinal study on a large sample of Australian children during the first three
years at school and found that children subsequently diagnosed as readers
with learning difficulties were deficient at the beginning in a broad range of
cognitive skills, wereas those with a specific reading difficulty had a more
limited range of problems, mainly involving phonological processing skills.
The finding of Rutter and Yule that there is a different prognosis for members of the two groups is an interesting one. One could argue that readers
with learning difficulties will improve in reading at a rate commensurate
with their intellectual development, in the same way as normal readers.
Those with a specific reading difficulty, by contrast, will continue to dete-
riorate relative to their intellectual development and therefore urgently
need remediation. The study by Jorm *et al.* implies that these children with
a specific reading difficulty would benefit from a remediation programme
involving the training of phonological skills and the chapter by Margaret
Snowling offers advice on how this might be achieved. Furthermore, Beech
(1989) outlines theoretically why these and others skills are related to future reading progress.

A Case Study

There now follows an account of the assessment of a child which incorporates some of the types of assessment already discussed and some of the
procedures to be discussed in subsequent chapters. The assessment begins
with a psychologist following up a request made by the child's parents
through their GP, as a result of informal evaluation both by them and the
child's teachers. It commences with an IQ test which is a typical first approach made by psychologists following a hypothesis testing model (a largely summative approach). However, it includes informal evaluations of
reading, writing and mathematics which could also be made by teachers. It
concludes with criterion-referenced and diagnostic assessment which is
teacher based. It should be stressed that this is only one approach, but it
should be useful for teachers in attempting to follow-up on similar psychological assessments. Another approach would be simply for the teacher to
use criterion-based and diagnostic assessment with its emphasis on formative assessment which is of immediate benefit to the child. However, in missing out IQ we might also miss out important information on the child's
potential.

Christopher is eight years one month old. His parents are concerned because he is not getting on well at school. In fact he is below average in all
subjects yet he seems intelligent. They think he is 'hyperactive' and they are
also concerned that he is unable to keep friends. His teacher is also a little
concerned but thinks he is slow to mature especially as his reading has improved with remedial help over the last few months.

In assessing such a child it was thought to be important to find out, first,
whether he was really under-attaining and how severe this was. This assessment would be carried out by a psychologist since many of the tests would
be available only to them. It involves a comparison of Christopher's scores
with those of his peers (that is, it is norm-referenced assessment). However, these results might also give some important clues to specific learning
difficulties, which might be further assessed by the teacher.

Box 1.1

Christopher's performance on the Wechsler Intelligence Scale for Children (WISC-R)

Verbal Scale	Scaled score	**Performance Scale**	Scaled score
Information	15	Picture Completion	11
Similarities	12	Picture Arrangement	10
Arithmetic*	7	Block Design	9
Vocabulary	15	Object Assembly	16
Comprehension	13	Coding*	3
(Digit Span)*	7	(Mazes)	7
Verbal IQ	106 (Average)	**Performance IQ**	97 (Average)
Full-scale IQ	101 (Average)		

Freedom from distractibility factor (Digit Span, Arithmetic, Coding), scaled score 6.

Note that a scaled score of 10 is average for the general population and the range of scores is 1–20.

* Significantly low score.

On the Wechsler Intelligence Scale for Children – Revised (WISC–R), Christopher obtained the result shown in Box 1.1. According to Kaufmann (1979) such a result should not be taken at face value. Christopher might be thought to be average, however, three subtest scores (Arithmetic, Digit Span and Coding) are significantly below all others (a difference of three points from the average of other subtest scores within a subscale is considered significant). These three subtests go up to make the Freedom from Distractibility factor (Kaufmann, 1979) and a low score here indicates that Christopher has a problem with attention. It might also be noted that when Digit Span and Arithmetic scores are taken from the Verbal Scale; results on the other subtests would yield a Verbal IQ of 124 which is in the superior range.

As the WISC-R does not cover all abilities which might be of interest, certain subtests in the British Ability Scales (BAS) were also given. These are shown in Box 1.2. As the average T-score is 50 for these subtests (with average range 40 to 60), the results indicate that Christopher has a problem in the area of visual memory. From the results in the WISC-R it might be expected that Christopher would attain a performance in the average range or possibly above average (given certain verbal skills). Box 1.3 indicates performance on certain attainment tests that were given to him. Apart from the normative assessment these results give information on the child's approach to a task, an informal evaluation. His written work is poor

Box 1.2

Christopher's results on the BAS subtests

	Ability score	T-score	Centile
Immediate visual memory	37	40	16
Delayed visual memory	28	38	12

Box 1.3

Christopher's performance on attainment tests

British Ability Scales – Word Reading

Ability score: 86   T-score: 35   Centile: 12
Reading age: 6 years 11 months

Neale Analysis of Reading – Form C

Accuracy of reading   Reading age: 7 years 1 month
Comprehension   Reading age: 8 years 2 months

British Ability Scales – Basic Number Skills

Ability score: 86   T-score: 35   Centile: 7
Mathematical age: 6 years 10 months

for an eight year old. He usually has good ideas but letters are poorly formed, do not stand straight and spelling is very poor.

These results indicate that Christopher is about a year behind in attainment when compared with his peers which answers the question posed at the beginning of this section. Furthermore:

1.   There is evidence of distractibility which might relate to the 'hyperactivity' problem expressed by his parents.

2. He has difficulty with visual memory and possibly other visual motor skills (note the relatively low score on Block Design and poor writing).
3. He understands what he reads, which reflects his level of intelligence.
4. The types of errors made in reading (for example some reversal errors, 'down' for *bread*, 'from for *for*) indicates that there might be a visual-motor problem. (The fact that Christopher attempts to guess on the basis of first letter for most of the time rather than using context gives an indication of his stage in learning to read, for example 'smart' for skates, 'special' for string, 'nice' for nest).
5. The types of error made in Arithmetic and Basic Number Skills also give an indication of problem areas, for example, in Arithmetic he started making errors where numbers near to ten had to be held in the head. The type of task could be: 'a man had 17 newspapers and he sold 11 of them, how many did he have left?' Difficulty here might indicate a memory problem but might also indicate the stage in mathematical development of the child.

These results give us important clues towards further investigations where the purpose is to find out more about the child in order to help him/her in the future. This incorporates informal evaluation, norm-referenced tests, diagnostic assessment and criterion-referenced tests. The results also imply that if there is a real problem in the visual-motor area the best method of teaching this particular child to read would be through the verbal-kinaesthetic channel (using phonics) rather than through the visual channel (look and say).

The areas which might be pursued are:

*   Further investigating the visual-motor deficit.
*   Further assessment of distractibility and social problems in the school.
*   More detailed analysis of reading and mathematics in order to give some guidance as to further teaching.

Christopher's visual-motor problem arose as he was noted to be clumsy during PE at school. This area would be more appropriately assessed by the methods indicated by Sheila Henderson.

According to Christopher's mother his overactivity is decreasing as he gets older, but it currently appears to be contributing to difficulties in his relationships with peers. He has a loud voice and tends to be over-exuberant, talking over people a lot. This area warants assessment in the ways discussed by Sue Spence. Perhaps his distractibility could be managed by manipulation of the school environment in ways suggested by Geoff Lindsay.

It seems that memory might be a problem area in arithmetic. He also mistook the plus sign to be a minus sign (but see Ridgway and Harding's chapter for further discussion). However this was not further investigated, but the reading difficulty did receive attention. The *Macmillan Diagnostic Reading Test* for Stage 2 (Reading Age equivalent six to seven years) yielded the profile shown in Box 1.4.

Box 1.4

Christopher's scores on the Macmillan Diagnostic Reading Test for Stage 2

(Reading Age equivalent six to seven years)

	Score out of 10
100 key words	9
Consonant blends: Recognition	7
Reading	5
Single consonants and vowels	8
Blending 2–3 letter words (sound blending)	9
Spelling 2–3 letter words	10
Transcribing sounds	9
Reading accuracy	10
Reading comprehension	10

Note: A child with this reading age should get 10/10 for each subtest before he or she proceeds to the next stage.

At this level of reading, compatible with previously assessed reading age, Christopher still has some difficulties. He does not know all sounds and in writing reverses b and d and even c occasionally. He has few difficulties with single consonants and vowels although there is some confusion over e/a and e/i. His errors included reading went as 'want', will as 'well'. He had difficulty in reading words with the following consonant blends: ld, ct, st, nk, nd, sk, but could read other blends such as sw, sm, pr, and fl. This gives an indication of which aspects need to be taught next if a phonics programme is being followed. This would be a criterion-referenced assessment, but it does not give a complete picture of all that is needed in teaching the child to read. Further assessment procedures are given in Margaret Snowling's chapter; for example, it seems likely that this child does not use context cues, and this needs further assessment.

The assessment method used here required two hours over two sessions and provided information in three different ways:

1. Norm-referenced assessment indicated the child's skills/abilities in relation to peers.
2. Diagnostic assessment produced a profile of the child's individual strengths and weaknesses.
3. Criterion-referenced assessment indicated the current position of the child in terms of his development within a hierarchy of skills required for learning to read.

Conclusion

There is a wide range of procedures available to help with the assessment of the primary school child. Not all are available to both teachers and psychologists. As a general rule, tests which require knowledge of the normative basis and interpretation of statistically significant differences (say between subtest scores) are only available to qualified psychologists. Those tests which do not require statistically based interpretation (for example, many reading tests and criterion-referenced assessments) are available to teachers. As will be apparent in the following chapters, many would argue that the latter are the more relevant types of assessment.

The teacher, the psychologist, other professionals and of course parents – whose contribution has too often been overlooked in the past – must combine their skills and experience in order to draw together all relevant pieces of information in the assessment of the whole child. Some of these are relationships and behaviour within the family and with peers; classroom behaviour and attainment; and performance on tests. They will be able to evaluate the different performances of the child in different contexts. One child may score well in a one-to-one relationship (for example, the IQ test given by an office-based psychologist) and yet be quite unable to concentrate on work in the classroom. Such an apparent discrepancy is often seen in highly distractible childen. Another child will be affected by high anxiety and perform less well on the isolated IQ test than in the relaxed classroom atmosphere or at home. Some children perform better in a highly structured classroom than in the less formal one and vice versa. The intention of this volume is to encourage those engaged with children in primary education to recognize the value and importance of applying different types of assessment, and of assessing the child within different contexts.

References

Ames, T. (1984). *The Macmillan Diagnostic Reading Pack*. Basingstoke: Macmillan.

Beech, J.R. (1989). The componential approach to learning reading skills. In: Colley, A.M. & Beech, J.R. (Eds) *Cognition and Action in Skilled Behaviour*. Chichester: Wiley.

Elliot, C.D., Murray, D.J. & Pearson, L.S. (1983). *British Ability Scales*. Windsor: NFER-NELSON.

Hegarty, S., Pocklington, R. & Lucas, D. (1981). *Educating Pupils with Special Needs in the Ordinary School*. Windsor: NFER-NELSON.

Jorm, A.F., Share, D.L., Maclean, R. & Matthews, R. (1986). Cognitive factors at school entry predictive of specific reading retardation and general reading backwardness: a research note. *Journal of Child Psychology and Psychiatry, 27*, 45–65.

Kaufmann, A.S. (1979). *Intelligence Testing with the WISC-R*. New York: Wiley.

Lloyd-Jones, R. & Bray, E. (1986). *Assessment: From Principles to Action*. London: Macmillan.

Nash, R. (1976). *Teacher Expectations and Pupil Learning*. London: Routledge and Kegan Paul.

Neale, M. (1956). *The Neale Analysis of Reading*. Basingstoke: Macmillan.

Neale, M. (1989). *Neale Analysis of Reading Ability: Revised British Edition*. Windsor: NFER-NELSON.

Rutter, M. & Yule, W. (1975). The concept of specific reading retardation. *Journal of Child Psychology and Psychiatry, 16*, 181–97.

Sumner, R. (1987). *The Role of Testing in Schools*. Windsor: NFER-NELSON.

Wechsler, D. (1974). *The Wechsler Intelligence Scale for Children: Revised*. Sidcup: The Psychological Corporation.

Yule, W., Rutter, M., Berger, M. & Thompson, J. (1974). Over and under achievement in reading: distribution in the general population. *British Journal of Educational Psychology, 44,* 1–11.

Assessment in the Reception Class

Tricia David and Ann Lewis

The topic of assessment is one that has become increasingly important in the early years of education. This is shown by comparing what the Plowden Report (1967) had to say on the topic with the views expressed in *'Education 5 to 9'* (GB.DES, 1982). A teacher is unlikely to have an anti-assessment conversation, as one of us did ten years ago, with an LEA inspector who maintained that 'Weighing the pig doesn't make it any fatter'. We would reply that it should, however, lead to appropriate action.

During the past year, a great deal of anxiety has been generated by Government plans to introduce national testing of children aged seven. The stated aim is the elevation of standards, the communication to parents of their children's abilities and the comparison of performance of all concerned. The furore caused by the suggestion that seven year olds should be tested, and scores for children, teachers and schools be available for comparison, has resulted in greater debate than ever before about the nature of assessment and testing. Experts, for example, Margaret Brown and Harvey Goldstein of London University (1987) and Clare Burstall of the NFER (1987), have explained that tests which grade children and schools cannot be used simultaneously to assess the capabilities of children and offer pointers to their future learning needs by indicating where weaknesses lie.

This chapter focuses on the assessment and evaluation of children in the early years in primary school, with particular reference to the reception class. The terms 'assessment' and 'evaluation' are used deliberately, since it is thought that the two processes are inextricably linked (Shipman, 1983). In much of our discussion, the term assessment is used to cover both processes, operating in conjunction for the child and teacher in the early stages of education. This involves the collecting of information about a child's knowledge, skills and attitudes, as well as judgement, interpretation and planned action. Assessment as an enterprise demands caution. It is not possible to make definitive, certain statements about what a child so young can and cannot do; any assessments will be the result of 'best guesses'. We can strengthen our assessments by maintaining a flexible view of what we expect and by listening to the contributions of others, especially the parents and the children themselves.

The Preschool Years

In the child's early years, a host of informal assessments will have been made by those closest to the child (see Box 2.1) – parents, grandparents, siblings, parents' friends, as well as preschool workers. Some of the last group may also have carried out formal assessments of the child's progress – for example, the doctor and health visitor may have performed hearing, sight and other tests and a nursery teacher may have completed a profile of some sort (for example, Bate and Smith, 1978).

Box 2.1

An example of an informal assessment by the family

Clare was the younger of two preschool sisters, aged four and two. An aunt came to stay and at the end of two days with the family, left the mother stunned by her parting remark that it was such a pity Clare was not yet able to talk. At first the mother decided the aunt was somewhat at fault in being unable to understand Clare's utterances, but the more she thought about the remark, the more she realized that the elder sister was doing much of Clare's talking for her, while at other times the family were all anticipating her needs. Of course, she might have progressed perfectly well in any case, but the incident made the family resolve to give Clare greater opportunities to speak for herself.

The example in Box 2.1 illustrates the kind of ongoing awareness needed by those involved with young children. This applies particularly to teachers with a class of 20 to 35 four and five year olds.

Transition

A child who has attended some form of preschool group will usually find the transition to the reception class less stressful than will a child who has come straight from home. There may be a number of reasons why a child did not attend a preschool group: lack of facilities, rural location and parental choice (sadly this reason is most often the case in families where the child and parent would benefit from group involvement (Shinman, 1981)). The evaluative study of starting school by Barrett (1986) indicates that a complex web of factors influences the match between children's preschool experiences and expectations of statutory schools.

Other studies of transition (for example, Cleave et al., 1982) have shown that reception class teachers have few contacts with preschool establishments and pay little or no attention to information passed on about individual children. Reception class teachers need the opportunity to spend time at the end of the school year visiting homes and preschool groups. By observing the children, teachers will have a clearer idea of (a) what each new entrant can do, (b) what the parents and preschool colleagues expect of the child, and (c) how the child behaves with other children and adults in a familiar setting. Similarly pre-entry visits to the infant school are vital for children, parents, and nursery workers. The parents know the individual children best and should be encouraged to realize the valuable role they have to play to participating in the education of their children, including the opening of a school profile folder containing the parents' account of the children's lives so far.

Assessment and Evaluation in Reception Classes

WHY ASSESS LEARNING

The first reason for trying to assess children's learning in schools is to match learning opportunities to children's development and needs. Research (for example, Bennett et al., 1984) and surveys by HMI (GB.DES, 1978, 1982) have indicated that teachers' estimates of children's attainments have sometimes been inaccurate for more able pupils. This has been less true of infant teachers than of teachers working with older children. This may reflect the reception class teacher's recognition of the diversity of preschool experiences, which provide the base-line for work in the infant school. However, some investigations of procedures used to identify young children thought to be 'educationally at risk' have indicated that while teachers of young children were able to identify the group of 'less able' children, the teachers were much less sensitive to those children's levels of attainment on particular tasks. This point leads to a second purpose in assessing children in the reception class. Children with special needs, including children who are particularly gifted, may be identified at this point, when they come for the first time into the formal, full-time education system. A third purpose for assessing reception class children concerns the importance of providing a framework of formative and summative assessments, within which the daily teaching and learning activities will be monitored by teachers. This is part of the professional role of reflective practitioners.

WHAT DO WE WANT TO ASSESS?

It is unrealistic to attempt to assess everything about a child. Aspects which we regard as the most important must be assessed most assiduously but this must not blind us to the fact that the children will bring with them other gifts, abilities and interests which we should value. Questions concerning what teachers are, or should be, assessing about children in reception classes leads to an examination of educational aims.

Deciding what skills and concepts children may be expected to learn during the early years in school can be a focus for group discussions between colleagues. This point is discussed further later. Such action is consistent with a developmental approach if the task is viewed with the acceptance that teachers of young children need to be open and flexible, so that they do not miss learning opportunities created and acted upon by the children themselves. Indeed, such flexibility can be a strength, for the ability to recognize such an event and note it, dated, to be included in the children's profile folders should be part of the process too. This type of entry is likely to arise out of general observations of the child during activities in the classroom or in the outdoor environment.

HOW SHALL WE ASSESS THE CHILDREN'S LEARNING?

Bruce (1987) has provided a set of ten principles, derived from educationalists such as Froebel, Susan Isaacs and the Mcmillans, which underlie ideas about the teaching and learning of young children. These principles include, for example, an emphasis on links between areas of learning, and the importance of child-initiated learning. Ways of assessing young children need to take such principles into account. These principles have been endorsed and extended in research by developmental psychologists (reviewed in Meadows and Cashdan, 1988). Some of these ideas will be highlighted here as they have implications for how we assess children in reception classes.

Firstly, assessment should take into account both what the child can do unaided and what he or she can do with help. The difference between the two is what Vygotsky (1978) termed the 'zone of potential development' and is the area of the child's development at which teaching should focus. For example, if a child can count five objects unaided, can count to eight when an adult takes the child's hand and moves the sixth, seventh and eighth objects into line, but the child cannot continue this process beyond eight, then teaching should aim at that middle level. This illustrates a second point, that assessment and teaching are inter-related. The formative kind of assessment described above, is valuable when teaching, as it marries together an assessment of what the child can do with what he or she needs to be taught. The corollary of this is that isolated, summative assessments fulfil a different purpose which is less closely related to teaching. A standardized test, such as a vocabulary scale, has its uses but it lacks direct relevance for planning teaching. Drawing on the work of post-Piagetians (such as Donaldson, 1978), a third point, central to the TGAT (Task Group on Assessment and Testing) Report (1988), is that assessment should be a meaningful part of the child's usual learning activities. If we want to know whether or not a child should have a book to read, is it better to give the child a 'reading readiness' test (these now tend to be included in 'reading skills inventories'), or to observe the child playing in the book corner? Given a sound framework for the observations, the latter will provide a more valid and reliable measure of emergent reading, and will assist the teacher in deciding whether to prompt the child into reading a particular book.

Finally, an answer to the question of how should assessment of young children be carried out, needs to take into account the social context of learning. Several studies, following the work of Doise and colleagues (1975), have shown the importance of interaction with other children when assessing children's learning. Assessments of children working alone, as in the traditional formal test situation are (aside from possible difficulties concerning the unfamiliar environment and tester) likely to underestimate what children are able to do, compared with situations in which children work in pairs or small groups on a common task. This has been found to be particularly true of conversational abilities which, in a sense, can never be validly tested in a formal situation. This was a difficulty with which the Assessment of Performance Unit (APU) assessments of oral language have had to grapple and which has aroused controversy (Maclure et al., 1988). Concern for continuity and for familiarity with the principles of early years education mentioned above, lead reception class teachers to engage their pupils in learning through structured play and integrated learning.

WHAT ASSESSMENT INSTRUMENTS SHOULD WE USE?

It will be clear from what has gone before that we favour the use of observational measures of children's development. However, these, as noted earlier, need to be structured in some way. Several approaches to observational assessment of children's attainments have been used in the past. These fall broadly into three overlapping groups: developmental check-lists, series of criterion-referenced tests, and observational check-lists. These three may also represent a continuum from summative to formative assessment, although one assessment instrument may fulfil both summative and formative assessment purposes; a point which will be explored further below.

Developmental check-lists have been well known and widely used. These norm-referenced approaches include Sheridan's development items (1976), upgraded versions of scales devised by Sheridan et al. and others (for example, Bellman and Cash, 1987), and compilations of various types of items (for example, National Children's Bureau, 1977). Bate et al. (1976) have carried out an extensive review of these and similar scales. Developmental check-lists provide broad norms for children of reception class age, (for example, a 'normal' five year old should be able to: skip on alternate feet, copy a square, give their home address, and use a knife and fork competently; Sheridan, 1976). As a form of summative assessment used at the end of the school year, for example, they may provide a crude measure of a child's progress. However, there have been two difficulties in translating these developmental scales for use in reception classes.

First, they often do not, and were not intended to, relate immediately or clearly to the school curriculum. If an item appears in a developmental check-list, should it be taught directly (for example, should the children be taught to memorize their home addresses), or is the developmental item a 'soil test', not to be taught directly, but used as an indicator of wider things? If the developmental item is to be taught directly, what should precede or follow it in the learning sequence? And how should all these activities fit together to make a coherent and meaningful curriculum?

Secondly, items from developmental check-lists are often broadly phrased and there is disagreement about definitions of 'pass' on certain items. For example, teachers and other professionals might disagree about what they will accept as a 'square' – will any shape (with four sides/curved sides/two equal sides, and so on) be deemed acceptable? Does it matter if the shape is drawn with a chunky crayon or must it be a pencil? Similarly, can the teacher take into account the child's home background/ethnic group in the assessment of proficiency in handling a knife and fork?

The first of these main criticisms has been taken into account in the development of series of criterion-referenced tests. These have been developed within schools and LEAs and are likely to become more widespread and specific in the wake of the implementation of the National Curriculum. Examples of series of criterion-referenced tests (CRT) for young children have emerged in work on procedures to identify children with mild or moderate learning difficulties (see Lindsay and Pearson, 1986). Unlike developmental check-lists, CRT, especially when drawn up by teachers in a particular school, have been devised to link with the school curriculum. The CRT represent a sampling of the development which the curriculum aims to promote. For example, CRT used by reception class teachers might include items relating to children's ability to: tie shoe laces, recall the three primary colour names, recognize the three secondary colours, find the way to the headteacher's room alone, accurately repeat a message orally to another teacher, cooperate in a game with other children, operate a computer game successfully, discuss a joint activity with another child, write their first name legibly, walk along the school's balance beam on their own, offer three similarities and three differences between, say, a dog and a cat, and so on. The detail of how these are assessed will reflect the factors described in the previous section. Particular CRTs will reflect the school population – perhaps including varied items relating to both mother-tongue (where it is not English) and English language development in a school with bilingual pupils.

Although approaches to assessment using CRT may be both summative and formative and, unlike developmental items, may link well with the school's curriculum, they do raise problems concerning validity and relia-bility. One mechanism to improve these is through extensive moderation and networking among groups of teachers, working in different schools and different catchment areas.

This is also important in relation to the third form of assessment used in reception classes – structured assessment schedules. (See, for example, Dowling, 1988, for suggestions of schedule contents.) Structured assess-ment schedules consist of items selected by the teachers themselves, with the intention of observing either individual children or the use of play acti-vities by the class.

It can sometimes be difficult for a teacher of young children to perform extended observation of one child, due to the high demand for adult invol-vement in their work at this stage, but it should be possible for the teachers to observe fairly closely for a series of shorter bouts and then to use a sampling technique of a different kind to give a 'picture' of the child's school day. This method of examining the child's use of time requires the teacher to glance at the target child say, every fifteen minutes and note what he or she is doing. Such a record can be reviewed at intervals during the term and is vital if the teacher wishes to be able to reflect on the way children in the class spend their time. In one nursery study (Clark and Cheyne, 1979), observation revealed that some of the children were spending up to a quarter of their time in aimless activity. Another study (Hutt et al., in press) demonstrated that young children spent a great deal of their early months in nursery provision simply watching others. Later in their nursery careers, this activity had diminished and children were more frequently observed engaged in play activities. Such examples highlight the importance of recording the patterns of all the children, since observation of only a few might lead the teacher to conclude that this group were under-involved, while a child who was still spending·substantial amounts of time looking around or watching others after six months in a class might need extra help in overcoming shyness. Teachers should decide beforehand what their observations are for – a general jotting of events may be useful as described above, alternatively, if they wish to assess the frequency with which a particular behaviour occurs, they may need a check-list ready made to tick off predetermined categories. Staff might discuss the relative merits and uses of different types of observation and their implications.

One of the main issues to bear in mind when deciding on a school-con-structed observation check-list or record sheet is the need for items to be as objective as possible. For example, one teacher classified Edward as cheeky and precocious, this teacher's attitude towards him, had he been in her class, might have resulted in a loss of self-esteem and subsequent undermining of the intelligent work of which he was capable. Two other members of staff, who taught Edward, felt very positive about him and encouraged what they interpreted as freshness and a lively, enquiring mind, needing conversation with adults.

WHEN SHALL WE MAKE ASSESSMENTS?

Teachers in the reception class are continually making spontaneous judgements about their pupils. Teachers who are most adept at making accurate assessments are the ones who have become able to monitor the class and use their observations. Although friends have sometimes thrown up their hands in horror at the idea of comparing a race-horse trainer with a teacher, one of the writers has found that the qualities which have made a successful trainer appear to be the same as those needed by an effective teacher. Some very successful trainers have described how they watch the horse, its habits, preferences, moods, and so on, and then select not only the most appropriate training programme each day, but the type of race track, the time of year, and so on at which to expose the horse to its 'summative assessment' situations. They have been carrying out formative assessments all the time, even to the point of changes in feed!

Parents with summer-born children, finding their children still, on average, behind their older class-mates after over two years in school, rejoiced at the recent increase in the number of LEAs admitting children to reception classes at the beginning of the school year in which the children were five years old. This rejoicing implicitly focused on the quantity, rather than quality, of the schooling.

Such admissions policies have created many complications, one of which has been professional difficulties for many reception class teachers. The majority of those involved in early years education advocate the introduction of such admissions policies only when and where such practices can be justified by the appropriate staffing levels, resources, space and teaching methods, equivalent to those found in a nursery unit. Early entry is seen by many as a way of satisfying parent voters, offering under-fives provision 'on the cheap', yet in reality, failing the children. Most reports of what is happening in practice (for example, Stevenson, 1987) show that, far from providing a 'flying' start for four year olds, inappropriate treatment, with emphasis on 'the three Rs', rather than experiential learning, can result in difficulties for the summer-born children. In schools where staff have been sensitive to the children's needs and aware of their own inadequacies (though these are through no fault of their own), there has been an attempt to convey to parents the importance of the quality of provision, not simply the quantity. What this means is that early years teachers in most parts of the country have been evaluating their own practices, often forming networks to provide mutual support. They are aware of the importance of allowing children time to settle in the reception class, helping other teachers in the school appreciate the special needs of the youngest pupils, and cooperating with others to make sensitive assessments.

HOW SHALL WE ORGANIZE THE RECORDING OF ASSESSMENT?

Detailed record keeping is usually extremely time-consuming. As Shipman (1983) has commented, the time taken in compilation is rarely matched by the time taken consulting such documents. Yet they can form the basis of discussion with parents and colleagues, from both within the staff team and outside it, for example, bilingual teachers, psychologists, social workers, medical and health professionals. The records can also help the class teacher analyse what he or she is doing in relation to a particular child and with the class as a whole. The most useful record sheet will be one which the staff team have devised, used and adapted, themselves. However, teachers of the youngest pupils might like to use a published document as the basis for their initial discussions, for example, the *Keele Preschool Assessment Guide* (Tyler, 1978) or *Early Learning: Assessment and Development* (Curtis and Wignall, 1980) or the suggestions in Dowling (1988), with modifications related to further extentions of the children's work where appropriate, in the reception class. Teachers will obviously need to reflect on the demands made by the guidelines for the National Curriculum and the attainment targets, as well as maintaining the broad curriculum, the provision for spontaneity and flexibility so characteristic of early childhood education.

Other aspects of the proposed profile folder will include scores from norm-referenced tests, work-book check-lists, specific test results, and examples of work, either to illustrate a significant point, or to act as markers of the child's progress. Other materials becoming increasingly common as part of school activities, but not yet widely used as part of pupil profiles, are audio-cassette and video-tape recordings. Videos of 'everyday' sessions in which the camera becomes part of the classroom furniture, can be reviewed during staff discussions. Photographs, produced to illustrate work on a particular project, may be added to a child's profile folder because they show the child in the process of creating or achieving a product. Once children can write, they too can be invited to comment on their achievements and difficulties. Younger children could be encouraged to talk about themselves for a tape recording. Even children of four are able to elucidate, to someone at home, if not to the teacher, who can do what in their class and why they themselves are able/unable to perform certain tasks.

THE CONTEXT OF ASSESSMENT OF CHILDREN IN RECEPTION CLASS

Assessments and attainments do not take place in a vacuum. They are the result of interaction between the child (including family background and experiences), the teacher, the curriculum and the context. The context in which assessment takes place includes the other children in the school, available resources, and values promoted by the school.

Of course, it will be argued that the assessments in the case study in Box 2.2 differed because they were subjective and that this case study illustrates the dangers of impressionistic judgements. However, our contention is that the assessment of young children should be based on teachers' professional judgements. These evolve in the day-to-day interaction with pupils and can provide a more useful barometer of children's attainments and educational needs than do standardized tests. Naturally this requires some defence

---

Box 2.2

Case study illustrating contrasting assessments

Danny was described by one adult as producing very good written work. Danny independently compiled a 'nature diary' of a street, illustrating this with pictures, captions, and reports of natural objects found in the street during one week. He had received little direct teaching, but a lot of encouragement during this work. At the same time a second adult made a completely different assessment of Danny's written work. She described it as 'poor, showing little imagination and not finished off properly'. Danny's handwriting was not well formed or clearly legible. These two adults had very different ideas about what was valuable, and this was reflected in their assessments. One adult was Danny's parent, the other his class teacher. It is not relevant here to discuss which adult matched which assessment, the point is that their subjective assessments of Danny's written work varied widely, reflecting their own values and other contextual factors.

---

against the charge of subjectivity and superficiality and we would argue that it is important for teachers undertaking such assessment and evaluative work to examine contextual factors, for we cannot assess the child without recognizing those issues.

Teachers must be aware of the need to assess themselves, the classroom and the whole school environment. If the assessment is to provide as 'true' a picture as possible of the child's levels of attainment, then it must be carried out in ways that will ensure that the child feels at ease. Assessment situations must either match the everyday classroom environment or they should take place in the classroom with continuity of the usual climate. Furthermore, teachers' attitudes, values and behaviour have been shown to have a bearing upon their pupils' attainments, particularly in relation to gender, race and class. Similarly, sociologists have argued that children designated as having special requirements reflect teachers' anxieties, rather than children's needs. Prejudice may also work to favour some children. To wrongly overestimate a child's needs may be as damaging as to underestimate them. It is interesting that children, even in the early years of schooling, rapidly pick up teachers' assessments of class-mates' abilities (Crocker and Cheeseman, 1988) and that children live up or down to these expectations. Since a great deal of this influence occurs through the hidden, rather than overt, curriculum it can be unconscious and particularly insidious.

HOW WILL THE INFORMATION BE USED?

Discussion with colleagues in school
In addition to those uses already described, for the class teacher, on-going assessments of children provide evidence about those children's progress, whether from day-to-day or year-to-year. These can be used as bases for 'case study' meetings in which all the staff in a school meet together to discuss individual children. In some schools staff meet regularly, once or twice a week, for a short time, either before or after school, and individual tea-

chers take it in turn to present a review of the progress of certain children. Sometimes the discussion may focus upon a group about whom there is concern, but generally every child will be reviewed at some time. This forum provides as base for evaluating the usefulness of the records maintained, examining patterns in the development of individual children, and liaising with parents and other professionals.

Discussion with parents.

We have already indicated that we believe parents should be involved in the school's profiling arrangements. The stress placed by the present government on parental participation, though contested as a ploy by some, has in fact hit upon one spot in which schools were not, in general, communicating enough detailed information to parents. Studies (such as Wikely, 1986) indicate that what parents want most is clear, detailed information about what their children can do and how they can help their children be happy and competent at school. They are often made to feel they are pushy and interferring, yet what they seek is a fair share in the consultations and decisions made about their own children. (Equally, studies show that most parents are not interested in committee work, making curricular decisions or managing schools.) Parents who are perceived as equal partners with teachers in an on-going process, can assist in later transitions, from class to class or school to school. However, the evidence seems to indicate that the insights of many parents fall on deaf ears, or are apparently so unwelcome they are not given (see Box 2.3). A 1986 survey by the National Consumer Council (1986) reported that about a quarter of all parents felt they could not visit their children's schools unless specifically invited, or for a specific problem, while half of the parents questioned would have liked more detail on their children's progress.

Box 2.3

Case study illustrating poor parent–teacher communication

Susie attended a primary school where there were two open evenings a year for parents. At an early autumn open night, Susie's new class teacher told her parents that the previous teacher had made a mistake with Susie's end of year reading age, since she had come up with a far lower result. Susie's mother, a teacher herself and therefore in a professional dilemma, felt unable to explain that Susie was a child who took time to feel relaxed with a new adult. She had especially liked the previous teacher. Susie's mother knew that the first reading age score was the correct one, and was afraid this new teacher would reduce her expectations of Susie.

By involving parents fully in a partnership which includes the profiling of their children we are hopefully producing a more rounded system, since parents can help us assess children's potential learning styles and keep us informed of the joys and pains we may be unknowingly inflicting on our young charges! We are also preventing the mistrust which is engendered by closed, or secret documents. Such practices have excluded from power those people who should have a hand in decisions about future plans – the children themselves and their parents (ILEA, 1987). As the report of the ILEA Committee of Enquiry into Freedom of Information in Education points out:

> School records on pupils should be open to the pupils themselves, regardless of age, as well as parents.

Discussions with other professionals – both intra- and inter-professional work.
Support for all early years teachers, in the form of groups like the proposed TGAT networks could develop quite rapidly and, as with whole school staffs, become a forum for the examination of effective and efficient assessment and records. (One reservation in such a proposal is the amount of undirected time experienced teachers are already giving in order to fulfil the demands being made of them.)

A good example occurs in Warwickshire, where four year olds in School Support Groups began in 1986, as a spontaneous response to the news that reception classes were to admit, with no extra staffing, all the year's intake of children in September. These groups meet regularly and include local nursery teachers as valuable participants. A system, which required infant teachers to begin a programme of work in which pressure from a prescribed curriculum and tests to be administered at seven years of age made them feel vulnerable, could be damaging to infant teachers who have struggled to ensure that they are offering young children sensitive and appropriate provision. From the evidence we have at present (for example, Jowett and Sylva, 1986) it appears likely that children taught through guided play and through a broad and rich curriculum do in fact perform well in quite formal tests and young children do not benefit from a longer time spent in formal, didactic instruction during the early years. The type of test proposed by TGAT (1988) are of the kind which require children to have worked experientially and since this is an approach which is widely supported by educationists, there is much hope that the recommendations will continue to be supported by the Secretary of State.

This espousal of structured play and integrated learning might appear to have been challenged in an article in the *Times Educational Supplement* (20.5.88) following the publication of the Thomas Coram team's research on children in inner city infant schools (Tizard et al., 1988). The article was sensationally headlined 'Test them at five'. Barbara Tizard argued that by assessing children early in their school careers teachers can focus on those children most needing their attention. The headline confused the issue. Informal teacher assessments are always needed whereas tests are needed rarely. Some years ago one of the writers was a member of a group of headteachers who called for an end to an LEA policy of testing seven year olds. The tests used were summative, norm-referenced tests, supposedly aimed at identifying those children who would require 'remedial' support in their junior school years. The headteachers argued that teachers in the infant classes were professionally able to identify children needing greater support at an earlier age than seven, through formative evaluation of the processes and products of the children's activities, together with the teacher's intimate knowledge of the context in which the children were developing. They argued further, that the LEA testing was diverting teaching support away from the early years, where it was not needed and could be more effective, and that the labelling of the child as 'remedial' in junior classes was consolidating, rather than ameliorating the opinion of such children, by themselves, by teachers and by peers. In order to convince others that such professional assessments are respectable, early years teachers must have more than the out-dated 'I carry it all round in my head' approach. By developing their own expertise, they will be opening up possibilities for children, becoming consciously aware of omissions in children's experiences, rather than the feared labelling of their pupils. Intra-professional liaision relating to assessment may also involve class teachers coordinating their teaching with the work of peripatetic specialists.

In order for the time spent in school by any advisory staff to be spent most effectively, comprehensive profile folders are essential (see Box 2.4).

Box 2.4

Case study of inter-professional liaison

A bilingual teacher, called to a school to work with an ethnic minority child who seemed to be experiencing severe learning difficulties, found that on questioning the child about work covered by the teacher, detailed in the child's profile record, that his difficulty was not with the work itself, but in active use of English. The action which could then be taken was an extension of the work learned through mother tongue teaching and strengthening of English language work with the child, in the classroom.

In cases where the educational psychologist is asked to provide support, staff no longer expect the expert to come into school and wave a magic wand or remove the child to a special school. They expect to provide the psychologist with information about the child as well as some analysis of staff action. This can then be used as a basis for discussion about approaches to the child's difficulties, or the teacher's difficulties.

Conclusion

The assessment and evaluation of children in the infant and first school is an essential part of the teacher's role. Since effective practice in the early years is based on a developmental tradition, the importance of flexibility in reviewing the child, the curriculum, the teacher and the context, norm-referenced tests are seen as offering little of value to a profile folder. However, it is important to recognize that the National Curriculum attainment target results, which will form part of the profile, will be the responsibility of the class teachers and their colleagues in the local moderation network. This indicates an acknowledgement of the valuable on-going assessments teachers are able to make.

Such records can be strengthened where teachers take on the role of action researchers in their own classrooms, developing the kind of reflective analysis discussed by Pollard and Tann (1987). We are in frequent contact with many class teachers who see an important aspect of their work as that of teacher-researcher, reflecting on their own practice at all times, using empirical, interpretive and critical methods to do so. Furthermore, despite the constraints imposed by time and by staff:pupil ratios, many early years teachers are attempting to improve practice by seeking to diagnose children's difficulties and misunderstandings by ensuring meaningful teacher–pupil discussions, thus employing the research findings of others (for example, Bennett, 1987).

Although we would also expect teachers to keep other records of their work with the children in order to evaluate their own needs, both in terms of professional expertise and development and in terms of the environment and staffing, we have not detailed these in this chapter, since our focus has been the individual child. Our greatest concern is that while teachers are expected to maintain such full records, including the discussion and creation of appropriate record sheets, they may be subject to the criticism that their judgements are invalidated by being subjective and untested in the wider community. We hope that by forming networks they will be enabled to support each other and provide the expected moderation; their efforts will ensure that the proposed testing does not result in a return to 'teaching to the test' and damaging competitiveness in place of cooperation.

References and Suggested Reading

Barrett, G. (1986). *Starting School: An Evaluation of the Experience.* London: AMMA.

Bate, M., Smith, M. & James, J. (1976). *Review of Tests and Assessments in Early Education.* Windsor: NFER-NELSON.

Bate, M. and Smith, M. (1978). *Manual for Assessment in Nursery Education.* Windsor: NFER-NELSON.

Bellman, M. & Cash, J. (1987). *The Schedule of Growing Skills in Practice.* Windsor: NFER-NELSON.

Bennett, S.N., Desforges, C., Cockburn, A.D. & Wilkinson, B. (1984). *The Quality of Pupil Learning Experiences.* London: Lawrence Erlbaum.

Bennett, N. (1987). The search for the effective primary teacher. In: Delamont, S. (Ed.) *The Primary School Teacher.* Lewes: Falmer Press.

Brown, M. & Goldstein, H. (1987). Letter in the *Guardian,* 27.10.87.

Bruce, T. (1987). *Early Childhood Education.* London: Hodder and Stoughton.

Burstall, C. (1987). Letter in the *Guardian,* 3.11.87.

Clark, M.M. & Cheyne, W.N. (1979). *Studies in Preschool Education.* London: Hodder and Stoughton.

Cleave, S., Jowett, S. & Bate, M. (1982). *And So to School.* Windsor: NFER-NELSON.

Crocker, A.C. & Cheeseman, R.G. (1988). Infant teachers have a major impact on children's self-awareness. *Children and Society, 2, 5,* 3–8.

Curtis, A. & Wignall, M. (1980). *Early Learning.* London: Macmillan.

Doise, W., Mugney, G. & Perret-Clermont, A. (1975). Social interaction and the development of cognitive operations. *European Journal of Social Psychology, 5,* 367–83.

Donaldson, M. (1978). *Children's Minds.* Harmondsworth: Penguin.

Dowling, M. (1988). *Education 3 to 5.* London: Paul Chapman.

Great Britain. Department of Education and Science. (1978). *Primary Education in England: A Survey by HM Inspectors of Schools.* London: HMSO.

Great Britain. Department of Education and Science. (1982). *Education 5–9.* London: HMSO.

Hutt, S.J., Tyler, S., Hutt, C. & Foy, H. (in press). *A Natural History of the Preschool: Play, Exploration and Learning*. London: Routledge and Kegan Paul.

Inner London Education Authority. (1987). *Informing Education*. London: ILEA.

Jowett, S. & Sylva, K. (1986). Does the kind of preschool matter? *Educational Review*, 28, 21–31.

Lindsay, G. & Pearson, L. (1986). *Special Needs in the Primary School: Identification and Intervention*. Windsor: NFER-NELSON.

Maclure, M., Phillips, T. & Wilkinson, A. (1988). *Oracy Matters*. Milton Keynes: Open University Press.

Meadows, S. & Cashdan, A. (1988). *Helping Children Learn*. London: David Fulton.

National Children's Bureau (1977). *National Children's Bureau Development Guide*. London: NCB.

National Consumer Council (1986). *The Missing Links Between Home and School: A Consumer View*. London: NCC.

Plowden Report. Great Britain. Department of Education and Science. (1967).

Central Advisory Council for Education (England). (1967). *Children and their Primary Schools*. London: HMSO.

Pollard, A. & Tann, S. (1987). *Reflective Teaching in the Primary School*. London: Cassell.

Sheridan, M. (1976). *Children's Developmental Progress from Birth to Five Years* (Revised). Windsor: NFER-NELSON.

Shipman, M. (1983). *Assessment in Primary and Middle Schools*. London: Croom Helm.

Shinman, S. (1981). *A Chance for Every Child*. London: Tavistock.

Stevenson, C. (1987). The young four year old in nursery and infant classes: challenges and constraints. In: NFER/SCDC Seminar Report *Four Year Olds in School*. Windsor: NFER/SCDC.

Task Group on Assessment and Testing (1988). *A Report*. London: HMSO.

Tizard, B. (1988). Test them at five. *Times Educational Supplement*, 20.5.88.

Tizard, B., Blatchford, P., Burke, J., Farquhar, C. & Plewis, I. (1988). *Young Children at School in the Inner City*. London: Lawrence Erlbaum.

Tyler, S. (1980). *Keele Preschool Assessment Guide*. Windsor: NFER-NELSON.

Vygotsky, L.S. (1978). *Mind in Society*. London: Harvard University Press.

Wikely, F. (1986). Communication between parents and teachers. In: Hughes, M. (Ed.) *Involving Parents in the Primary Curriculum*. Exeter: Exeter University Occasional Papers/Perspectives.

The Assessment of Cognitive Abilities

Geoff Lindsay

The testing of children's cognitive abilities has a long tradition within the education system. In practice the main approach to this task has been by the use of intelligence tests of one form or another, including those given to groups of children and those administered individually. This approach has been the subject of much criticism in the recent past. Psychologists and teachers have raised objections to the use of such tests on a variety of grounds, for example, their bias against specific groups of children, and their lack of usefulness. The education system as a whole probably makes less use of such standardized tests since the decline of the 11-plus examinations, although some schools continue to use them on their own account.

In this chapter the issue of the assessment of children's cognitive abilities will be examined from several perspectives. The development of a more integrated form of assessment of the child within his or her context, is proposed as a desirable alternative.

The Use of Standardized Tests

The measurement of cognitive abilities has been a corner-stone of educational psychology and teaching for a long time. Early experimental psychologists devised a variety of methods to attempt to assess individuals' ability to think, plan and reason. It is well known that other psychologists and educationists saw the possibility of using such tests, and developments of them, to assess young children. The early work of Binet and Simon in France, is a familiar example.

From these early beginnings a whole movement and industry have been developed. In the United Kingdom, Cyril Burt, the first educational psychologist, promulgated the use of intelligence tests to aid the London County Council in its allocation of children to forms of education. Later, the 11-plus test made use of forms of intelligence tests in addition to assessment of attainment. Local authorities and individual schools have used intelligence tests to decide how children should be grouped within schools (for example, streaming) and to identify those requiring some special provision. In the USA also the use of intelligence tests 'took off'.

Later years (particularly in the 1960s in the USA and the 1970s in the UK) saw the development of variants of these ability tests. Whereas intelligence tests were designed to provide overall, global assessments of cognitive ability, interest has developed in attempts to identify and assess more specific abilities. At this time, therefore, there was much interest in more specific language, perceptual, motor and perceptuo-motor abilities; research and experience had shown that many children failed at basic educational tasks such as reading, despite good levels of general intelligence as measured by IQ tests.

In addition to the broadening range of types of standardized assessment techniques, this period also saw an increase in the use of more detailed and intensive individual assessments. The 11-plus examination and many forms of intelligence tests available to teachers were designed to be given to classes or schools at a time. To provide a more detailed, extensive, and intensive examination of an individual child requires individual assessment. The need to carry out such assessment was urged and the increase in the numbers of specially trained staff (educational psychologists in particular) allowed this to occur. The 'grandparent' of intelligence tests developed for use with children, which is still in use, in the *Stanford–Binet* (see Reviews section). It provides measures of mental age and IQ. The *Wechsler Scales* (*WPPSI* and *WISC-R*) and the *British Ability Scales* provide additional information and are each based on different models of intelligence (group and specific factors, in addition to 'g', a general measure of ability). These are also reviewed.

The test results alone are not the only information potentially available. To give the whole test takes about 45–60 minutes. During that time it would be possible to observe working processes. For example, does the child go very methodically, but slowly, checking every move, so leading to lower scores on subtests which give bonus points for speed? Therefore, the assessment period could give information on both the process and product of the child's approach. On the other hand, such a test is not enough. Of itself each gives no *direct* insight into the child's approach to the tasks at which he or she is failing (for example, reading). Neither does it give information on the classroom, teaching style, curriculum materials and so. There are several tests of general cognitive ability available to teachers, for example, *Raven's Matrices, Cognitive Abilities Test* and the *Richmond Tests*. These are limited is so far as they do not cover all aspects of intelligence (see test reviews). However, the *Stanford–Binet, Wechsler Scales* and the *British Ability Scales* are all well developed and standardized approaches to the assessment of individual children's cognitive abilities. Historically, the tests reflect the increasing interest in going beyond assessments of general intelligence alone (although this can still be useful) to assessing more specific abilities or groups of abilities.

Other tests were designed to supplement and extend the use of IQ tests. Although the *WISC* had been found useful in providing a breakdown of scores, this did not cover areas that some psychologists and educationalists had found important. Such tests as the *Frostig* and *ITPA* proved popular in the 1960s and 1970s. Unfortunately reviews of their technical quality and particulary of the lack of obvious success of the training programmes based upon them (for example, Larsen et *al.*, 1982) led to their going out of fashion for psychologists. However, teachers have developed interest in the assessment of abilities exemplified by these two instruments. One test, the *Aston Index* (Newton and Thomson, 1976) has much in common with these initiatives. It also has a suggested programme of intervention, the *Aston*

Portfolio (Aubrey *et al.*, undated). Unfortunately, the evidence on the *Index* is not encouraging (see Lindsey, 1984).

The use of the major intelligence tests has a long and well-recorded history. The extension of interest into standardized tests of more specific abilities is generally less positive. Whatever doubts we may have about intelligence tests (see below) there are many more about the ability tests mentioned here.

The Flight from Assessment

Historically, then, intelligence and IQ have had a central position in the assessment of children. Theories of intelligence, and the concept of underachievement, whereby a child's attainment in, say reading, is compared with that predicted by IQ and age, were covered in teacher training. Group tests were also used in schools, particularly when the 11-plus was common. Psychologists have had considerable experience in this theory and practice. For both groups, teachers and educational psychologists, intelligence was seen as a central theoretical construct, and its assessment was a necessary endeavour. More recently this emphasis has changed, and both groups appear to spend less time on intellectual assessment, either in training or practice, although intelligence testing certainly has not disppeared entirely. There are several reasons for these developments, but I shall focus here upon those which are scientific/empirical in nature.

BIAS

Much concern has been expressed, particularly over the past 10 to 20 years, on the supposed bias which is inherent in intelligence tests. A landmark in this debate was Kamin's publication *The Science and Politics of IQ* (Kamin, 1974). Were IQ tests fair, or did they discriminate against particular groups, for example, females, ethnic minorities and working class children? To what extent was such apparent discrimination a result of the theory of intelligence, the construction of the instrument and its standardization, or the administration of the test and its interpretation?

Of particular relevance in Britain is the work of Mackintosh and Maskie-Taylor (1985) in their contribution to the Swann Report. In this paper, the authors consider the possible explanations for the differences found, over many studies, between the mean IQ scores of different groups. Their analysis of UK studies suggests that we would be unwise to accept the view that there are proven differences in ability between racial groups *per se*. First, it appears that the scores of the children tested were related to their length of stay in the UK (many of the ethnic-minority children were recent immigrants). Second, when social class was controlled the differences between groups reduced considerably. When more social variables were included in the analysis, the difference between mean scores reduced still further. These variables included overcrowding, number of parents, size of family and neighbourhood. The review by Mackintosh and Maskie-Taylor therefore, suggests a more complex scenario. There is evidence that mean scores between racial groups differ, but these differences appear to relate to social factors, and:

when they are taken into account, the difference between West Indian and indigenous children is sharply reduced, to somewhere between I and 7 points...

(Mackintosh and Maskie-Taylor, 1985, p. 147)

USEFULNESS

The other major criticism of IQ tests has been that they have limited usefulness. This is a pragmatic concern, and represents an interesting shift from an earlier position when IQ and similar tests were considered very useful. This shift highlights the purpose of the assessment, and in particular its degree of specificity. IQ tests, by their nature, give a general assessment of intellectual functioning. As such they can only serve as a basis for similarly general decisions, usually about classification and placement. Thus, IQ has been used to place children in grammar schools or schools for what were then termed the 'educationally subnormal'. However, in addition to the technical concerns regarding the reliability of such assessments and the consequent placement decisions, the nature of the questions has also changed. We are now much less concerned with placing children in new settings; instead our intention is to enhance the child's development within the situation that exists. This change has been due in part to the moves towards integration of children with special educational needs. Teachers in mainstream schools now need more guidance on the nature of a child's needs and appropriate strategies to help meet these.

The use of IQ tests has been regarded as of limited usefulness for the kinds of assessment which are linked directly to teaching (see below). However, it is arguable that this move away from IQ type asessments has been made at the expense of clear analyses of the child's relevant abilities. In my view it is not enough to assess and control the curriculum and its presentation, there is still a need to examine the individual child's approach to learning, even though the IQ-related approach may no longer be appropriate.

UNDERACHIEVEMENT AND SPECIFIC LEARNING DIFFICULTIES

For many years the practice of assessing children's IQ and attainments, in order to determine who was underachieving, was a prevalent activity among educational psychologists, and remedial teachers. Educational systems had been developed, which required a distinction to be made between children of low ability and attainment and children whose attainment is lower than that predicted by ability for the child's age. For example, a ten-year-old child with a reading age of eight years and an IQ of about 80 would be considered to be 'working to potential'. The assumption was that at this level of intelligence, we should expect attainment to be below the average and these scores are in line with expectation. On the other hand, a similar child with an IQ of 120 would be considered to be underachieving. Here the expectation was that the child's attainment scores should be above the mean, to match the level of intelligence. A reading age of about 12 years would be expected. On the face of it, this sounds reasonable. Unfortunately it is based upon the assumption that IQ and attainment *should* be closely matched. We don't have the same expectations of the relationship between IQ and ability to play sport or to understand a car engine. Indeed, there are strange, inverted relationships, which are often declared. Some intellectually able people are not only not ashamed, but even proud of their inability to change a car wheel, use a computer, hang wallpaper, and so on. However, these approaches were necessary as different systems were set up for children who fell into categories of having learning difficulties or having specific reading difficulties.

Research evidence has raised many doubts about this practice. The assumption that the children with specific reading difficulties were, in a sense, more in need in that they had a discrepancy which must be rectified, has been challenged on two grounds. First, the allocation of extra resources is, in part, a moral question. What makes these children more deserving? Second, the research does not reveal that these children improve more than children with learning difficulties. Early studies of remedial classes and centres showed consistently that even where there were short-term gains, these usually 'washed out' once the chid returned to the mainstream setting.

There also appears to be a considerable overlap between children with learning difficulties and those with specific reading difficulties (for example, Van Wissel, 1987). There is no denying the existence of children with specific learning difficulties, but they do not form one homogenous group. They show a variety of patterns of strengths and needs, which can lead to their being put into groupings, but these are far from satisfactory. For example, some children show significant problems with short-term memory. Given a set of four digits aurally they are unable to repeat them orally. This inability relates to blending sounds to form a word; if the child can't remember four sounds, how will he or she blend four or more together? But other strategies may be relevant. Can the child group information to reduce the effective number of items, or make use of the context to have a good guess at the total word? Thus, even having similar problems in one area, does not necessarily lead to identical treatment.

There are other difficulties with an approach which attempts to fit a child to a category on the basis of test results. Is a child with an IQ of 150 but a reading quotient of 120 'disabled' and does this child have special needs? What is the difference between having a disability and an incompletely developed ability? There are also statistical problems with expected scores. For example, the 'expected' reading quotient of a 12-year-old child with an IQ of 140 on the *British Ability Scales (BAS)* is 124. For such a child the reading quotient would need to be as low as 103 on the BAS reading scale before the score is sufficiently unusual for it to be considered very significant psychologically. At this point fewer than one in 25 would achieve such a discrepancy. Thus, in this case, a child of very high general intelligence (well within the top one per cent) needs to have a reading age, which is average.

This example is extreme, and some would argue that I am too conservative in my cut-off point to indicate psychological significance. Nonetheless it does indicate the danger of superficial examination of differences on tests leading to over-hasty judgements.

However, these problems should not deflect us from the main question. What is the nature of the child's abilities, how do these influence the area under consideration and how must the child's learning be structured in order that it be optimized? This approach does not end with a simple categorization, whether it uses a simple formula comparing IQ with Reading Quotient, or a more complex formula, as used in parts of the USA (see Board of Trustees of the Council for Learning Disabilities, 1987, for a critique). A continuation of assessment techniques and methods may, however, be useful in pointing the way to a teaching programme.

Curriculum-based Assessment

Dissatifaction with IQ and other ability tests has developed over the past decade. Teachers and psychologists have increasingly turned to curriculum-based assessment (CBA) in preference to the use of such tests. This approach shifts the emphasis away from the child onto the curriculum and the teacher. It is associated with a revamping of the curriculum itself. This has been redefined as a series of more specific objectives, arranged hierarchically. Assessment, therefore, becomes a task of examining where on the series of objectives the child has reached and their subsequent progress. As Cameron (in a later chapter) describes it, this may include an assessment of the child's acquisition (for example, the number of words learned from a list) and fluency (the rate at which the child performs the task at hand).

In many ways, CBA can be seen as a reaction against assessment procedures which were too remote from the requirement of the job at hand. However, it would be wrong to see CBA simply as a reaction to the failings of the previous model. It has a coherence and value in its own right. In addition there is now a large body of evidence which supports the use of the various components of this approach. It is not surprising, therefore, that special educators and psychologists in particular, have been at the forefront of advocating that assessment of children should not only include CBA, but that CBA should be the only type of assessment used in this area. Such protagonists have argued this on two grounds:

- The use of intelligence tests, and other assessments of children's abilities has been discredited.
- The use of CBA provides all that it is necessary to know in order to help the child's progress optimally through the curriculum.

However, there are several points which must be considered before we move wholeheartedly to CBA. First, the notion of the curriculum is not without difficulty. It has not been found possible to break all the curriculum into objectives, particularly in behavioural terms. The division into the 'open' (for example, aesthetics, not amenable to this approach) and 'closed' (for example, basic skills areas) curriculum goes only some of the way to meeting this objection. This quotation from an educator from a very different school of thought is worth considering at this point:

> Education as induction into knowledge is successful to the extent that it makes behavioural outcomes of the student unpredictable.
>
> (Stenhouse, 1975, p. 82)

Second, the practical difficulties of conducting task analyses, devising sequences and precision teaching probes, and developing the necessary materials are major. Some commercially developed materials are now available, but these can never, by their nature, be totally comprehensive. Each skill and each child's development of that skill is unique and, potentially, will need a slightly different programme. Third, many teachers find the style of CBA off-putting, particularly mainstream primary staff. There is a wide gulf between it and the modern primary approaches. Fourth, there is a danger of putting the cart before the horse. Teachers may teach that which can be assessed most easily.

Fifth, the focus on the child and the child's interaction with the minutiae of the curriculum is open to question. As was stated above, there are other factors which affect children's learning (for example, the nature of the classroom ecology) and these are often ignored. There is still the question of the child *per se*. CBA assumes a behavioural model of the child where what matters is what the child does, not what he or she thinks, feels or values. Does this truly give all the information necessary to ensure a child's optimum progress and nurture?

New Developments in Cognitive Assessment

The development of curriculum-based assessment has much to recommend it, but one glaring omission is a consideration of the child as a learner. Could it be that the dissatisfaction with concepts of intelligence, with IQ tests and other ability measures, and the benefits of CBA have led to that familiar tendency involving infants and bathwater? I now intend to consider alternative developments which in my view should lead to a reconsideration of this position.

CONCEPTS OF INTELLIGENCE

Critiques within the teaching literature have often confounded concern about methods with that of the underlying construct. Clearly it is possible to be highly critical of an IQ test while still supporting the idea that intelligence is a useful concept. However, concern has also been expressed about the concept of intelligence itself. Unfortunately, intelligence is in many ways a slippery concept. The essence of this problem has been shown most clearly in a recent book by Sternberg and Detterman (1986) entitled *What is Intelligence?* This contains 24 essays by leading researchers in the field, all of whom were asked this 'simple' question. Their replies are as interesting for their diversity as for their erudition. Some authors focused on biological definition, others stressed a social interactionist perspective. The two editors provide a most useful taxonomy, essentially a form of hierarchy of concerns or, in their terms, loci of intelligence.

For teachers the main interest lies at the individual and the environmental levels, in the Sternberg and Detterman typology. If we return to the discussion of curriculum-based assessment, it can be seen that what is omitted, by this focus, includes the whole level, which is particularly concerned with cognitive processes 'inside' the head, as opposed to the behavioural processes, relevant to interaction with the curriculum.

REUVEN FEUERSTEIN'S MEDIATED LEARNING THEORY

It must be recognized, however, that it is just this 'process' or 'ability' approach which has been criticized in the past, as I described above. However, once more it must be stated that this previous failure need not be directly due to the model, but perhaps to its implementation. For example, the work derived from the ideas of Reuven Feuerstein has much in common with these approaches, but there is some indication of positive findings (see Burden, 1987; Messerer et al., 1984). The method makes use of the *Learning Potential Assessment Device (LPAD)* where the intention is to focus not on what the child knows or can do, but on what the child is about to learn, their immediate potential. This is a procedure which covers a large number of areas, examining how the child sees the world, processes information and communicates results. This approach uses a test–teach–test method, hence there is no one-off assessment session.

Feuerstein has developed from his *LPAD* a form of teaching he calls 'Instrumental Enrichment'. Here youngsters (the main focus has been on secondary pupils) are taken through exercises to overcome the deficits highlighted and develop their abilities. In short, 'intelligence can be taught' is the message. The method develops specific knowledge and skills. For example, one task is to classify a large number of animals given certain criteria (for example, all animals living in water need a pool, those that can fly need a cage with a top). But the particular thrust of this approach is on the *mediating* processes, planning, organizing thought and material, for example.

Feuerstein's work has much in common, at one level, with the ability training programmes criticized above (for example, Frostig). However, it is considerably greater in breadth and depth, and based upon a theory of human development which is more general. Research is limited despite its having 'taken off' in many countries, due at least in part to the charisma of the originator. However, studies are now appearing and the Department of Education and Science has sponsored a research project in Britain. At this time it is necessary to suspend judgement, but of interest in the present context is that this programme, while having redefined the curriculum and provided materials, also places the child's individual abilities at the centre of the endeavour.

STERNBERG'S TRIARCHIC THEORY OF INTELLIGENCE

This variegated approach to intelligence can also be seen, on a smaller and more restricted scale, in the work of two particularly influential authors: Sternberg and Gardner.

Sternberg has proposed a triarchic theory of intelligence which he has described in several publications (for example, Sternberg, 1985). Rather than concentrating on an individual's internal processes *or* the environment, the theory relates processes *to* the person *in* the environment. There are three sub-theories. The first sub-theory relates intelligence to the internal world of the individual. The second relates intelligence to the experience with both the internal and external worlds of the individual. The third relates intelligence to the world external to the individual. Within each sub-theory there are further elements which can be considered (for example, how knowledge is acquired and how performance is carried out).

Sternberg's work is grounded very much in cognitive psychology. The question for us, therefore, is does it have any application in education? I would suggest that it does, and I shall try to give some examples. It should be stated, however, that being a 'grand theory' (that is, trying to encompass a whole area of human activity) it is not possible to do more than refer to some parts of it here. (Also, for a very useful introduction to the theory's application to learning disabilities see Kolligian and Sternberg, 1987.)

The first part of Sternberg's theory is focused on what happens 'in the head of the individual child. One area of concern is the ability of children to plan, organize, monitor and evaluate their own performance. Children vary in their ability to carry out such tasks, and this general and higher-order ability appears to be particularly related to general intellectual ability. That is, children with lower general intellectual ability tend to be poorer in this area, even if they have other strengths. This area is of great importance, which has been recognized by Feuerstein. As described above, his work has paid particular attention to developing these skills. His programme has built-in assessments but a teacher could devise ways of assessing and developing these areas. Indeed, it is such abilities which are often helped by 'thinking skills' programmes.

The second area to be considered is that of how children acquire knowledge. The learning of single words in reading is an example. Does the child simply learn each word in isolation, or is learning facilitated by relating one to another. For instance, the teaching of spelling often makes use of short lists which have a common property. This might be simply a letter configuration, for example, 'sl', 'dr' words. It might include meaning, for example, ex- or and anti- words. Can the child make use of meaning in the latter examples?

A third example will be taken from the second sub-theory, that which relates the child's intelligence to previous experience. For example, the child will need to relate present experiences to those from the past. How competent is an individual child at doing this? Is each day's mathematics exercise a complete surprise, even though it is identical with those of the past three weeks? Can the child adapt to an old task in a new setting, for example, if given a mixture of addition and subtraction sums on one sheet having previously only encountered them at separate times. To what extant is the child automatic in processing new information? Take for example the child who reads word by word, even when each is known with 100 per cent consistency. Such children often are still analysing each word singly. They have not become automatic in their response to the word as a whole.

As I stated above, Sternberg's work has much to offer. At present it is necessary to construct most of the assessments which would be required although some standardized tests can be seen to match some of the components of his theory. However, there is a rich source here to guide our approach to assessing children's approaches to learning.

The Way Forward

In this chapter I have reviewed the development of the assessment of children's cognitive abilities. There was a time when intelligence was seen as a useful concept, and IQ tests were used widely. Recently we have seen disenchantment with both. (For a particularly critical review of the usefulness of the concept of intelligence see Howe, 1988.) At the same time there has been the positive development of curriculum-based assessment, and newer approaches to conceptualizing cognitive abilities. What, then, is the way forward?

My proposal is for the development of a more integrated and integrative form of assessment. The intention would be to assess the child within a context. This differs from other approaches which have either focused upon within-child abilities (for example, IQ tests), or on the curriculum, or at best the child–curriculum interaction, partially examined by, for example, precision teaching.

AN APPROACH TO ASSESSMENT

The research evidence available suggests that a full assessment of a child could have at least the following components. These are portrayed here as separate components and also as interactions.

The child

There are times when an overall, global assessment of intelligence is useful. However, for most children causing concern to teachers such global IQ scores give no new information. What is needed is a more finely developed, extensive and intensive range of approaches for the assessment of specific elements of cognitive functioning. The structure given by Sternberg is useful here. Assessments might include a child's general planning and organizational abilities, strategies used when learning new material, and flexibility to new learning demands. The cognitive style of the child is an important consideration. Does the child approach a task methodically, but slowly, or quickly but carelessly. Both can be 'good' or 'bad'. (For a recent review of cognitive style research see Miller, 1987.)

Take, for example, the teacher who tells the class to 'take your time and produce your best work' and the colleague who wants 'this work to be completed in ten minutes'. Each teacher's approach will give a differential advantage, or disadvantage, to different children. And, of course, as teachers we have often made both demands of our classes ourselves! An assessment of the child's style, and flexibility of style is important.

Related to this is the child's resistance to distractions. Some children with learning difficulties have great problems resisting distractions. These may be in the classroom (for example, noise, movement), or on the page (such as writing in the wrong place, or being distracted by other material). Such tendencies need careful assessment by manipulating the environment or the presentation of work to assess the child's problem and give guidance to action. In some extreme cases, children can be helped by placement in quiet distraction-reduced environments for part of the time when maximum learning is required. Thus there is a wide range of areas of the child's cognitive ability which is potentially useful to assess. At this time this will require a combination of both standardized tests and other home-made and experimental procedures.

The curriculum.

Assessing the child, however, is not enough. What is the curriculum 'diet'? Recent increase in interest in special needs has led to a greater awareness of the importance of considering a whole-school approach to this issue. Curriculum should not be seen as something for the majority plus a different set of activities tacked on for the 'slow learners'. Rather, the aim now is to integrate not only children but also the curriculum. This requires teachers to re-examine their teaching and their curriculum.

Within the field of special education much has been done. There have been many initiatives, both commercially published and home-grown, to produce specific curricula for children with special needs. However, this is not enough. These curricula are aimed at the development of specific skills and abilitites (for example, spelling programmes). What is still needed is the development of the same approaches in other areas (such as project work at primary level) and subject specialism at secondary. There is much importance, therefore, at assessing the curriculum itself in the context of assessing a child.

Of particular importance are interest and motivation. The learning tasks may be fascinating to 90 per cent of the class, but not a particular child. Motivation will then be impaired. I have already criticized many of the materials used by those who have constructed objectives-based curricula; the task may be broken down with admirable logic but be presented with dire consequences for enjoyment.

Child–curriculum interaction.

Analysis of the first two areas is not enough. It is not sufficient to use research evidence to determine the likelihood of optimal teaching methods, for example. Rather it is important to examine the actual interaction between a particular child and the curriculum in its widest sense. Thus, it may be that the general findings of research in, for example, introversion–extraversion will give some indication of likely optimal outcomes, but the position taken here is that we should not accept uncritically such evidence, based on general findings summated from large numbers of children.

The class.

Wheldall et al. (1986) have shown the importance of a variety of factors in the classroom environment. The work emanating from the Oracle project (for example, Galton et al., 1980) has also indicated how classrooms can vary with respect to the teacher's preferred style of operating. They identified four types of teaching style and, in a second publication (Galton and Simon, 1980), showed how teacher style was differentially related to the pupils' academic performance in different subjects.

Thus, in order to assess a child fully, it is important to assess also that child's learning environment. This calls for a collaborative exercise. The teacher is in the best position to assess many aspects, but is also possibly 'too close'. An outside perspective may be useful: the combination of the two even more so.

Child–class interaction.

Beyond the classroom per se it is also necessary to examine the child's interaction with the environment. Some reference to this was made above when I discussed the child's resistance to distractibility, for example. The learning environment must be assessed to check its match with the child's needs.

Another area of examination is the child's reactions to his or her perceived position or status in the class. For example, a child may thoroughly enjoy the 'special' work given if in a withdrawal situation, but feel stigamatized if given the same work in class. An excellent child–curriculum match may be disastrous in this setting.

The school.
Assessment of children in clinical settings has been criticized by teachers and educational psychologists for many years. Some examination of the school, and classroom, has been advocated in order to understand the child's context for learning. More recent research has provided evidence for school effects on learning and so this approach now has more than face validity. For example, Bickel and Bickel (1986) have reviewed evidence from studies in the United States to show which factors in schools and classrooms optimize children's learning. Mortimore et al. (1988) have researched school factors in a UK setting and produced similar findings. Educational leadership, orderly school climate, an emphasis on basic skills, for example, have been shown to correlate with success as shown in school differences in the progress of pupils, even when factors such as social class have been taken into account. The relative standards of attainment, for example, of the individual child and the norm of the school are relevant. It may be significant to one child's development to be an able pupil in a very low achieving school, or a child of modest ability in a high achieving establishment. The 1988 Education Act emphasized these effects. Schools may find themselves going in and out of favour as results are published and 'market forces' lead to changes in over- and under-subscription. The nature of the school, therefore could change year by year, a situation already happening in some parts of the country. Without an assessment of this it is not possible to understand fully the child's activities and progress. There is therefore a case for another interaction, child and school.

Society.
Finally, there is a need to assess the nature of the wider society. This is probably the least likely to be practised in any other than a general manner. However, the effects of poverty or racism, for example, in the neighbourhood may be of particular relevance. Consider, for example, the ability of children to learn when their journey to school each day is fraught with danger. Further, there are the wider socio-political dimensions which interact with the processes described in earlier stages. The IQ debate was considered earlier in this chapter in terms of perceived bias. We must also be sensitive to such issues interacting with the other aspects of the assessment approach considered here.

IMPLICATIONS

This model of assessment is clearly much more complex than that which we normally consider. However, it will be seen that many of the elements are already part of practice, but are conceptualized as different procedures.

For example, the assessment at the level of the school is common, but usually leads to generalized aggregated scores and overall descriptions of the school as a whole.

It must be accepted that this is not an easy approach to implement. However, some teachers and psychologists have been attempting to carry out such a procedure, albeit in a tentative manner, for some years. The tendency has been, however, to focus on different parts of this model, some developing curriculum-based assessments, others working to develop in-school analyses of their successful practices.

In my view, the task now is to develop further both the skills of assessment of cognitive abilities required of this model, and their necessary integration into one assessment approach. Although my focus here has been the assessment of the individual child, albeit within a context, there are spin-offs for the assessment of other areas of concern, for example, the school as an institution.

References

Aubrey, C., Eaves, J., Hicks, C. & Newton, M. (undated). *The Aston Portfolio*. Wisbech: LDA.

Bickel, W.E. & Bickel, D.D. (1986). Effective schools, classrooms and instruction: Implications for special education. *Exceptional Children, 52,* 489–500.

Board of Trustees of the Council for Learning Disabilities (1987). The CLD Position Statements: Use of discrepancy formulas in the identification of learning disabled individuals. *Journal of Learning Disabilities, 20,* 349–50.

Burden, R. (1987). Mediated learning theory: The challenge to the school psychologist. *School Psychology International, 8,* 59–62.

Cornwall, K., Pumfrey, P. & Hedderley R. (1983). Specific learning difficulties: The 'specific reading difficulties' versus 'dyslexia' controversy resolved? *Division of Educational and Child Psychology Occasional Papers, 7,* 3.

Department of Education and Science (1987). *National Curriculum: Task Group on Assessment and Testing.* London: HMSO.

Galton, M. & Simon, B. (Eds) (1980). *Progress and Performance in the Primary Classroom.* London: Routledge and Kegan Paul.

Galton, M., Simon, B. & Croll, P. (1980). *Inside the Primary Classroom.* London: Routledge and Kegan Paul.

Howe, M.J.A. (1988). Intelligence as an explanation. *British Journal of Psychology, 72,* 349–60.

Kamin, L.S. (1974). *The Science and Politics of IQ.* Chichester: Wiley.

Kolligian, J. & Sternberg, R.J. (1987). Intelligence, information processing and specific learning disabilities: A triarchic synthesis. *Journal of Learning Disabilities, 20,* 8–17.

Larsen, S.C., Parker, R.M. & Hammill, R.D. (1987). Effectiveness of psycholinguistic training: A response to Kavale. *Exceptional Children, 49,* 60–6.

Lindsay, G. (1984). *Screening for Children with Special Needs.* London: Croom Helm.

Mackintosh, N.J. & Maskie-Taylor, C.G.N. (1985). The I.Q. question. In: *Education for All: The Swann Report,* 126–163, Cmnd 9453. London: HMSO.

Messerer, J., Hunt, E., Myers, G. & Lerner, J. (1984). Feuerstein's instrumental enrichment. A new approach for activating intellectual potential in learning disabled youth. *Journal of Learning Disabilities,* 322–5.

Miller, A. (1987). Cognitive styles: An integrated model. *Educational Psychology, 7,* 251–68.

Mortimore, P., Sammons, P., Stoll, L., Lewis, O. & Ecob, R. (1988). *School Matters; The Junior Years.* London: Open Books.

Newton, M. & Thomson, M. (1976). *The Aston Index.* Wisbech: LDA.

Stenhouse, L. (1975). *An Introduction to Curriculum Research and Development*. London: Heinemann Educational.

Sternberg, R.J. (1985). *Beyond I.Q.: The Triarchic Theory of Intelligence*. Cambridge: Cambridge University Press.

Sternberg, R.J. & Detterman, D.K. (1986). *What is Intelligence?* Norwood, NJ: Ablex.

Tansley, P. & Panckhurst, J. (1981). *Children with Specific Learning Difficulties*. Windsor: NFER-NELSON.

van der Wissel, A. (1987). I.Q. profiles of learning disabled and mildly retarded children. A psychometric selection effect. *British Journal of Developmental Psychology, 5,* 45–52.

The Assessment of Written Language Skills

Margaret J. Snowling

Throughout their daily lives, children are immersed in language. However, on entering school, many are for the first time faced with a more formal language system than the one which suffices for interaction with their peers and for communication within the family. They will have to use this system proficiently when listening and talking with their teacher, when following instructions and, especially, when learning to read and write. It is not surprising, therefore, that school achievement is largely determined by verbal ability and that vocabulary is an excellent predictor of educational potential. The corollary of this is that children with language difficulties are 'at risk' of educational failure in the classroom. This chapter is particularly concerned with a variety of difficulties which children face when acquiring written language skills, namely, reading, spelling and writing and how these might be affected by deficits in underlying spoken language. In short, it deals with the interface between spoken and written language processing and aims to show how a range of different literacy problems can be effectively assessed.

In carrying out the detailed assessments needed to pinpoint the reasons for a child's difficulty, it may be necessary to examine functioning of the underlying spoken language system. For instance, children with speech-articulation difficulties (sometimes called 'dyspraxic') have inordinate difficulty with the sound processing skills required for spelling (Snowling and Stackhouse, 1983). In contrast, children who have difficulty with language concepts are 'at risk' of reading comprehension deficits (Snowling and Frith, 1986). The speech therapist and teacher working in collaboration are ideally placed to carry out such assessments using a range of standardized tests and clinical procedures (Klein, 1985; Stackhouse, 1985).

Similarly, a multiprofessional approach will be important when assessing the needs of bilingual children. The reading difficulties of these children may be attributable to differences between the sound system they use and that of English, or to a restricted command of the language, leading to problems with reading comprehension and throughout the curriculum. A judicious selection of standard and non-standard procedures can always be used to analyse the most subtle of written language difficulties, provided that the tester has theoretical understanding of reading and spelling development. One framework is that proposed by Frith (1985) who sees the child as passing through three phases during literacy development.

Assessment of Literacy Skills

A comprehensive assessment of written language skills should always include an evaluation of both reading and spelling. This is important because some children with early reading problems may overcome these to be left with severe spelling difficulties. Moreover, groups of children who experience spelling difficulty (dysgraphia) in the absence of reading impairment have been described by Nelson and Warrington (1974) and Frith (1980) amongst others. The opposite pattern, that of reading difficulty in the absence of spelling deficit, has rarely been reported, although it is not so unusual to find children whose reading and spelling is proficient at single-word level, but who have problems in understanding what they read. This emphasized the fact that reading assessment should explore comprehension as well as decoding strategies. A sample of free writing should also be examined during a comprehensive assessment for a number of reasons. First to make an assessment of writing fluency and handwriting skill. Second, to estimate the frequency with which spelling mistakes normally occur and, importantly, to make a qualitative assessment of the child's spontaneous use of language when writing.

Ideally written language assessment should make use of both standardized and non-standard procedures (Snowling, 1985). Standardized tests are useful for screening purposes, particularly, for deciding whether or not a child is performing at the age-appropriate level. In conjunction with a test of general ability, these tests are frequently used to decide whether a child is generally shown in their reading and spelling development or whether they have specific learning difficulty which is impeding progress (Hulme and Snowling, in press; Yule and Rutter, 1985). When followed up with qualitative analysis of reading and spelling strategies, using criterion-referenced tests, the assessment can produce a baseline from which to recommend teaching programmes and against which to monitor progress (see Figure 4.1).

The choice of standardized test is a matter of preference, no hard and fast rules can be set. This chapter will deal with some tried and tested instruments, which illustrate a useful and informative approach to assessment. We shall begin with an approach to the testing of reading, which is capable of unveiling at least two types of problem, one with decoding and one with comprehension strategies. We shall discuss two contrasting cases showing how these deficits can be traced to problems in different underlying language skills.

READING AS A DECODING SKILL

Arguably, the quickest and most efficient means of testing reading is by using a graded single-word reading test. Most teachers and psychologists will be familiar with these and may use them routinely to estimate a child's Reading Age. They can also be used as an initial way of gaining insight into a child's reading difficulty. Well-known tests such as the *Schonell Graded Word Reading Test*, the *Burt (Rearranged) Word Reading Test* or more up-to-date versions such as the *British Abilities Scales Word Reading Test* (available only to psychologists) can, if used systematically, give enormously useful information over and above the 'standard score. The careful examiner can take

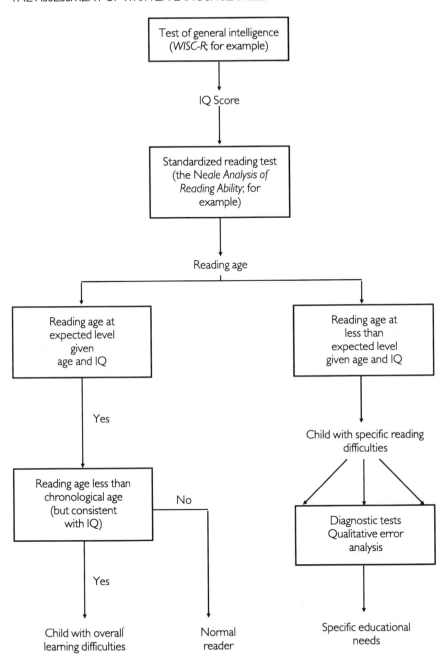

Figure 4.1: Flow diagram to elucidate the steps involved in reading assessment

note of the words which the child reads automatically. If these are pronounced correctly, then it can be assumed that they form part of the child's sight vocabulary (Boder, 1973), that is, that the child has some initial image or representation of that word. If an incorrect reading is given, then errors can be analysed to see whether they share visual similarity with the targets, as would be expected in the early phase of development, or whether this approach is atypical given the level of attainment the child has reached. If the examiner also notes the words which are read following analysis of their sounds, a judgement can be made about the proficiency of 'word attack' or phonic skills.

To illustrate, let us examine the reading errors of two children, both with specific reading difficulties, who were reading at the seven-year level on the BAS Word Reading Test. The first, Lynn, aged 11 years, gave fast responses to the words she read correctly, suggesting reliance on a sight vocabulary. However, while automatic, many of her responses were incorrect; she read at as 'that', men as 'man', dig as 'big', skin as 'sky', climb as 'club', chain as 'chair' and beard as 'bread'. She used 'word-attack' skills only rarely and she was never successful. She read travel as 'tra', glove as 'glow' and calf as 'kaf'. Her difficulty with these so-called 'phonological' reading strategies was borne out when she was explicitly asked to pronounce nonwords which, by their very nature, she had never seen before. She found this extremely difficult and made many errors even with simple syllables such as zuk, tig.

The second child, Tom, aged 10 years, displayed a very different approach. He seldom responded quickly when faced with a word. He did make a few visual errors (for example, he read army as 'arm', chain as 'chin') but primarily, he sounded-out words. He was often successful although errors included pronouncing gate as 'gat', coat as 'kort', heel as 'hill', ladies as 'laddies', leather as 'lever' and lawn as 'loan'. Tom's nonword reading was relatively good, attesting to the proficiency of phonological reading strategies.

These observations suggested that, while both Lynn and Tom were struggling to attain reading skills, they had adopted different approaches. Teaching factors may have had a role to play, although, to date, we have little empirical evidence on this point. Specifically, Lynn was relying heavily upon a visual approach. She required help with decoding skills, perhaps with an emphasis upon a phonic approach. Tom, however, required a different teaching strategy. He was already relying heavily upon alphabetic skills and indeed, he would frequently sound-out words. He needed to increase his sight vocabulary so that reading would become more automatic. This could perhaps best be done through a paired-reading technique supplemented by explicit training to expand his sight vocabulary, or through a 'real books' approach introduced at this stage. Analysis of Lynn and Tom's performance on the single-word reading test tells us nothing about their ability to understand what they read or about whether they can use context to facilitate decoding. Unfortunately, the standardized tests which are available for examining such skills would have to be used cautiously with these children. Since their reading is still at a relatively low level of proficiency, they need to devote considerable attention to the decoding aspect of reading. Thus, a failure to understand what they read may reflect capacity limitations rather than comprehension problems per se. In this instance, a test of listening comprehension can provide useful information. Essentially, if the children can report back what they have heard when they have listened to, rather than read, a story of equivalent difficulty, then it is reasonable to conclude that they have no genuine difficulty with the language skills which are needed to read for meaning.

ASSESSING 'VISUAL' AND PHONOLOGICAL READING STRATEGIES

Before moving on to examine ways of testing reading comprehension, I should like to mention some psycholinguistic tasks which are useful in conjunction with standardized reading tests, to firm-up a tester's opinion that the child being seen is using visual and/or phonological reading strategies. These tasks (abbreviated forms are shown in Box 4.1) are based on those devised by cognitive psychologists to test various component processes of a model of reading (Ellis, 1984).

Box 4.1		
Psycholinguistic tasks for the assessment of reading strategies		
Test 1		Test 2
Regular	Irregular	Non-words
grill	flood	plood
lime	pint	jint
task	dove	pove
hatch	bread	cread
plug	bowl	nowl
cask	vase	jase
match	breath	freath
bitter	double	louble
organ	lever	dever
mixture	colonel	polonel
thimble	biscuit	kiscuit

Test 1 requires subjects to read aloud sets of regular and irregular words, matched for frequency and number of letters. Regular words are words containing consistent grapheme–phoneme correspondences. They can be read either by phonological means (by letter–sound translation) or, if they are familiar, by visual means. In contrast, irregular words contains inconsistent or unusual spelling patterns and, if read by letter–sound translation are mispronounced, for example broad read as 'brode'. Children who are in the first phase of reading development should have equal chance of reading regular and irregular words correctly provided they are matched for frequency of occurrence, whereas children at a later stage should find regular words easier because they can be read phonologically. When seven-year-old readers were tested, we found that they read 56 per cent of regular and 31 per cent of irregular words correctly, suggesting they could use phonological reading strategies to supplement their visual sight vocabulary.

Test 2 requires subjects to pronounce printed nonwords derived from the irregular words in Test 1 by changing one phoneme, usually the initial one. Nonword reading provides an excellent test of alphabetic competence. We found that seven year olds reading at a level consistent with their age could pronounce some 50 per cent of one-syllable and 30 per cent of two-syllable nonwords correctly when we counted either rule-based ('hig-nu' for *hign*) or analogic ('hine' for *hign*) responses to be counted as correct.

To illustrate the use of these non-standard procedures and to show how a child's performance can point to the 'cause' of his or her reading problem, I shall mention two further cases, beginning with J.M., a child with developmental 'phonological' dyslexia (Snowling, Stackhouse and Rack, 1986). J.M. was referred to us with a history of speech difficulties. He had first been assessed by a speech therapist at three years and two months when he was not using sentences and his pronounciation of single words was unclear. He progressed well during six months of therapy and was discharged. When seen for educational assessment some some five years later, his speech was acceptable but a speech therapy opinion stated:

> Although J.M.'s speech is intelligible in everyday conversation, closer examination reveals residual difficulties of a phonetic and phonological nature. There is incoordination of the vocal tract leading to difficulties in particular with voice/voiceless contrast, articulatory and prosodic difficulties, and vocabulary limitations.

On the basis of his superior level of intelligence (IQ = 123) J.M.'s predicted Reading Age at that time was nine years four months but he had only reached the seven years five months level on the *Schonell Graded Word Reading Test*. Similarly, his predicted spelling age was eight years 11 months, but achievement measured at the six years seven months level on the *Schonell Graded Word Spelling Test*. In five minutes he could only produce a one line 'story':

> A little Roridn with a red best

Rather than dwelling upon his performance on standardized tests, let us turn to look at J.M.'s performance on the psycholinguistic tasks mentioned above. To assess the extent to which J.M. relied upon word-specific (visual) information during reading and how much he leant on phonological (phonic) reading strategies, we asked him to pronouce sets of regular and irregular printed words. When J.M.'s performance was compared with that of average readers who had reached the same level of reading on a standardized reading test (reading age-matched controls), there was a significant difference. As already mentioned, normal seven year olds read more regular than irregular words. However, this was not true of J.M. He did as well as them when reading irregular words but did not reap the same advantage when attempting the regular words. It would be argued that he was still operating at the early stage of reading. Moreover, his reading errors resembled their targets visually even though the letter order within them was not preserved. Some 47 per cent were of this kind (for example, he read sign as 'sing', bowl as 'blow', organ as 'orange'), and on 22 per cent of occasions, when he tried to use sound he ultimately made a guess (for example, he read flood as 'fault', bleat as 'built').

To confirm our impression that J.M. was relying upon visual reading strategies, we asked him to read aloud the nonwords derived from the real words he had already read. As predicted, J.M. had great difficulty. While average seven year olds could read approximately 50 per cent of single syllable non-words correctly, he had no success whatsoever. Many of his attempts were 'lexicalizations' (for example, he read plood as 'pool', hign as 'high', swad as 'want', wamp as 'warm'). So we could be certain that J.M. was still using visual strategies to access the lexicon.

From the point of view of remediation, we would want to know more precisely, where, in terms of sub-skills underlying reading, intervention should be made with J.M. Undoubtedly he was having difficulty in acquiring phonological reading strategies but where, exactly, was this difficulty located? To investigate this we first tested his ability to discriminate between minimal pairs of auditorily presented words (for example, pit–bit, goat–coat) using the *Wepman Test of Auditory Discrimination*. This was important because, if he could not tell sounds apart when he heard them, then he would certainly be unable to learn grapheme–phoneme correspondences. However, he gained a perfect score suggesting that he had no peripheral auditory perceptual problems. Next, we asked him to decide whether pairs of spoken words rhymed or not for example, rope–soap, brown–bone (see Box 3.2). Rhyming is thought to be one of the basic sound categorization skills required for satisfactory reading development (Maclean, Bryant and Bradley, 1987). On this test, J.M. made 5/24 errors, significantly more than to be expected considering his age and intelligence. Not surprisingly, he also had problems with the *Bradley Test of Auditory Organisation* (Bradley, 1980). This test asks the child to decide which of four spoken words is the odd one out. In one section, three are alliterative, the fourth begins with a different sound (for example, lick, lid, miss, lip). In two sections, three rhyme and one does not (for example, lot, cot, pot, hat). Performance on this test is known to be a good predictor of reading and spelling achievement and a child who has difficulties with it can benefit from training in sound categorization (Bradley and Bryant, 1983).

Box 4.2

Test of Auditory Rhyme Judgement

rope – soap	head – said
cash – wash	stood – blood
bird – word	cool – pull
gun – fun	pipe – ripe
cough – though	how – go
brown – bone	tree – bee

So, J.M. had difficulty with sound categorization and phoneme segmentation skills. His auditory short-term memory span was also limited and he had residual speech-articulation difficulties. I would like to argue that, in combination, these difficulties were preventing him from acquiring alphabetic skills. Interestingly, some four years later, his difficulties have altered little (Snowling and Hulme, in preparation). He has increased his reading age, as measured by word reading, but he still makes visual errors and his nonword reading remains poor. He has received excellent remedial help in the intervening time, pointing all the more to the intransigence of his problem. There is therefore a need for screening and assessment procedures to be administered as soon after school entry as possible.

J.M.'s case represents just one possible profile on the non-standard tests. A contrasting one was seen in the case of P.F, a nine year old whose reading age was seven years six months, similar to that of J.K. P.F. was referred with a history of fluctuating hearing loss. However, when assessed, her hearing was found to be within normal limits. Standardized testing showed that P.F. had specific reading difficulties, with decoding affected more than comprehension skills. Thus, on the *Neale Analysis of Reading Ability*, she gained a reading age of seven years 11 months for accuracy, nine years five months for comprehension. First, P.F. was asked to read the regular and irregular words attempted by J.M. and normal controls. She showed a marked regularity effect, reading 89 per cent of regular but only 26 per cent of irregular words correctly. Moreover, her reading errors confirmed her extreme reliance on phonological decoding strategies, she read sword as 'sw-ord', bowl as 'bowel', bread as 'breed' and wand as 'wanned'. Next P.F. attempted the nonwords which were derived from the words she had already read. She did extremely well on this test, pronouncing 84 per cent correctly. Thus, her performance was markedly better than that of J.M. and, interestingly, also better than reading age matched controls in the sense that she was using phonetic decoding skills more than them. In actual fact, this was the basis of P.F.'s problem. In the face of a slow start with reading, probably because of her hearing problems, she had been introduced to a strict phonic teaching regime. It would now be necessary to take the emphasis away from this piecemeal approach, to introduce her to higher-order grapheme–phoneme correspondence rules rather than simple letter–sound correspondences, and to help her to build a sight vocabulary.

Thus, the non-standard tests shown in Box 4.1 can be used to confirm the type of reading strategy a child is applying and thereby to specify educational needs. Children who perform like J.M. on these psycholinguistic tests have been described as 'developmental phonological dyslexic children', while those who perform like P.F. have been termed 'developmental surface dyslexic children'. At present, we know most about the etiology of the first 'type' of dyslexia and remain uncertain as to whether these children differ in terms of their underlying language skills from the children with surface dyslexia, or whether the difference is a superficial one associated with teaching factors (Hulme and Snowling, in press). In P.F.'s case, at least, this seems to be a possibility.

READING AS A COMPREHENSION SKILL

Testing reading comprehension can be undertaken in a number of ways. At the most basic level, children might be asked to choose one of several alternative printed words to correspond with a definition which they also read (for example, an exact copy is a: dungeon, doubt, deposit, draughty, dumpling, duplicate). The SPAR Test (Young, 1976) utilizes this procedure and is popular because it can easily be administered to groups of children. However, if by reading comprehension is meant the ability to extract meaning from text and to integrate this with general knowledge as the 'story' unfolds, then the SPAR has grave limitations. Many practitioners like to use cloze procedures whereby the children will independently read a text and, at intervals, complete a 'gap' with an appropriate word. For instance, 'there was a chest of...and a cupboard to put things...' The Gap Test is a good example (McLeod, 1970). The major disadvantage of this technique is that it taps production as well as reading ability. So, a child reluctant to write, perhaps because of a spelling problem, will be penalized. Hence, if time permits, the individual administration of a test in which the child reads a story and then discussses its content is preferred.

Standardized testing of prose reading is the Neale Analysis of Reading Ability (Neale, 1958; Revised Edition, 1989). Children read aloud short passages and are then asked questions about them. Separate measures of reading accuracy and reading comprehension are obtained and a reading rate can also be derived. The test has three parallel forms which is advantageous for the purposes of retesting. An alternative test, is the New Macmillan Reading Analysis (Vincent and de la Mare, 1985). The test is similar in principle to the Neale, producing age equivalent scores for both accuracy and comprehension measures.

V.C. was an eight-year-old child, thought by her teachers to be good at reading and spelling. On the British Ability Scales Word Reading Test, she scored at the eight years eight months level and her reading errors were quite characteristic for someone of her age. In line with this, she gained an age equivalent score of between eight years six months and nine years seven months on the New Macmillan. However, comprehension of what she read was weak. According to the test norms her comprehension age was within the range seven years five months to nine years two months. Observation of her performance suggests that it was more realistic to place her ability at the lower end of this range. When asked questions concerning the content of what she had read, V.C. was at a total loss. Had she not been told to look back over the text for the answer, she would seldom have given any response. As it was, Vicky could sometimes locate the answer by virtue of her decoding skill and, when she did, she would simply read out the relevant section from the passage. This strategy suggested that Vicky was unable to integrate the details of the text as she read it and was not, therefore, following story meaning. A nice feature of the New Macmillan (also the new edition of the Neale) is that one of the comprehension questions asks the child to make an inference based on what they think should happen next or to speculate about the reason why something happened. In no case was V.C. able to do this. She was unable to go beyond the information given and could only report story-content by scanning back over what she had already read. To illustrate, V.C. read the following passage making only two minor errors (given in parentheses):

> It was late at night and Alex was on her way home. The roads were silent and empty and all the houses were dark. It was then (when) she heard tremendous (trendous) noise about her. Alex looked up into the night sky. She could hardly believe her eyes. Some kind of huge aircraft was hovering above the town. It had flashing lights in many different colours. What she saw next she would remember all her life.

When asked what was the first unusual thing to happen she said 'There was an aircraft in the sky'. Not only was this the incorrect answer but also, it would seldom, in reality, be an unusual thing. She did not know what was unusual about the aircraft but, when asked how she could tell something exciting happened after Alex saw the aircraft, she read out verbatim from the text; 'it had flashing lights in many different colours'. She thought the aircraft had come from 'the sky', a literal answer where a speculative response, such as 'from Mars' was required. So, V.C.'s responses illustrate her difficulties with what might be called 'on-line' story processing. Moreover, it seemed that she totally misconstrued the nature of the reading task. She could read aloud well but, in so doing, devoted all her attention to the decoding process, ignoring the story as it developed.

The developmental dissociation between decoding and comprehension skill, hinted at with V.C., is more striking when one compared J.M. (described above) with S.H. These two boys were seen when they were 12 and ten years respectively to assess their educational needs at that time. First, it is important to point to the specificity of the boys' reading problems. Both were of above average intelligence; J.M.'s WISC-R IQ score was 123 which is within the superior range, S.H.'s was 112 which is bright average. Moreover, both did better on performance than on verbal tests, the discrepancy being greater in the case of S.H. (132 versus 94) than J.M. (128 versus 113).

However, on the *Neale Analysis of Reading Ability* (1956), they obtained contrasting profiles. (Please note that the Revised Edition of the *Neale Analysis* was not available when the study was carried out.) J.M. gained a reading age of nine years two months for accuracy and 11 years one month for comprehension — he had a specific decoding difficulty but, nonetheless, could understand what he read well. In contrast, S.H. achieved a reading age of 11 years one month for accuracy but only eight years ten months for comprehension — he had a specific comprehension problem.

The differences in the their performance can perhaps best be illustrated by examining their responses when asked to read one of the passages of the *Neale*. We will concentrate here upon the first half of a story about the slaying of a dragon. The story goes:

> The fearful roaring of the dragon guided the knight to the monster's territory. As the intruder crossed the dreaded marshes, the dragon charged furiously, whipping its enormous tail around the legs of the knight's steed. The knight now realised that he must attack when the creature was off-guard...

On this section of the test, J.M. made the following reading errors: he read territory as 'terror', intruder as 'intricate', charged as 'changed', its as 'his', steed as 'steer', collapsed as 'elapsed'. S.H. made far fewer errors; he read the as 'a' and whipping as 'whipped'. It was therefore astonishing to find that S.H.'s comprehension was much less good than that of J.M. When asked how the knight knew exactly where to find the dragon, J.M. replied 'By his fearful roar', S.H. replied that he didn't think he did. In response to 'What kind of land did the knight have to cross over?', J.M. correctly said 'Dreaded marshes', S.H. said 'Unknown territory'. Finally, J.M. said that a good moment to attack the dragon would be when he was off-guard, S.H. thought when he was asleep. Hence, J.M. had a much better grasp of story content than S.H. despite the difficulty he had in actually reading the text aloud. Moreover, on diagnostic tests of sentence and text processing, J.M. performed relatively better than younger average readers of similar decoding skill (Snowling and Hulme, in preparation). S.H., on the other hand, performed less well than children with a mild reading difficulty whose mental age was around seven years (Snowling and Frith, 1986).

In S.H.'s case it was unlikely, given his IQ, that a lack of general knowledge could account for his comprehension difficulty or for the superficial way in which he was processing the text. In principle though, his difficulty could still have arisen for any one of several reasons. Perhaps it was that he read too fast to make sense of the text. Alternatively he may have had difficulty with the meanings of the individual words, with the syntactic structures of the sentences or maybe he simply forgot what he read. An examiner would almost certainly want to go on to explore these various possibilities to determine best how to help him. Together with Hazel Dewart, I did just this and we would argue that S.H. had specific problems with semantic retrieval. I shall now try to show how we came to this conclusion.

EXPLORING THE REASONS FOR COMPREHENSION FAILURE

From the outset we felt certain that S.H.'s problems were not related to memory deficits. On WISC-R Digit Span, a test of auditory memory, he gained a scaled score of 12 which is high average. This contrasts dramatically with J.M.'s scaled score which was only seven ('dull average'). S.H. could remember six digits forwards and four in reverse order, a normal verbal span for his age. WISC-R subtest scores gave us a further lead; for Similarities (a test of verbal reasoning and concept attainment) S.H. achieved a scaled score of seven which is 'dull average', compared with J.M. who gained a very superior score of 16. For Vocabulary, a test in which words have to be defined, S.H.'s scaled score was six, again 'dull average' while J.M.'s was 13 'bright average'.

Considering S.H.'s poor performance on these verbal tests relative to overall IQ, we explored his underlying language skills further. Specifically, we focused on this knowledge of word meanings and how easily these could be accessed within semantic memory. To this end, we administered three standardized tests. His performance on BAS Word Definitions confirmed the difficulty he had on the previous vocabulary test – this time he scored only at the first centile. Next his Verbal Fluency was tested using another of the British Ability Scales' tests. He was asked to bring to mind as many animal names and as many foods as he could, given one minute for each task. Responses were slow and effortful, he could think of very few items in either case and his score fell at the fifth centile. It was clear, therefore, that S.H. had semantic problems but still not clear whether his difficulty was one of lack of knowledge (this seemed unlikely given his general intellectual level), or one of a failure to bring to mind the information he had available.

To investigate this, we tested his receptive vocabulary, that is his ability to match spoken words with pictures, to see whether he would do any better when he did not have to express himself verbally. We used the *British Picture Vocabulary Scales* (Dunn et al., 1982) in which one of four alternative pictures has to be selected to correspond with an auditorily presented word. On this test, S.H. did much better; he gained a standard score of 107 which is at the 68th centile. This is more in line with IQ. Finally, to check that S.H. could understand the range of syntactic structures which he might encounter during reading, he was administered the *Test of the Reception of Grammar* (Bishop, 1982), known as *TROG*. In this test, one of four alternative pictures has to be matched with a spoken sentence for example, 'the boy chasing the horse is fat', 'the pencil is above the flower'. He scored at the 50th centile on this test, which is perfectly average for his age. Therefore a specific problem with the comprehension of syntactic structures could be ruled out. This was not true in the case of V.C. mentioned above, who scored below her age-expectation on the *TROG* test.

So, the results of standardized testing suggested that S.H. had a sizeable vocabulary for his age. However, he had great difficulty in accessing this word-knowledge. This was especially true when time limits were imposed, for example, when his verbal fluency was tested. Informal observations made by his teacher bore out this characterization. Thus, when asked by her what 'amuse' meant he said 'I know what amusing means – interesting, like and an amusing room...well, no, I don't know what amusing means'. When asked to define 'capture' he said, 'I saw a capture programme' then, 'I have a cage for a capture' then, 'I catched...catchured...can't do it'. He seemed to have difficulty in reaching the precise meaning of words which, none the less, he could discriminate from distractors. We predicted that this would affect his reading considerably. His proficient decoding skill would allow him to reach the pronounciations of words on the page quickly but he would inevitably be slow to access their meaning. This mismatch between decoding and comprehension speeds would result in comprehension failure. To improve his reading skill we suggested that he would benefit from language therapy aimed at improving vocabulary and expressive language skills. More importantly, when reading, he needed to slow down his rate of decoding, and to focus on the meaning of the text as it unfolded. This might be done by using cloze procedures or, less formally, by promoting dialogue around the story as it developed.

Returning to J.M., he had no difficulty whatsoever with the language tasks which S.H. had failed. On an experimental definitions task (Snowling, Van Wagtendonk and Stafford, in press), he failed to define only four relatively obscure words (stethoscope, abacus, balalaika, gondola) producing a score of 62/66. The test was discontinued with S.H. after 33 items, 21 of which he was unable to define.

The Assessment of Spelling

Discussion so far has focused upon reading and the skills which are presumed to underlie it. While reading experience is undoubtedly crucial for the satisfactory development of spelling, spelling is in fact an independent process and failure to assess this important production skill will seriously limit the usefulness of educational assessment. For the purposes of spelling assessment, it is important for the examiner to make reference to a theoretical model of the spelling process. It is widely held that there are at least two processes by which a word can be spelled. The first involves directly accessing an internal dictionary or 'lexicon' in which spelling information is abstractly represented. If the spelling of a word is known, then it can be automatically written on the basis of this information. Children who are in the early stage of learning will of course not have many words represented in this way. Thus, in order to write they will have to rely heavily upon a second, indirect, route which makes use of letter–sound rules. The use of this phonological route requires phoneme segmentation and sequencing skill and therefore will pose a challenge to children with auditory processing problems.

It is necessary to distinguish at least three sorts or error; phonetic errors, which when read back sound correct, non-phonetic errors which do not correctly portray the sound sequence of the word and semi-phonetic errors which contain characteristic developmental immaturities (Ehri, 1985). Examples of these various error types are shown in Box 4.3.

Box 4.3		
Spelling Errors		
Phonetic errors	Semi-phonetic errors	Non-phonetic errors
young/yung	mind/mid	health/helef
thumb/thum	train/chan	direct/bricet
does/dose	help/hep	final/finial
white/wite	friends/freds	chemistry/camaste
umbrella/umbreler	contented/cotentid	numbering/nundrin
calculator/calqulater	cigarette/sigret	geography/gohhary

The distinction between phonetic and non-phonetic errors is relatively straightforward. However, it is more difficult to decide which errors can be classified as semi-phonetic. We have argued elsewhere that these are the types of errors which all children make when they are still relatively inexperienced with respect to spelling conventions (Snowling et al., 1986).

Thus, they will predominate in the spelling of beginners. Read (1986) observed that young children at this stage will tend to simplify consonant clusters in their writing for example, test for tent, fez for friends. These errors can still be found in the spelling of polysyllabic words by children under nine years of age (for example, refreshmet for refreshment, instucted for instructed). Similarly, children tend to omit unstressed syllables in a rule-governed way (fing for finger, sigret for cigarette) and to misrepresent vowel sounds. It should be stressed that, if the majority of a child's spelling errors are semi-phonetic, it is likely that they are progressing normally and, with increasing reading experience, spelling will improve. These errors are quite different from the non-phonetic ones made by children with genuine spelling difficulties. Remedial work need not, therefore, be centred around them.

So, when assessing spelling performance, the main question to have in mind is whether the child has normal use of phonological (alphabetic) spelling strategies. If they have, then their spelling errors will be phonetic or in some instances semi-phonetic, and it can be concluded that their phoneme segmentation and sequencing skills are normal. If, on the other hand, spelling is primarily non-phonetic, then difficulties with phonological processing skills are to be anticipated. Different forms of remediation are required in the two cases.

STANDARD TESTING OF SPELLING

Ideally spelling ability should be evaluated in at least two settings: formally by means of a spelling test and, informally, through scrutiny of free writing. This is because some children will spell well when their full attention is devoted to the task but will make errors when they are concentrating upon getting their ideas down onto paper. Alternatively, an instrument like the *Diagnostic Spelling Test* (Vincent and Claydon, 1982) taps a range of spelling skills. This test (suitable for seven to 11 year olds) comprises seven subtests as shown in Box 4.4. They follow the theoretical work of Peters (1967) and seek to indicate directions which practical work might take.

Thus, in the Homophone Test, the child has to choose between two alternative spellings:

for example, I want to write/right a story

Box 4.4

Diagnostic Spelling Test

(Vincent and Claydon, 1982)

Test 1 Homophones	Test 5 Nonsense Words
Test 2 Common Words	Test 6 Dictionary Use
Test 3 Proof Reading	Test 7 Self Concept
Test 4 Letter Strings	Diagnostic Dictation

Children who do poorly on this test are relying heavily upon the phonological strategies characteristic of the alphabetic phase. The Common Words Test invites children to complete sentences to comply with picture and first letter clues:

> for example, The door to my...is painted black

It is a criterion-referenced test, the results of which can be analysed qualitatively and in conjunction with the results of a diagnostic dictation, which is also included. Tests three to five tap the ability to analyse words in terms of their visual characteristics (letter-by-letter structures). Remedial prescriptions follow directly from these as they can from the Dictionary Test which requires the child to find target words in alphabetically arranged lists.

Two of the most popular spelling tests in the UK at present are the *Schonell* and the *Vernon Graded Word Spelling Tests*. Both require the examinee to write down single words to dictation, a sentence context being provided in the case of the Vernon. It is important, however, to add a definition to some of the *Schonell* words to avoid confusion between homophones (for example, see, fare). However, the results of a spelling test (usually described as a spelling age), on their own, tell us little about the reasons for a child's difficulty or about the type of remedial assistance they require. To this end, examiners should carry out a qualitative analysis of spelling errors, placing them in the context of spelling development and thereby identifying typical and atypical processes.

In the literature, the claim is often made that reading and spelling strategies can be different in nature, that is, children may use phonological strategies efficiently for spelling but not for reading or, that a child might rely heavily upon sound-based strategies for reading but make non-phonetic spelling mistakes. Nonetheless, there is frequently a coincidence between the types of strategy that children use for the two tasks. Take Lynn and Tom, children with specific reading difficulties mentioned at the beginning of the chapter. Just as their approach to reading differed, so did their spelling. Both gained spelling ages of around seven years on the *Vernon* test but observation of their approach, together with analysis of their errors, suggested that Lynn had segmentation difficulties precluding the use of phonological rules, while Tom relied upon phonological spelling strategies. The children's attempts at the words they spelled incorrectly are shown in Table 4.1.

ASSESSING SPELLING STRATEGIES

One disadvantage of graded spelling tests is that the examiner is generally discouraged from continuing above the child's 'ceiling'. This can mean that the sample of words they will attempt is biased according to frequency of occurrence and, in particular, syllable length. A beginning speller, for example, would seldom be asked to attempt words of six or more letters. This limits the information which can be gleaned about the proficiency of underlying sub-skills. To illustrate, in the case of Lynn and Tom, our picture of their strengths and weaknesses was confirmed quickly by asking them to spell the words cigarette, umbrella, contented and refreshment, having first assured them that these were especially difficult words just for them to

Table 4.1: Spelling errors made by two children who gained similar scores on the Vernon Graded Word Spelling Test

Target	Lynn	Tom
head	hurd	hed
paint	pater	pant
chair	chain	chere
young	youne	yug
pencil	piensh	pensill
thumb	pham	thum

'try'. Lynn's spellings were as follows: seiulgret, unrleler, coted, feshmun, confirming the problems she had with sound segmentation and sequencing. Tom's spellings were, in contrast, easily deciphered: sigeret, umbreler, contentard, refreshut. There was therefore no reason to suspect that he had phoneme segmentation problems. On the contrary, development appeared to be along normal lines, even though it was proceeding slowly.

Thus, if a standardized spelling test is to be used to measure spelling attainment, it is important to supplement it with a non-standard procedure to increase diagnostic power. Typically, I would administer 10 one-, two- and three-syllable spellings and look at the phonetic accuracy with which the

---

Box 4.5

Diagnostic Spelling Test

(Snowling, 1985)

One syllable	Two syllables	Three syllables
pet	apple	membership
lip	puppy	cigarette
cap	packet	catalogue
fish	trumpet	September
sack	kitten	adventure
tent	traffic	contented
trap	collar	refreshment
bump	tulip	instructed
nest	polish	umbrella
bank	finger	understand

child could spell these (Snowling, 1985; see Box 4.5). However, what is most important is that an examiner selects a number of words of varying structure which they routinely administer so that they can use these systematically to observe the approach and strategies of different children. For instance, returning to J.M. and S.H., they attempted an identical set of non-standardized three- and four-syllable words. Given J.M.'s phonological difficulties, we can anticipate that his errors will be primarily non-phonetic. In contrast, there is no reason to suspect S.H. to have a spelling problem given that his difficulties were primarily related to comprehension processes.

Table 4.2. shows, as expected, that not only was S.H. a better speller than J.M. but also that his spelling errors were primarily phonetic. This attests to the normality of his phonological skills. S.H.'s spelling had developed at the expected rate but this had not been possible for J.M. because of his problems with phoneme segmentation, auditory sequencing and short-term memory. This forces us to suggest that J.M. needed help with basic auditory-phonological skills, a similar conclusion to that made from observation of his reading performance.

Table 4.2: Spellings of three- and four-syllable words by J.M. and S.H.

Target	J.M.	S.H.
membership	menbership	/
understand	unstand	/
cigarette	cigeret	ciggaret
catalogue	carherlog	caterloce
September	septenber	/
adventure	adventer	/
contented	/	/
refreshment	refeashment	/
instructed	intertdie	instrukted
umbrella	unbeller	/
mysterious	missdeos	misterios
machinery	misshieote	/
politician	poeotison	politition
congratulate	conrolate	/
geography	geogren	/
magnificent	megnifsent	magnifisant
calculator	cowoleter	calcuator
discovery	dishavere	/
radiator	radeator	radeator
automatic	atormatic	/

Specific spelling problems.

The other major subgroup of children with spelling problems are those whose spelling is perfectly phonetic but does not obey English orthographic conventions. The difficulties of this group of children are poorly under-stood. Some people think they are simply 'lazy' while others ascribe their problems to the illogicality of the English spelling system. Clinical observa-tion suggests that these individuals often have a higher Verbal than Perfor-mance IQ (Nelson and Warrington, 1974) but there are no hard and fast rules about this.

Frith (1980) has suggested that, although they are usually good readers, they in fact read differently to good readers who also spell well. Specifically, they pay less visual attention to the 'unimportant' parts of words. They will, for example, miss more of the unstressed e's in e-cancellation tasks than good spellers, whilst checking the same number of stressed e's. Similarly, they are poor at proof-reading. Their problems may therefore be to do with the allocation of visual attention during reading, even though it is their spelling which is specifically impaired.

Simon was boy with just such a spelling problem. I saw him when he was 16 years old and undoubtedly a young man of above average intelligence (*WAIS* IQ = 117). Simon was reported to have had reading problems at an earlier age, but now his problem was specifically with spelling and this was detracting from his work. On the *Schonell Graded Word Spelling Test B* he a gained spelling age of 11 years six months, which was well below expected level. However, without exception, his spelling errors were perfectly phonetic. These are given in Table 4.3.

Table 4.3: Spelling errors made by a bright 16 year old with a specific spelling deficit

Target	Response
stayed	staied
headache	headake
copies	coppies
library	libary
patient	pationt
appreciate	appresheate
familiar	fermiller
sufficient	sufishent
apparatus	apperatous
amateur	amerter

The pattern of phonetic spelling perfomance characteristic of Simon, can be seen at all levels of spelling attainment. Individuals with this type of spell-ing problem need systematic introduction to the spelling patterns and rules of English. This is usually best done using a multisensory teaching approach

(Hornsby, 1985). However, if the individual concerned has already reached a relatively high standard of proficiency, then a remedial programme may most profitably be directed toward teaching the technical vocabulary required for school work or for future career development. Moreover, these days, the use of a word-processor with a 'spell-check' facility can improve the lot of specifically disabled spellers immeasurably.

Creative Writing Skills

It would be inappropriate to complete a chapter on the assessment of written language skills without stressing the importance of examining a child's creative writing ability. The procedures available for doing so however, lag markedly behind those available for the systematic testing of reading and spelling. The examiner must rely primarily upon experience and clinical skill until such time as linguists provide us with more valid and reliable tests. Nonetheless, by adopting a systematic approach, it is possible to begin to specify the nature of a child's writing difficulty (if any) and to decide where intervention is required. Ideally, a timed sample of free writing should be obtained so that a judgement can be made about writing rate, often crucial for the consideration of how a child will fare in an examination setting. As rule of thumb, I normally allow a child between five and ten minutes to produce written work to a previously discussed title. Amongst children with reading or spelling problems, it is astonishing to see the variety of written work which is produced. First, by way of a yardstick, consider the work of Chris, an 11 year old of average intelligence. In five minutes he wrote:

> Manya's dream was to become a scientist but the scientist said, 'Science is for men not for girls, I'll put you down for cookery classes.' Manya went out in a huff and slammed the door. In such countries as France in Paris girls worked just like boys in the same room.
> Manya live(d) in Poland, but in Russia and Poland that was that.

In contrast, Lynn, although of the same age and ability as Chris produced only the following:

> My cat is a sopey (soppy) cat. He is 12 yaers (years) old. I am 11 years old. I like my cat he is my cat not my sister cat or my mum cat or my dad cat. They like my cat veary (very) mash (much).

Chris' work was average for his age. The content was reasonable. He used a variety of sentence structures, including direct speech punctuated appropriately and he sampled a range of vocabulary. Mistakes could be caracterized primarily as slips of the pen. In contrast, Lynn's work was extremely limited. She stuck with one basic sentence structure. Punctuation was restricted to the use of capital letters and full stops, with some indication that she would begin to forget these as time proceeded. It is also noteworthy that Lynn sampled only few vocabulary items, possibly as a way of avoiding spelling mistakes.

The written work of J.M. and S.H. illustrates a further point. It will be recalled that these boys experienced different patterns of language deficit. Taking his expressive language difficulty into consideration, it was anticipated that S.H. would find it more difficult to express himself on paper than

J.M. To an extent this was true, the content of his work was very poor, ideas were limited and vocabulary use was minimal even though he had no reason to avoid words on account of a spelling problem. Thus, in five minutes he wrote:

> If I had won a million pounds I would go out and buy a car and everything else what you possible buy and go home and be rich very rich. Then the next day I would buy the same thing and stuff and be rich very rich. Then the next day I would do the same until I will have no money left.

J.M.'s written work was richer in content but it contained an inordinate number of syntactic and spelling errors, rendering it difficult to decipher. It did not in any way reflect the ability which J.M. showed in spoken communication. In seven minutes he wrote:

> London is the catobal (capital) and (of) England in the street there are (a)lot of black Taxi and larger (large) biling (buildings) The Queen living in london and the street (streets) are cramd (crammed) with people. (A) lot of train (s) come in andout of london to(o) and it verg (very) attpensif (expensive). I think london is a noisey pease and if I live(d) in london I would go mad with all the beep(ing) and bezzing (buzzing) but is had (has) lot(s) of buitfeel (beautiful) porseaton (positions).

Noteworthy were the problems with grammatical endings. He wrote 'living' for lives and omitted the affixes -s, -ed and -ing at various points. He did not make these errors in his speech and therefore, it seemed important to teach him to proof-read his work carefully to avoid them during writing.

To reiterate, standard procedures have not yet been worked out for assessing creative writing skills. However, a sample of free writing can provide a rich source of data for evaluating a child's spelling ability and the skill with which words can be used in writing. Moreover, if the examiner has in mind a 'check-list' for systematic use, a criterion-referenced testing procedure can be devised, against which to monitor progress. In this regard, it would seem important to allow children a specific amount of time in which to write. Attention should then be paid to their writing fluency and rate, the content of their work (the ideas), their use of syntactic structures, vocabulary and punctuation. The extent to which the individual uses planning and checking procedures should also be taken into account. Lastly, presentation both in terms of spelling and handwriting will require evaluation if a teaching programme attuned to individual needs is to be devised.

Conclusion

To conclude, this chapter has dealt with the assessment of reading, spelling, writing and language skills, especially as applied to the child with *specific* written language difficulties. What of the child with overall learning difficulties − the slow learner, whose reading and spelling development will be affected, as will performance in other academic areas? In essence, the same prescriptions apply to these children. There is nothing to rule out the use of the above tests with them. While a slower overall rate of development can be anticipated in this group of children, there are still likely to be wide individual differences, as amongst children of average intelligence. It is not unusual to find problems with reading comprehension associated with poor vocabulary development. However, many other constellations of deficit are possible and as yet, little explored in the research literature.

Please note that the Revised Edition (1989) of the *Neale Analysis of Reading Ability* was not available at the time when this chapter was written.

References

Bishop, D.V.M. (1982). *T.R.O.G. Test for Reception of Grammar.* Abingdon, Oxfordshire: Thomas Leach.

Boder, E. (1973). Developmental dyslexia: a diagnostic approach based on three atypical reading-spelling patterns. *Developmental Medicine and Child Neurology, 15,* 663–87.

Bradley, L. (1980). *Assessing reading difficulties.* London: Macmillan Educational

Bradley, L. and Bryant, P. (1983). Categorising sounds and learning to read: a causal connection. *Nature, 301,* 419.

Dunn, L.M., Dunn, L.M., Whetton, C. & Pintilie, D. (1982). *The British Picture Vocabulary Scale.* Windsor: NFER-NELSON.

Ehri, L. (1985). Sources of difficulty in learning to spell and read. In: Wolraich, M.L. & Routh, D. (Eds) *Advances in Developmental and Behavioural Paediatrics.* Greenwich, CT: Jai Press Inc.

Ellis, A.W. (1984). *Reading, Writing and Dyslexia.* London: Lawrence Erlbaum.

Frith, U. (1980). Unexpected spelling problems. In: Frith, U. (Ed.) *Cognitive Processes in Spelling.* London: Academic Press.

Frith, U. (1985). Beneath the surface of developmental dyslexia. In: Patterson, K.E., Marshall J.C. & Coltheart, M. (Eds) *Surface Dyslexia.* London: Lawrence Erlbaum.

Hornsby, B. (1985). A structured phonetic/linguistic method for teaching dyslexics. In: Snowling, M. (Ed.) *Children's Written Language Difficulties.* Windsor: NFER-NELSON.

Hulme, C. & Snowling, M. (in press). The classification of children with reading difficulties. *Developmental Medicine and Child Neurology.*

Klein, H. (1985). The assessment of some persisting language difficulties in the learning disabled. In: Snowling, M.J. (Ed.) *Children's Written Language Difficulties.* Windsor: NFER-NELSON.

Maclean, M., Bryant, P. & Bradley, L. (1987). Rhymes, nursery and reading in early childhood. *Merrill-Palmer Quarterly, 33,* 255-82.

MacLeod, J. (1970). *GAP Reading Comprehension Test.* London: Heinemann.

Neale, M.D. (1958). *Neale Analysis of Reading Ability.* Southampton: Macmillan Educational.

Neale, M.D. (1989). *Neale Analysis of Reading Ability: Revised British Edition.* Windsor: NFER-NELSON.

Nelson, H. & Warrington, E.K. (1974). Developmental spelling retardation and its relation to other cognitive abilities. *British Journal of Psychology, 65,* 265–74.

Peters, M. (1967). *Spelling: Caught or Taught?* London: Routledge and Kegan Paul.

Read, C. (1986). *Children's Creative Spelling.* London: Routledge and Kegan Paul.

Snowling, M.J. (1985). *Children's Written Language Difficulties.* Windsor: NFER-NELSON.

Snowling, M. & Frith, U. (1986). Comprehension in 'hyperlexic' readers. *Journal of Experimental Child Psychology, 42,* 393–415.

Snowling, M. & Hulme, C. (in preparation). J.M.: a longitudinal case study of a phonological dyslexic.

Snowling, M. & Stackhouse, J. (1983). Spelling performance in children with developmental verbal dyspraxia. *Developmental Medicine and Child Neurology, 25,* 430–7.

Snowling, M.J., Stackhouse, J. & Rack, J.P. (1986). Phonological dyslexia and dysgraphia: a developmental analysis. *Cognitive Neuropsychology, 3,* 309–39.

Snowling, M., Van Wagtendonk, B. & Stafford, C. (in press). Object naming deficits in developmental dyslexia. *Journal of Research in Reading.*

Stackhouse, J. (1985). Segmentation, speech and spelling difficulties. In: Snowling, M.J. (Ed.) *Children's Written Language Difficulties.* Windsor: NFER-NELSON.

Vincent, D. & Claydon, J. (1982). *Diagnostic Spelling Test.* Windsor: NFER-NELSON.

Vincent, D. & de la Mare, M. (1985). *New Macmillan Reading Analysis.* Basingstoke: Macmillan Educational.

Wepman, J. (1958). *Auditory Discrimination Test.* Chicago, IL: Language Research Association.

Young, D. (1976). *SPAR Reading Test.* Essex: Hodder and Stoughton Ltd.

Yule, W. & Rutter, M. (1985). Reading and other learning difficulties. In: Rutter, M. & Hersov, L. (Eds) *Child and Adolescent Psychiatry.* Oxford: Basil Blackwell.

The Assessment of Mathematical Skills

Jim Ridgway and Leonora Harding

The education system in England and Wales is in the midst of a dramatic reform whose long-term outcomes are uncertain. The major force by which these reforms are to be brought about will be the assessment system to which children are subjected. It is easy to underestimate the boldness of the changes which have been proposed; this is the first time that attempts have been made in the UK to bring about large scale, assessment driven, curriculum change. It is appropriate, therefore, to review the variety of educational assessment methods which have been employed in the past and to relate these to the sorts of assessment procedures which will be necessary in the future. A policy of assessment-driven curriculum change requires clear statements about:

- long-term educational goals,
- detailed specification of aims and objectives for pupils of different ages and abilities, together with definitions of exemplar tasks which epitomize these definitions and give them meaning,
- educational guidelines which relate test scores to future possible remedial actions.

Mathematics for ages 5 to 16 sets out the proposals of the Education Secretary for the National Curriculum. The document comprises the Report of the Mathematics Working Group with appropriate appendices, and significant qualifying remarks from the Secretaries of State. We shall begin the chapter with some of the proposals from the Working Group, which contain implicit (and sometimes explicit) theories of the development of mathematical knowledge, and clear statements about the aims and objectives of mathematical education. Mathematical content was considered under six headings: number, algebra, measures, space and shape, and handling data.

An individual pupil's progress was to be reported as scores on each of three profile components (PCs): one relating to knowledge, skills and understanding of number, algebra and measures; one relating to knowlege, skills and understanding of shape and space and handling data; and one relating to practical applications of mathematics.

The Working Group emphasized the importance of PC 3, and recommend that it should be given a higher weighting in the report of overall progress than either PC 1 or PC 2. The Secretaries of State were less impressed. They argued that 'the attainment targets suggested for practical applications should be re-examined and, where possible, should be combined with attainment targets in Profile Components 1 and 2' and 'We...expect to see much greater weighting attached to Profile Components 1 and 2 than the Working Group suggested' (page iii).

Mathematics in the National Curriculum (1989) sets out the statutory orders relating to mathematics teaching, and defines just 2 profile components set out below. A pessimistic interpretation of this change is that the views of the Working Party on the importance of practical applications of mathematics (which echoed the Cockcroft Report) have been set aside. An optimistic interpretation of this modification is that practical applications are to be woven inextricably throughout the mathematics curriculum. It will be interesting to observe the long-term educational implications of this important change.

Table 5.1: Attainment targets and associated statements of attainment for key stages 1 to 4

Level	Description	Example
Knowledge, skills, understanding and use of number, algebra and measures		
AT 1	Using and applying mathematics	Use number, algebra and measures in practical tasks, in real-life problems, and to investigate within mathematics itself
AT 2	Number	Understand number and number notation
AT 3	Number	Understand number operations (addition, subtraction, multiplication and division) and make use of appropriate methods of calculation
AT 4	Number	Estimate and approximate in number
AT 5	Number/Algebra	Recognize and use patterns, relationships and sequences, and make generalizations
AT 6	Algebra	Recognize and use functions, formulae, equations and inequalities
AT 7	Algebra	Use graphical representation of algebraic functions
AT 8	Measures	Estimate and measure quantities, and appreciate the approximate nature of measurement
Knowledge, skills, understanding and use of shape and space and data handling		
AT 9	Using and applying mathematics	Use shape and space and handle data in practical tasks, in real-life problems, and to investigate within mathematics itself
AT 10	Shape and space	Recognize and use the properties of two-dimensional and three-dimensional shapes
AT 11	Shape and space	Recognize location and use transformations in the study of space
AT 12	Handling data	Collect, record and process data
AT 13	Handling data	Represent and interpret data
AT 14	Handling data	Understand, estimate and calculate probabilities

Fourteen Attainment Targets (ATs) have been specified in the National Curriculum for mathematics (Table 5.1), which relate to mathematical content, and to more general mathematical skills. ATs are defined as 'the knowledge, skills and understanding that pupils of different abilities and maturities are expected to have by the end of each key stage' (page i of *Mathematics for ages 5 to 16*, DES, 1988). The descriptions offered are broad, general descriptions, and not 'attainment targets' in any real sense. They only begin to attain the status of 'targets' in subsequent descriptions of *levels* of attainment within each attainment target; each of AT 1 to AT 14 is associated with a number of levels (usually 10) that appear to provide a developmental hierarchy of mathematical skill. Illustrations of levels 1 to 5 (which roughly cover the attainment range found in primary school) are shown for AT10 (Table 5.2), together with exemplar tasks. An average pupil is expected to reach level 2 by age seven, level 4 by age 11, level 5/6 by age 14 and level 6/7 by age 16.

Table 5.2: Pupils should recognize and use the properties of two-dimensional and three-dimensional shapes

Level	Statements of attainment, pupils should:	Example
1	• Sort 3-D and 2-D shapes	Sort a collection of objects of various shapes and sizes
	• Build with 3-D solid shapes and draw 2-D shapes and describe them	Make various constructions from a range of materials
2	• Recognize squares, rectangles, circles, triangles, hexagons, pentagons, cubes, rectangular boxes (cuboids), cylinders, spheres, and describe them	Create pictures and patterns using 2-D shapes or 3-D objects Select from a collection of 3-D objects those which have at least one flat surface
	• Recognize right-angles corners in 2-D and 3-D shapes	
3	• Sort 2-D and 3-D shapes in different ways and give reasons for each method of sorting	Sort shapes with a square corner, shapes with curved edges shapes with equal sides or faces
4	• Understand and use language associated with angle	Know acute, obtuse and reflex angles, parallel, perpendicular, vertical and horizontal, etc.
	• Construct simple 2-D and 3-D shapes from given information and know associated language	Construct triangles, rectangles, circles, nets for cubes, pyramids and prisms
5	• Understand congruence of simple shapes	Group together congruent shapes from a range of shapes
	• Explain and use angle properties associated with intersecting and parallel lines and triangles, and know associated language	Identify equal angles in a diagram

The ATs contain a strong implicit theory of the nature of mathematical development and are intimately linked with the statutory programmes of study.

There will be two kinds of assessment; Standard Assessment Tasks (SATs) and Teacher Assessments. SATs will be taken nationally by all pupils in a particular age cohort. Because of the large range of ATs, SATs will sample but a few ATs (14 in all). It will be Teacher Assessments that provide 'continuing and detailed coverage of the progress of individual pupils over an extended period'. The role of SATs will be to moderate Teacher Assessments nationally. It follows that SATs will be balanced across ATs within Profile Components, sampling at least one-third of ATs at each reporting age. SATs may be set in a range of contexts, to enable schools to choose contexts appropriate to pupil culture locally. SATs are presented as a series of activities taking from 15 minutes to an hour (for a group of four children).

SATs for seven year olds form the basis of assessment in English, mathematics and science and will be presented to children as part of normal school work. Teachers are asked to introduce the work and carry out the tests over a few days in such a way that comparisons across classes could be made fairly. Pupils respond orally, via diagrams and drawings and the construction of objects, as well as in writing.

Tasks include, for example, a shopping activity, 'play' at shops, calculating change, weighing and so on; and activities that involve assembling and displaying information of a descriptive nature (hair colour, height and so on), the design of performance measures, data recording and collection (time to run 50 metres, number of digits that can be remembered, and so on). The design and form of these tasks will have a direct effect upon the kinds of classroom activities they stimulate. A number of research and development groups have been invited to design these tasks, since almost no systematic work has been done before to develop such tasks for seven year olds.

If schools and teachers are to be judged on the basis of pupils' attainment on a set of tests, they will devote a significant amount of time to teaching for these tests. If these tests are constructed from a principled view of the nature of mathematical knowledge and its development, all might be well. However, to reflect mathematical knowledge broadly, the tasks themselves are likely to be heterogeneous in terms of time scale (since extended pieces of work must be included), administration (to include oral and practical work) and the performances required from pupils. The time taken to administer appropriate tests to cover each subject in the National Curriculum would be enormous. Trials run in the summer of 1990 confirmed this guess. There was widespread teacher dissatisfaction, and a demand for far simpler testing methods. The Secretary of State now envisages that pupils will take at most 50 tasks spread over a ten-day period (compared with 200 to 250 tasks taken during the trial period). The foci of these tasks will be reading, writing, mathematics and basic scientific skills. Fourteen ATs will be covered instead of the original 32 ATs, which correspond to the programmes of study set out in the National Curriculum. Six of the 14 ATs for seven year olds in mathematics will be assessed (AT 7: algebra, is designed for older pupils).

Newspapers (for example, *Guardian*, 19th October, p. 1) report that the Prime Minister favours an exclusive focus as 'simple paper and pencil tests'. The actual restrictions in the range of tests used, and the political pressures for even greater narrowing, are both pressures for a 'back to basics' movement of the sort explicitly warned against in the Cockcroft Report.

If public judgements about schools are to be made on the basis of pupils' basic number work, and rather little else, then schools are likely to focus heavily on teaching such skills. A major purpose of establishing a National Curriculum was to specify each pupil's entitlement to a clearly defined and varied mathematics curriculum. Failures to resolve the associated assessment problems are a genuine threat to education as a whole.

At age 11 years, a much wider range of assessment methods will be used, and extended tasks will be supplemented with both long and short tasks. The 'Milk Crate' problem from Leone Burton's *Thinking Things Through* was given as an example, along with a logical puzzle (A, B, C, D, E, are all to play Badminton together, but are not all free the same day. B and C cannot...and so on) and an interesting spatial problem. The short tasks return to more familiar ground, with examples from ILEA's *Checkpoints* and questions from Suffolk LEA. Trials of these materials were not completed at the time of writing.

Uses of Different Types of Test

There is a dramatic gap between current curriculum ambitions and the tests now available to assess mathematical attainment. A National Curriculum supported by regular testing at ages seven, 11, 14 and 16 is likely to have a dramatic negative backwash on pupils' learning experiences, if tests are conceived narrowly or are ill-chosen. A large number of psychometric tests are available which have apparently been designed to satisfy goals similar to those of the National Curriculum – regular monitoring, comparison of standards between schools, diagnosis of pupil problems, and the criterion referencing of pupil attainment. An analysis of the uses of such tests is valuable in itself, and can also provide pointers to the problems of designing assessment methods which are intended to satisfy a number of different goals.

PSYCHOMETRIC TESTS

The three most common forms of tests used in educational contexts are norm-referenced tests; criterion-referenced tests; and diagnostic tests.

NORM-REFERENCED TESTS

Norm-referenced tests report a pupil's standing in comparison with peers. The nature of the basis for this comparison is often not specified, and can only be judged by an inspection of test items. For example, Test Y1 in the *Y Mathematics Series* focuses heavily on basic mathematical operations on numbers. *Tests in Basic Mathematics* deliberately sample a wide range of mathematical domains. Unlike tests proposed in the National Curriculum a number of currently published tests are seriously deficient in that they provide no specification of what it is that is being measured other than some loose lables such as 'mathematical ability', and because they fail to provide adequate information about the samples of pupils on which test norms are based. Included in this category are the *Group Mathematics Test*, the *Leicester Number Test*, the *Nottingham Numbers Tests*, the *Senior Mathematics Test*, and the *Y Mathematics Series*. These tests are discussed in *A Review of Mathematics Tests* (Ridgway, 1987).

NFER-NELSON publish three sets of norm-referenced mathematics tests namely the *Basic Mathematics Test* series, the *Mathematics Attainment Test* series, and its replacement *Mathematics 7–12*. Too many tests (but not *Mathematics 7–12*) report pupil attainment as a single score, rather than as a score band. The obvious virtue of a score band is that the error inherent in measurement is made clear to the user, thereby reducing the likelihood of them overestimating small differences in test scores between pupils.

Some tests report pupil attainment on a single dimension. Others categorize performance in terms of scores on different subsets of items. These subscores are sometimes referred to as scales or subscales. A collection of such subscores or the aggregation of scores from a number of different tests when brought together is referred to as a profile because the collection reflects the relative strengths and weaknesses of each pupil with respect to some larger sample; *Mathematics 7–12* provides profiles, for example. These profiles need to be treated with great care for two distinct reasons. Firstly the reliability of subscores is considerably lower than the reliability of complete tests, and apparently large differences in subscores on different components can reflect nothing of any real importance. This difficulty can be overcome if profiles are not presented as a single collection of scores, but rather are presented as a collection of score bands where the width of the score band reflects the standard error of measurement of each subscore.

The process of thinking about pupils' attainment in particular topic areas, especially when considered across all the pupils in the class, is likely to bring about some teacher reflection on the current balance of mathematics taught. Users can also be encouraged to consider group performance on individual items, to stimulate reflection about the roots of problem difficulty in mathematics.

A second problem associated with the interpretation profiles is that what they report is only the relative standing of a pupil compared to national averages. It is illusory to believe that these represent differences in any absolute levels of performance; indeed the very idea of assessing the absolute difficulty of a geography test compared to say a history test is wrong; all that can be done is to compare the relative standings of pupils compared to their peers on each test.

CRITERION-REFERENCED TESTS

Criterion-referenced tests set out to provide clear statements about the nature of the criteria which are to be satisfied and the tasks which indicate that these criteria have been adequately met. Such tests have often been designed as a reaction to norm-referenced tests in that they provide a statement about achievement which can be understood by pupils, teachers, parents, potential employers and the like. The specification of criteria is somewhat problematic, however, and this is highlighted by the Secondary Examinations Council (SEC) statements on National Criteria published for GCSE. Expressions such as 'understands', 'estimate', 'approximate', 'apply and interpret', 'organize and interpret' and many of the other phrases used are not criteria in the sense implied by criterion-referenced tests. They still have the status of aims and objectives and will continue to have this status until a large collection of tasks and associated scorings of them is produced to exemplify these criteria which can be analysed in some detail.

A second problem with criterion-referenced tests is that as the criteria become more detailed, their number increases dramatically. Since evidence on each criterion must be provided from several items, the implications for test construction and test administration are considerable. For example, the *Yardsticks* series of tests (now out of print), which set out a large number of criteria in mathematics, extended to six booklets and 2245 test items. It could be seen as an extensive resource pool of items which addressed a set of clearly stated behavioural objectives. Pupils recorded their own progress, and so these behavioural objectives might have helped pupils to reflect upon the nature of mathematical knowledge and their progress in acquiring it. However, the scheme (and others like it) had some serious deficiencies. First, it offered a logically based, 'bottom up' view of mathematical knowledge in which pupils had to be technically proficient in arithmetic before they handled applied problems such as giving change or sharing sweets. The idea that there should be a simple progression from techique to understanding is quite wrong, both conceptually and pedagogically. If pupils are to see some point in technical mastery they need experience in dealing with applied situations in which formalisms can be helpful. An emphasis on mastery learning is welcome, but one can have serious reservations about the view that pupils should master every aspect of every topic since the implications for the education which children will receive are dire.

A virtue of criterion-referenced tests for example *The Profile of Mathematical Skills*, is that they enable positive statements to be made about what pupils can and cannot do rather than simply to draw attention to their rank orderings with respect to peers. One might argue that it is unsatisfactory to be told that in the first year one's score was 100, in the second year one's score was 100, in the third year one's score was 100, and so on. A statement of progress on the tasks that one can perform over these different school years is far more informative and, plausibly, has a more motivating effect on pupils.

Many of the purposes served by norm-referenced tests can also be served by criterion-referenced tests. For example, comparisons of the performance of different educational treatments, or different teachers within the same school year can be made. Pupil progress can be followed directly. A comparison can be made between schools on the basis of things which pupils within each school can do. Criterion-referenced tests also have the potential to identify strengths and weaknesses of individual pupils which can then be used both to design individual work plans, and when aggregated, can give the teacher an impression of class progress, strengths and weaknesses, and can identify topics which have been inadequately covered, and topics upon which no more time needs to be spent. A major role of criterion-referenced tests is that the form in which test scores are reported facilitates discussions with both pupils and parents. Pupils can be brought to reflect upon their own learning, and a statement of progress can be made quite directly to parents. In an analogous manner discussions of curriculum topics, and progress made in teaching can be facilitated within the school.

DIAGNOSTIC TESTS

These set out to present pupils with items deliberately chosen to reveal misconceptions, and on the basis of such items to identify the set of misconceptions which an individual pupil has. The clear implication is that teaching should be designed in such a way as to overcome these misconceptions which have been identified. For example, a pupil who when asked to add 0.3 to 7.9 writes 7.12, and who also asserts that 3.214 is bigger than 3.4 has not yet understood place value in decimals.

Diagnostic testing depends on a careful analysis of the patterns of mistakes which pupils make; tests are usually developed as a result of in-depth interviews with pupils followed by larger-scale studies of paper and pencil tests which derive from the interview studies. They can be used to; identify persistent and systematic pupil misconceptions (hopefully associated with ideas on how these misconceptions might be remediated); describe hierarchies of the development of particular conceptions and likely misconceptions en route which also have direct implication for teaching; form the basis of a discussion with parents, teachers and colleagues about appropriate action which should be taken. Scores can be derived from diagnostic tests in the same ways that they can be derived from criterion- and norm-referenced tests, and so many of the functions described earlier in terms of comparing different teaching programmes, different teachers, and different schools to each other can be performed by diagnostic tests.

Some tests are designed to cover in detail various mathematical areas, for example, the *Chelsea Diagnostic Mathematics Tests* consist of a number of tests aimed at the age group between nine and 15 (with some variations) on the topics of algebra, fractions, graphs, measurement, number operations, place value in decimals, ratio and proportion, reflection and rotation, and vectors. Diagnostic testing need not be confined to the use of diagnostic tests – rather, it refers to a style of test use. A good deal of diagnostic information can be gleaned from the way a child responds to test items on other maths tests.

One of the problems encountered in attempting to diagnose learning difficulties in mathematics is that many mathematical computations require for their solution the operation of a number of different skills or abilities. Cohn (1961) points out that long multiplication calls for: recognition of symbols, ability to order results, addition with carrying and places on both long-term memory (for tables) and working memory (carrying). A child may get the answer wrong through being unable to perform any one of these operations or several of them. A detailed analysis of such problems is given by Harding (1986). Some examples are given here to illustrate the wide range of difficulties which may be apparent from children's work, even in a very restricted set of tasks.

Difficulties with calculations
Calculation difficulties are quite common in children and may occur in any child because of temporary memory lapse. On the other hand, there are children who seem unable to learn how to perform certain calculations, and who make the same mistakes repeatedly.

Ward's (1979) survey showed the extent of the problems ten year olds have with calculation. Simple additions, for example 238 + 375, were correctly answered by the majority of children (87 per cent); subtraction was slightly more difficult with 439 - 284 being correctly computed by 70 per cent of children; multiplication and division were more difficult – only 55 per cent of 11 year olds got 283 × 7 correct.

Children's errors in calculation can often be accounted for as either mis-application of rules, or as problems of memory. Joffe (1980) gives the example of a child who begins by selecting the correct operation and then changes to another one half way through the calculation.

```
 236
 × 5        Multiplication changed to addition?
 ───
 380
```

```
 357
 −89        Initial addition changed to subtraction
 ───        and number carried incorrectly.
 476
```

A similar example is provided by Joe (aged 11). He computes the sum

```
  35                        235
  × 5      achieved by        5
 ───                        ───
 505                        505
```

In this case it would seem that Joe has correctly multiplied but then added the carried 2 to 3 to get 5. Perhaps half remembering a rule about putting a 0 where there is nothing to carry he put one in.

Carrying and re-grouping errors also occur in this context, especially when there is confusion over the number to be carried.
Two examples are given by Joffe:

```
  57
  × 8      The child carries 10 instead of 50.
 ───
 416
```

```
  42       The child has correctly multiplied 9 ×  2
  × 9      and obtained 18, but has carried the wrong
 ───       number (8 instead of 1).
 441
```

These illustrations show that children can make computational errors be-cause they have remembered computational sequences (algorithms) incor-rectly, or they confuse alogorithms, or get lost part way through. Incorrect algorithms are sometimes described as containing bugs (Brown and Burton, 1978) or mal-rules. An example of a series of computational errors with a common cause is shown below.

7	9	87	365	679	923	27,493
+8	+5	+93	+514	+794	+481	+1,509
15	14	11	879	111	114	28,991

The bug in the procedure is that, whenever the number is to be carried to the next column, the child writes down the tens digit (which should be carried) and simply ignores the units digit. No operations have been confused here. Badian (1983) illustrates a confusion, and shifting of methods by the failing attempts at a sum displayed by an 11-year-old boy of average intelligence. The boy made several attempts at the same sum, being correct at the fourth attempt.

$$\begin{array}{r} 309 \\ +\ 106 \\ \hline 903 \\ 309 \\ \underline{319} \\ 3 \end{array}$$

Confusion of addition and long multiplication.

Subtraction instead of addition (9 − 6 = 3).

Addition of zero.

$$\begin{array}{r} 309 \\ +\ \ 106 \\ \hline 963 \end{array}$$

Subtraction (9 − 6).
Addition (0 + 6, 3 + 6).

$$\begin{array}{r} 309 \\ +\ \ 106 \\ \hline 203 \end{array}$$

Subtraction.

$$\begin{array}{r} 309 \\ +\ \ 106 \\ \hline 415 \end{array}$$

Correct.

Analogous buggy algorithms are associated with calculations involving decimals and fractions. A common problem is in locating the decimal point – so pupils make errors such as $24.7 \times 0.2 = 49.4$ (achieved by counting for where the point goes from the wrong end? or perhaps from 'multiplication makes bigger, so it *can't* be 4.94') and for fractions, $\frac{1}{8} + \frac{1}{4} = \frac{2}{12}$ (adding as if they were ordinary numbers instead of fractions; cf. 'I got one out of 8 on Monday's maths test, and I out of 4 on Tuesday, so overall, I got 2 out of 12 right').

Many children have buggy algorithms which are overlooked because they often (say 90 per cent of the time) yield correct results. These incorrect algorithms become more and more firmly established via partial reinforcement. The child's mathematical bug can be found by careful observation and analysis of incorrect sums over a period of time, just as in the examples given here.

There *are* dangers in over-interpreting errors in computational procedures, in the way that we have just done. Logically, one cannot be sure about the cause of any mistakes made. If the same pattern of errors is found across problems, and persists with time, then confidence in the diagnosis of a buggy algorithm is increased. The analysis of a single problem or a single set of problems in terms of bugs and misconceptions needs considerable care. Computer scientists who try to model errors in performance via descriptions of algorithms with bugs have coined the phrase 'bug migration' to explain the observation that *different* patterns of errors are found when students tackle similar problems on tests a week apart! Advice on remedial teaching should include advice on increasing student reflections about algorithms, and the need to solve the same problem in different ways and to check answers, rather than simply on diagnosing and remediating particular errors.

With memory problems, two types of error are common, firstly forgetting multiplication tables, and secondly forgetting to 'carry' or 'pay back' in a computation. This second type can be thought of as forgetting of part of the algorithm. Badian (1983) refers to attentional–sequential dyscalculia (forgetting ordered information) in which children with this sort of problem are discussed, but there seems to be little evidence that this is a discrete type. Forgetting multiplication tables is quite common in children with reading difficulties. According to Miles (1970) many such children claimed to 'know their tables', but produced answers such as $7 \times 8 = 64$, $5 \times 7 = 25$. One child produced the same answer to two questions, that is, $7 \times 8 = 56$ and $6 \times 8 = 56$ and saw 'nothing wrong in it'. Miles (1983) notes the following types of error made by dyslexic children who, despite 'long and hard efforts', still made mistakes when reciting tables:

1. Loss of place (for example, 'Was it six sevens I was up to?').
2. Consistent errors in which a correct deduction is made from a faulty premise (for example, 'two eights are 15, three eights are 23').
3. A variety of slips such as changing from one table to another (for example, six eights are 48, seven nines are 63).

Memory is important for an number of other mathematical operations. As the mathematical problem gets more difficult, the memory factor is more important as the child has to hold more and more information in mind. Badian (1983) notes that some children are quite capable of performing single arithmetic operations, for example $7 \times 8 = 56$, but may seem to be unable to carry out this operation when it is involved in a more complex sum (say long multiplication), because of the additional memory load. Resnick and Ford (1981) also stress the role of memory in computation when discussing the correct execution of algorithms. Working memory carries out all the computational activity, retrieving necessary number facts (for example, $7 \times 8 = 56$) from long-term memory. During long calculations much of working memory will be occupied in keeping place in a long procedure and holding the numbers needed. If additional resources must be taken up in working memory by the computation of (say) 8×4, because this number fact is not known very well (is difficult to retrieve from long-term memory), then interference and the breakdown of the computational procedure is likely to occur. Hence, Resnick and Ford stress the importance of developing number fact knowledge to mastery level so these facts can be retrieved quickly and easily.

SPATIAL DIFFICULTIES

Spatial difficulties show themselves when children misalign numbers and fail to maintain place values. Some children also invert or reverse numbers, and may display learning difficulties on other spatial tasks such as reading the clock, measuring and geometry.

Children often have difficulty with reading and writing numbers which could reflect spatial problems, for example, Johnson and Myklebust (1967) note that the difficulty with reading and writing numbers mostly affects the numbers 2, 3, 5, 6 and 9. This is probably because 2 and 5 are confusable with S, and 3 confused with E as a mirror image. 6 and 9 are identical if rotated. The disturbance may also effect calculations, because a child cannot remember the appearance of numbers (for example, writing 2 for 5). One nine-year-old could do written work only with a wall clock available so that she could read the numbers. In older children written errors occur with more difficult notation.

Spatial difficulties are seen in the calculations performed by Ralph, an 11-year-old boy studied by Farnham-Diggory (1978). His mistakes in computation were mainly due to misalignment, as in this example:

$$
\begin{array}{r}
23 \\
+\ \ 5 \\
\hline
73 \\
\end{array}
$$

In the next example, he began writing from the left.

$$
\begin{array}{r}
19 \\
+\ 16 \\
\hline
215 \\
\end{array}
$$

An example of Joffe's (1980) shows that the problem can occur with more complicated calculations:

$$
\begin{array}{r}
236 \\
\times\ 142 \\
\hline
23600 \\
94\ \ 4\ 0 \\
47\ 2 \\
\hline
968702 \\
\end{array}
$$

Place values are often a source of difficulty in mathematics, as illustrated below (Joffe, 1980):

$$
3\,\overline{)\,609\,}^{\ 23} \qquad \text{Failure to insert 0}
$$

In the next example the child fails to treat the decimal point appropriately:

```
   2.4
×   .4
  4.8
```

Problems which have a spatial element were included in the survey of ten year olds carried out by Ward (1979). For the problem:

  Divide this shape into just four triangles

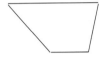

only 54 per cent of the children were correct, 23 per cent giving the answer as

Another type of wrong answer is obtained when John has difficulty with visualizing the situation: for example, a pie chart for the weather is given and the child is asked to estimate the number of hours of dry weather. He perhaps interprets the pie chart as a clock, with about 15 minutes when it is snowing (see Figure 5.1a). In the second example (Figure 5.1b), no account is taken of the relative size of the shaded portions.

COMPREHENSION PROBLEMS

Throughout the sixties and seventies, the importance of mathematical understanding was greatly emphasized. The general rationale was that many children were attempting to carry out mathematical computations without understanding any underlying principles, and thereby often were getting them wrong (Ward, 1979; Choat, 1980; Cockcroft, 1982; Denvir et al., 1982). Hart (1981) gave the example of two 12-year-old children who were slow to develop mathematical thinking. They were asked to choose the correct operation for a problem:

  A bucket holds eight litres of water. Four buckets of water are emptied into a bath. How do you work out how many litres are in the bath?

(Circle one answer)

8 × 4	4 ÷ 8
12 − 8	8 ÷ 4
8 + 4	4 × 8
4 + 4	8 − 4

(a)

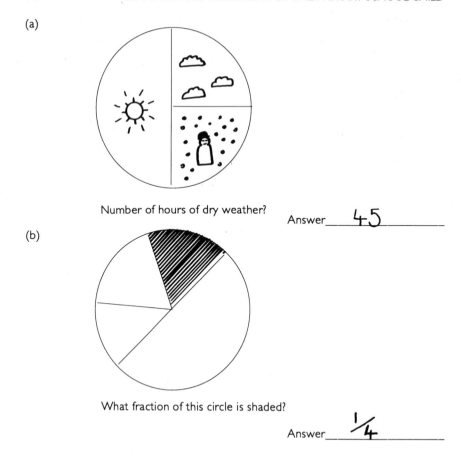

Number of hours of dry weather?

Answer___4.5___

(b)

What fraction of this circle is shaded?

Answer___¼___

Figure 5.1: John's difficulties in visualization

Neither child could do this or similar problems, which would suggest that they had difficulty in relating the numerical operation to the verbal problem and probably remained at Piaget's concrete operational level.

Another child, Billy, could not conceptualize the problem. This resulted in either (a) he didn't attempt the problem or (b) he had a vague idea of what he might have to do but it wasn't quite right. For example:

(a)   Karen wants to buy a guitar.
       She has saved £14.95.
       The guitar costs £25.
       How much more money does she need?
          Answer: £9.95

Billy probably worked out that there was a difference of almost £10 and that there was then another 5p to go somewhere and so he took it off. If he had checked back to see that the answer must be more than £10 he would have been correct.

   (b)   An empty box weighs 150 grams.
         When it is filled with paper it weighs 1 kilogram.
         How much does the paper weigh.
            Answer: 1150 grams

Either Billy doesn't seem to be able to conceptualize that the answer must be less than 1000 grams *or* he knows he has to do something with the two figures and so he rushes at it and gets the wrong answer.

DIFFICULTIES WITH THE LANGUAGE OF MATHEMATICS

Mathematical terms are often confused or misunderstood. This would seem to occur more often in children with reading difficulties than in those without. In a study by Joffe (1980) 50 per cent of children with reading difficulties were stuck when asked to find the total of two numbers, and this after having done eight addition sums correctly. They did not grasp the meaning of the word 'total'. The difficulty is seen mostly in mathematical problem solving, especially where there is no clue as to the mathematical operation to be performed. For example, take the problem:

> 'If Alice, Emma and Rosemary have 33 conkers altogether and each has an equal share, how many does Rosemary have?'

Many children failed to see that this was a division problem.

   Wheeler and McNutt (1982) have made a systematic study of the effect of language development on children's ability to solve mathematical word problems. They gave low achieving 11 year olds sets of word problems graded for three levels of difficulty in sentence structure (easy, moderate and hard). The problems themselves were at the same level of mathematical complexity. The children could do many more of the easy and moderate problems than the difficult problems. An example of an easy problem is:

> 'Jim likes to bake cookies for his family. Last night he baked 50 cookies. He gave 24 of them to a friend. How many cookies will his family have to eat?'

An example of a difficult problem is:

> 'If it is 23 miles on a bicycle from Anne's home to Jane's home by staying on the streets and it is 15 miles shorter by cutting through the park, how long is the trip the shorter way?'

Difficult problems are those that contain either a compound sentence and a complex interrogative sentence or a compound/complex interrogative sentence (as in the example above).

Diagnosis and Criterion Referencing

It might appear that diagnostic assessment is superior to both criterion-referenced and norm-referenced tests because of the need to key them directly into statements of what pupils can and cannot do, and the suggestions of what remedial activity might be appropriate. However, this appealing analysis is too simple. The power of diagnostic tests is bought at the cost of a great narrowing in the scale of assessment which can be made. Diagnostic tests usually cover a very narrow part of the curriculum and make no attempt to produce overall statements of general attainment.

A weakness of the tests from teachers' viewpoint is that, although levels of understanding and misconceptions are identified, little advice is given on what to do about the ways these things can be remediated. There is little point in diagnosis without some notion of future action. A sensible adjunct to these tests is the work of Alan Bell and his colleagues at the Shell Centre for Mathematical Education into the development of diagnostic teaching. Alan Bell's work couples an analysis of pupil misconceptions with classroom materials intended to remediate these misconceptions.

A similar problem arises when one sets out to establish criterion-referenced tests; broadly specified criteria are more like aims and objectives, while well-specified criteria require volumes to write out. Published criterion-referenced tests usually require a lot of items to cover a rather small range of mathematical skills. Implicit in the criteria is a hierarchy of progress which can be followed. In the National Curriculum, ATs are more globally specified, and guidance on appropriate classroom activities are correspondingly more general. For example: 'Activities should bring together different areas of mathematics'; 'The order of activities should be flexible'; and 'Activities should be balanced between tasks which develop knowledge, skills and understanding and those which develop the ability to tackle practical problems'.

Review

The National Curriculum has a strong implicit theory of the nature of mathematical development, of how mathematical development can be fostered, and of how it can be assessed. In some respects, the emphasis on a task-defined curriculum is strongly reminiscent of behaviourist traditions in education such as those associated with programmed learning, and with behavioural modification techniques. A worrying consequence of such traditions is that behaviour is divided into smaller and smaller units, with a resulting explosion in the number of tests which are developed. From the viewpoint of assessment, the National Curriculum takes mathematical education into unexplored domains; we simply do not know how to design extended tasks in such a way that pupils' abilities can be assessed across a variety of domains, reliably. Avoiding this challenge, and adopting a policy in which a curriculum is monitored via a collection of reliable, short tasks (which we already know how to design) might well have dire educational consequences of a heavy emphasis on the acquistion of decontexualized, fragmented skills.

Maths Microprobe: Computer administered diagnostic tests of addition and subtraction (Hagues, 1990) has been published since this chapter was written. Published by NFER-NELSON the progam diagnoses children's errors in addition and subtraction. *Practical Maths Assessments* (Foxman, Hagues and Ruddock, 1990) has also been published by NFER-NELSON. A diagnostic test, it also offers extension activities to remediate misconceptions and reinforce success.

References

Badian, N.A. (1983). Dyscalculia and non verbal disorders of learning. In: Myklebust, H. (Ed.) *Progress in Learning Disabilities 5*. New York: Grune and Stratton.

Bell, A. (1983). Diagnostic teaching – the design of teaching using research on understanding. *Zentralblatt fur Didaktik der Mathmatik, 83*, 2.

Brown, J.S. & Burton, R.R. (1978). Diagnostic models for procedural bugs in basic mathematical skills, *Cognitive Science, 2*, 155–92.

Burton, L. (1984). *Thinking Things Through*. Oxford: Blackwell.

Choat, E. (1980). *Mathematics and the Primary School Curriculum*. Windsor: NFER-NELSON.

Cockroft, W.H. (1982). Report of the Committee of Inquiry into the Teaching of Mathematics in Schools. *Mathematics Counts*. London: HMSO.

Cohn, R. (1961). Delayed acquisition of reading and writing abilities in children. *Archives of Neurology, 4*, 153–64.

Denvir, B., Stolz, C. & Brown, M. (1982). *Low Attainers in Mathematics 5–16. Schools Council Working Paper 72*. London: Methuen.

Department of Education and Science and the Welsh Office. (1988). *Mathematics for Ages 5 to 16*. London: HMSO.

Department of Education and Science and the Welsh Office. (1989). *Mathematics in the National Curriculum*. London: HMSO.

Farnham-Diggory, S. (1978). *Learning Disabilities*. London: Fontana/Open Books.

Harding, L. (1986). *Learning Disabilities in the Primary Classroom*. Beckenham: Croom Helm.

Hart, K.M. (Ed.) (1981). *Children's Understanding of Mathematics 11–16*. London: John Murray.

Inner London Education Authority (1976). *Checkpoints Mathematics Scheme*. London: Inner London Education Authority Learning Resources Branch.

Joffe, L.S. (1980). Dyslexia and attainment in school maths. *Dyslexia Review, Winter*, 12–18.

Johnson, D.J. & Myklebust, H.R. (1967). *Learning Disabilities*. New York: Grune and Stratton.

Miles, T.R. (1970). *On Helping the Dyslexic Child*. London: Methuen.

Miles, T.R. (1983). *Dyslexia: The Pattern of Difficulties*. St Albans: Granada.

Resnick, L.B. & Ford, W.W. (1981). *The Psychology of Mathematics for Instruction*. Hillsdale, NJ: Erlbaum.

Ridgway, J. (1987). *A Review of Mathematics Tests*. Windsor: NFER-NELSON.

Ridgway, J. (1988). *Assessing Mathematical Attainment*. Windsor: NFER-NELSON.

Ward, M. (1979). Mathematics and the 10 year old, *Schools Council Working Paper 61*. London: Evans/Methuen Educational.

Wheeler, L.J. & McNutt, G. (1982). The effect of syntax on low-achieving students' abilities to solve hard mathematical problems. *Journal of Special Education, 17*, 309–15.

The Assessment of Science

6

Wynne Harlen

Record-keeping and assessment in science at the primary level has been a neglected area (Clift et al., 1977) for two main reasons. First, until the recent discussions surrounding the development of a National Curriculum, the majority of teachers have not understood science as a central, or even essential, component of the curriculum (Harlen, 1987). Since a useful assessment is one which is closely related to the curriculum, clearly the fragmented and uneven practice of primary science did not lend itself to a well-constructed scheme of assessment. Second, assessment implies a framework of development; primary science has lacked agreement about such a framework, despite attempts of some curriculum developments to establish one.

The scene is changing swiftly, however. New legislation gives science a recognized place in the primary curriculum. At the same time it requires assessment of the pupils' achievements in learning science and establishes a framework for this assessment. However this does not mean that the problem of identifying the course of development in science has been swept away. The National Curriculum attainment targets provide a loose structure for assessment, sufficient for the reporting of attainment in the coarse profile components, but at the more detailed level required by teachers if assessment is to serve diagnostic purposes, the nature of progression is much less certain. The reasons for the difficulty in defining progression and identifying a satisfactory framework for assessment lie partly in the complexity of scientific activity. It is thus important to consider the nature of science and what is known of the course of development in scientific ideas, skills and attitudes.

A View of Science and Learning in Science

There are various views of science (see, for example, Ziman, 1968) but the one which underlies most current thinking in education, including that in the National Curriculum, is that it is the progressive understanding of the biological and physical aspects of the world. This implies both the process of coming to an understanding of the world – the testing of ideas and generalizations by scientific methods – and the ideas and generalizations which emerge from this process and which are used in making sense of objects and events arounds us. Current views of learning in science suggest that this is very similar in principle to the activity of practising scientists. The scientist uses existing theories (generalizations) to attempt to make sense of new phenomena or to predict events. If evidence shows that the theory or predictions based on it do not fit reality, then some change may be made to the theory or an alternative tried. In this way ideas and theories are modified so that they fit more of the available evidence and thus become more powerful in helping understanding of a wider range of phenomena.

In the parallel activity of learning science, pupils use their existing ideas in an attempt to make sense of their classroom activities and the events in their everyday lives and test their ideas against evidence in the same way as the scientist tests theories. Learning then becomes identified with change in ideas and those held at any particular point can be seen as part of a progression towards more powerful ideas. But the dependence of this development on the ways in which the ideas are tested is of considerable importance and provides the most convincing argument for an emphasis on the development of these skills. The skills in question are the ones involved in processing ideas and linking existing ideas to new situations, in using ideas to attempt to make sense of new phenomena and in deciding whether they fit the evidence. These 'science process skills' are essentially mental skills, though some manipulative skill is associated with their combination in investigative work. Lists have been proposed by various authors most of which differ little from that included in the National Curriculum. For children aged seven to 11 years of age this comprises the ability to:

- explore events and phenomena through direct observation and surveys,
- note patterns and regularities in their findings,
- suggest hypotheses and explanations which can be tested,
- plan fair investigations,
- carry out investigations systematically and safely,
- select and use suitable measuring instruments,
- make estimations,
- make justified inferences and conclusions (DES, 1988).

There is also a social dimension to the development of scientific ideas. Science is essentially an activity carried out by groups, thus the ability to share, cooperate and communicate with others is important to the outcome. In the National Curriculum these abilities are indicated in attainment targets relating to 'working in groups', 'reporting and responding' and 'using secondary sources'.

To complete the list of aspects of learning science there are, of course, the ideas developed through using science process skills and the social and communicative abilities just mentioned. These are now identified, in broad terms, in the National Curriculum, although the list is very little different from what is already covered in most comprehensive sets of curriculum materials and guidelines to good practice provided by some LEAs. The ideas are those at an appropriate level (see later for a discussion of this) relating to:

The variety of life	Forces
Processes of life	Information transfer
Genetics and evolution	Energy transfer
Human influences on the Earth	Sound and music
Types and uses of materials	Using light
Earth and atmosphere	The Earth in space

It is not forgotten that attitudes also play a part in learning, both attitudes of science and attitudes towards science. It is recommended in the TGAT report (GB.DES, 1988a) that attitudes should not be included in the national assessment because of their personal nature. Those which are less personal are very closely related to process skills and can be assessed in much the same way for teachers' use.

Scientific Development

It has been suggested in the last section that the activities of scientists and of learners of science are in many ways parallel. Both are using science process skills and abilities in communication and group cooperation to test out and extend the range of their ideas and theories. Yet there are obvious differences. The ideas of a nine year old about forces, for example, are clearly different from those of a sixth former, which in turn are different from those of a postgraduate physicist. Similarly the ability to investigate and communicate will vary for the average seven year old, nine year old and so on. What is the nature of these differences? What is the course of progression in learning? It is important to find accurate answers to these questions in order to establish a framework for assessment.

The development of a scientific concept can be regarded as the gradual change from ideas which apply to a few related objects only to ones which apply to many; from ideas which derive from superficial features of shape and form to ones which relate to less readily observable properties of function; from ones which are essentially concrete to ones which are abstract; from ones which merely describe to ones which have explanatory power. In terms of ideas about 'The Earth in space', for example, the average seven year old might be expected to be aware that the length of day and the position of the sun in the sky change during a year, whilst the average 16 year old might be expected to have an idea of the Earth as part of the solar system which explains annual changes in day length and average temperature. The steps between these two points are not easily filled in with any precision, but the general direction of change is clear and fairly well agreed.

In the case of the process skills, the notion of progression is complicated by the fact that there must be some content in relation to which they are used. In making an observation, planning an investigation, giving an account or contributing to a group discussion, there has to be some content – each has to be about something. What the 'something' is makes a considerable difference to the performance. The course of development has been described for process skill from empirical observations of children (Harlen et al., 1977) and from the (APU) survey findings. The result of work with 11 year olds leads to much the same description of development as does work with older children. This does not mean that there is no difference in the process skills of older and younger pupils, but that the difference shows in the ability to deploy skills at a certain level in relation to more sophisticated and complex subject matter. The 11 year old who can plan an investigation so that relevant variables are controlled when simple and familiar subject matter is involved would not be able to plan at the same level given a GCSE level problem, and the 16 year old who meets the same criteria for performance in planning as the 11 year old is none the less at a further point in development. The notion of development must, therefore, combine the level of process skill and the demand of the subject matter in which it has to be deployed.

Approaches to Assessment

This discussion of scientific development has made clear the interrelatedness of concepts and the process skills through which they are developed. But assessment must inevitably be analytical; it deals with various parts of children's performance, not the whole which is too complex. For only very few purposes (for example, school accountability) would it be useful to provide an assessment of children's science performance as a whole; it would certainly be of very little value to a teacher. However, in dealing at a more detailed level with the parts, that is, with separate process skills and concepts, it is important to see these in the context of the whole and to remember their interrelationship.

Assessment may cease to be valid (that is, it will not provide information about what it is intended for) if children are assessed in tasks which attempt to isolate a skill or concept from real experience. What this means in science is that children should be engaged in real scientific activity when assessed. The assessment may focus on only one part, one skill or one area of conceptual ideas, but the context of the whole is necessary for validity. In discussing these separately it is not suggested that they are performed separately.

PROCESS SKILLS

The influence of the subject matter on the way in which children tackle a science activity, noted previously presents a considerable problem for assessment. There seem to be two main ways round the problem. The first is to assess children's process skills across a range of subject matter, so that the differences associated with it are averaged out. This is the solution adopted in the APU surveys, where large banks of items assessing separate process skills were created for use in surveys. Such an approach is only possible within the context of a survey (where not every child has to take every item), for it is clearly impractical to assess every child in a class on a large number of items.

For the class teacher, the second approach to the problem is more feasible. This is to use the subject matter of the children's on-going activities and to combine results from assessing children over a number of activities. Such an approach automatically ensures that the subject matter of the as-

sessment is at an appropriate level and that the results can be used forma-
tively by the teacher. To be able to use any activity for this purpose is
rather an unrealistic ideal for not all activities provide opportunities for the
range of process skills to be used and so assessed. Consequently, it is
preferable to have some specially devised activities, which are designed to
provide the opportunities for children to use their skills and for teachers to
observe them. Such activities can be created by teachers within the context
of the topic being undertaken. Alternatively a bank of special activities
might be created (as has been mooted for the national assessment at certain ages) from which teachers can select the one fitting the children's work
at a particular time.

An example of an assessment activity within a common topic of 'Water'
might consist of the following. The task set to the children, working in their
normal groups, could be presented orally or on a workcard according to
practice for normal work:

> Use a dropper to make a drop of water fall onto a sheet of paper.
> Make some more drops, separated from each other. Are all the drops
> the same size?
> Look at them and then think how you might find out what makes a
> difference to the size of the drops. Plan out what you would like to
> do and what equipment you need. Write down your plan.

When the plans have been produced and the equipment gathered, the
children are told to start their investigation. By observing the children, reading their plans and later discussing their findings with them, the teacher
makes observations which enable yes/no answers to be given to items in a
check-list such as the following:

1.   Were relevant aspects of the phenomenon observed?
2.   Was the problem understood?
3.   Was a useful set-up planned?
4.   Was there reference to fair testing (at least one variable kept the
     same)?
5.   Was there a plan to observe/measure/compare something relevant?
6.   Were essential materials identified?
7.   Was the sequence of events planned?
8.   Was the investigation set up at the start as planned?
9.   Was at least one variable controlled (for fairness)?
10. Was at least one variable observation made?
11. Was an adequate set of observations/measurements made?
12. Were results recorded?
13. Were actions carried out in a useful sequence?
14. Were any results checked/repeated?
15. Were valid interpretations made of the results?
16. Were hypotheses proposed to explain findings?
17. Were predictions made?
18. Were predictions justified?
19. Were further investigable questions raised?
20. Were sources of error identified?

21. Were ideas shared among the group?
22. Were tasks shared among the group?
23. Was perseverance shown?

The list seems quite long, but each item is not difficult to decide because the task is structured to provide the information. If the task has been devised by someone other than the teacher some brief guidelines might be necessary, for example, to guide the discussion which is the basis for items 15 to 20.

The check-list could also be used at any time when normal activities present opportunities for the observations to be made. It is applicable to a range of activities and so provides a basis for combining information about a child from a number of different activities and social contexts. The assessment for any one activity may seem rather crude, but the combination of several results improves the precision. The detail in the check-list is sufficient for the teacher to use as a basis for identifying where a child needs help, whilst the items can be combined in various ways to give a summary assessment for other purposes. It provides information relating to most of the process skills in the National Curriculum and could readily be extended to include more attitude-linked items.

CHILDREN'S IDEAS

The gradual change in children's ideas, described earlier, implies that assessment involves gaining access to children's ideas, regarding them as points of development not as points of success or failure. The question to ask is not whether children have this or that idea but where they are in the development of this or that idea.

As before, the best situations of assessing children's ideas are those where the ideas are required as a normal part of their work. A test situation, which is quite separate from normal work, will not necessarily engage children in the thinking that it is intended should be assessed. For example, if children are asked about the conditions required for growing seeds, they may well give different answers if they are involved at the time in the investigation of various conditions on the growth of seeds than if they are not. Questions asked 'out of the blue' lack validity because they are decontextualized and further, since they are usually written, they are as much a test of reading comprehension as of anything else, as evidence from the APU surveys shows for 11 year olds (DES, 1985).

When teachers know what to look for, any activity (since it has subject matter and so involves ideas about it) can be regarded as a situation for assessing children's ideas. However, as for process skills, some specially structured elements can help. These should be seen by the children as normal parts of their work, not as test pieces, and should come at a point when children have had plenty of time for handling, exploring and discussing relevant objects and materials so that their thinking is already engaged. Then one of several ways can be used for gaining access to the children's ideas:

1. Asking them to draw what they think is happening.
2. Asking open questions so they are invited to explain their ideas and to use their ideas in making predictions.

3.   Initiating a class or group discussion about some event or object and
      listening to children explaining their ideas to each other.
4.   Asking them to keep a diary, or some other form of written record in
      which they feel free to express their own views.

Not all approaches are appropriate in all cases, but it is always possible to
find a suitable channel for children to express their ideas. As an example of
what can emerge, here are three drawings from children in a class where
hens' eggs were being incubated. The children were asked to draw what
they thought the inside looked like when the incubation started.

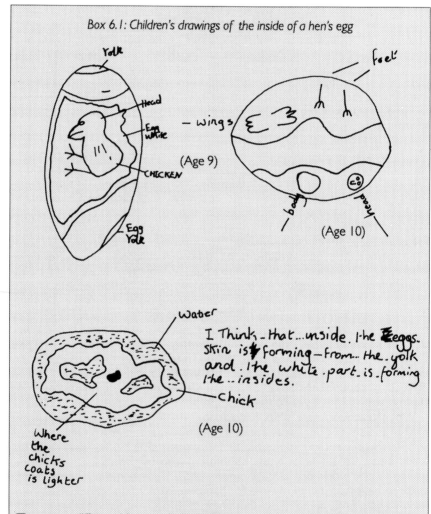

Box 6.1: Children's drawings of the inside of a hen's egg

Three very different ideas are indicated here, one where the chick is always recognizable in shape and grows only in size; one where the parts form separately
and come together later before hatching and one showing the beginnings of an
idea in which there is transformation of material as well as change in form.

Ideas about growth of a bean seed are revealed in this extract from a discussion between teacher and child:

> *Teacher.* Where do you think the leaves come from?
>
> *Child*: Out of the bean – they were inside the broad bean. We didn't see them when they were inside. They were curled inside.

A nine-year-old child's writing about growing seeds included the following (spelling preserved):

> The plant will need leaves to get air, it will need to clect food and water and a steam to carry the food to the flower.

This short sentence is rich in information about the child's ideas: the realization that plants grow, need air, water and food but also the misconception that food is absorbed from outside and carried up the stem, not made by the plant.

In these ways teachers can assess not only whether or not children have particular ideas (as required for assessing their progress towards the attainment targets) but what ideas they do have (as required for planning learning experiences which help their development). The question as to what ideas it is appropriate to expect pupils to have at various stages is a different one from the question of how children's ideas develop. The first of these has been tackled in the National Curriculum in terms of the levels of attainment in relation to ideas relating to the themes listed previously. For example, for 'Forces' it is suggested that children should:

> understand that pushes and pulls can make things move, stop and change (level 2, average age seven years).

> understand that when things are changed in shape, begin or stop moving, then forces are acting on them (level 3, average age nine years).

> understand that the movement of an object depends on the magnitude of the force exerted on it (for example, in the context of investigations with elastic and wind powered models).

> understand that the greater the speed of an object the greater the force that is needed to stop it (in the same time) and the significance of this for road safety.

> understand that the effect of a force depends on where it is applied in relation to a pivot.

> understand that things fall because of a force of attraction with the Earth (gravity) (level 4, average age 11 years).
>
> (DES, 1988)

It is useful to have these explicit statements so that teachers have an idea of the direction and level to aim for in the opportunities they provide for their pupils, but there is a danger of teachers regarding any ideas except these as 'wrong'. For example it seems to be common for children to regard the stopping of a moving object as implying the absence of a force rather than the presence on one opposing the motion. Ideas of this kind are part of a natural course of development towards the more scientific ideas. Until recently little work has been done at the primary level in mapping the course of development of children's ideas, but the SPACE project (Harlen, 1987; Russell and Watt, 1988) is filling this gap.

THE TEACHER'S ROLE

Carrying out assessment in the way suggested here makes considerable demands on the teacher. It includes; ensuring that opportunities are planned and provided for children to use process skills and develop their ideas; having in mind criteria relating to the development of process skills and concepts; developing the skills of observing children systematically and of interacting with them so that they share their ideas and to make the time to use these skills. Part of assessment is also recording and interpreting what is found and acting upon it. All this is a great deal more than would be involved in administering a ready-made written test, if such existed. But it is worth noting that the skills the teacher has to deploy for assessing pupils' development in science are a subset of those required for teaching science. This overlap is appropriate and indeed expected when assessment is regarded as an integral and supportive part of teaching, as it is in this chapter. Assessment which makes no demands on teachers is of no help to them or their pupils.

Summary

The National Curriculum has brought about a sharp change in the status of science in the primary school. It must be taught to all pupils and their progress has to be assessed and reported. Whilst keeping in mind the requirements of the National Curriculum, particularly with regard to the skills and concepts which are included, the focus in this chapter is assessment which is useful to the teacher by providing information about where children in their scientific development as a basis for providing further learning opportunities.

The nature and development in process skills and in concepts is discussed. Whilst the interrelationship of processes and concepts in learning is emphasized it is recognized that for the purposes of assessment it is useful to focus on separate skills and concepts. This can be done whilst children are involved in a whole investigation, either a part of normal work or one which has been specially devised to provide opportunities for a range of process skills to be used. An example is given of such an activity and of a check-list for use with it focusing on process skills. Suggestions are also made for assessing children's ideas and the extent to which those have developed in relation to levels proposed for national assessment.

An important message throughout is that assessment which is useful to teachers depends on their understanding of the nature of learning in science and on their ability to make and use observations of children involved in science activities, qualities equally relevant to both the teaching and the assessment of science.

References

Clift, P., Weiner, G. & Wilson, E. (1977). *Record Keeping in Primary Schools*. London: Macmillan Educational.

Great Britain. Department of Education and Science. (1985). *Science in schools: Age 11 Report No. 4*. London: HMSO.

Great Britain. Department of Education and Science. (1986). *Planning Scientific Investigations at Age 11*. APU Science Report for Teachers: 8. London: HMSO.

Great Britain. Department of Education and Science and the Welsh Office. (1988). *Final Report: National Curriculum Science Working Group*. London: HMSO.

Great Britain. Department of Education and Science and the Welsh Office. (1988a). *A Report. National Curriculum Task Group on Assessment and Testing*. (TGAT). London: HMSO.

Harlen, W. (1987). *What is Going on in SPACE?* Centre for Research in Primary Science and Technology, Department of Education, University of Liverpool.

Harlen, W., Darwin, A. & Murphy, M. (1977). *Match & Mismatch: Raising Questions*. Edinburgh: Oliver and Boyd.

Russell, T. & Watt, D. (1988). *Growth*. Report of the Primary Science Processes and Concept Explanation (SPACE) Project. Centre for Research in Primary Science and Technology, Department of Education, University of Liverpool.

Ziman, J. (1968). *Public Knowledge: The Social Dimension of Science*. Cambridge: Cambridge University Press.

The Assessment of Humanities

Alan Blyth

This chapter embodies a personal point of view about what kind of assessment might be possible, desirable and practicable in the part of the primary curriculum usually referred to as humanities, within the framework of the National Curriculum. Within that framework, humanities has some foundation status by virtue of history and geography, and some additional recognition because of the emphasis to be laid on economic awareness and on multicultural education. However, its position in schools, often denoted by a title no more specific than 'topic', has hitherto resulted in uncertainty about the kind of learning and assessment appropriate to primary humanities, and even about the legitimacy of including humanities as such in the primary curriculum at all.

In this chapter, it will be assumed that humanities is essential to children's full development, and that therefore the mode of assessment undertaken should be based on children's encounters with the ways of understanding that are characteristic of the major relevant disciplines – history, geography, economics, sociology and perhaps anthropology, politics and psychology – all at a level accessible to primary children, together with some knowledge about their own environment and its contexts. This is how, I believe, humanities should figure in what has come to be referred to as a process curriculum, or in what I prefer to call an *enabling curriculum* (Blyth, 1984). Assessment should then empower teachers to monitor this process of development; assessment should also enable children to extend their own powers of self-assessment and self-knowledge.

The ensuing discussion will use the basic terminology set out elsewhere in this book, with two additional distinctions. The first is between 'assessment', considered as something additional to normal teaching, and 'appraisal', which will imply everyday observations, systematically made by teachers. The other distinction is between 'recall' and 'transfer' that is, between playback of learning and its application first to similar situations (cognate transfer), and then to more sharply differentiated ones (general transfer) (Blyth, 1988).

It is now possible to consider actual approaches to appraisal and assessment in a process approach to primary humanities. Each of the major aspects of development will be considered in turn – skills, concepts, values and attitudes, and task procedures – followed by a reference to actual information or content. In this discussion it will be assumed that no rigid line can or should be drawn between assessment in humanities and assessment elsewhere in the primary curriculum. After a brief comment on record keeping, the chapter will be concluded with some more general observations.

Assessing Skills in Primary Humanities

REPRESENTATIONAL SKILLS

Humanities calls for distinctive representational skills. One of these concerns the use of maps. The ways in which children make and interpret maps – an issue on the borderline between geography and psychology because cognitive mapping is involved, – has been extensively studied and is well summarized by Catling (1979) and more generally by Bale (1987). Most teachers evolve procedures of their own for the assessment of map-making and map-reading skills and local groups of schools have developed linked policies, sometimes using guidelines such as those suggested by Catling (1980). As it happens, map skills have been central to studies of spatial perception and understanding, so that this is one aspect of humanities in which standardized testing has been developed, for example in the *Richmond Tests of Basic Skills* (France and Fraser, 1975) and the *Bristol Achievement Tests* (Brimer, 1969), both of which qualify for consideration in one of the standard test reviews (Levy and Goldstein, 1986). However, standardization is necessarily bought at the expense of the open-endedness involved in combining map skills is with the higher-order thinking skills to which reference is made in the next section. As soon as this move 'creative' application of skills introduced, it becomes necessary to forego the scoring advantages of test manuals and statistical procedures of the more traditional kind and to adopt instead the kinds of qualitative, intersubjective judgments developed for example by the APU in some of its work on written and oral language (APU, 1982).

Other forms of representational skills relevant to humanities have been substantially scrutinized, especially in relation to mathematical and graphical modes (for example, Boardman, 1983). In historical understanding, the obvious representational skill is the meaningful use of dating by the conventional time-scale, as distinct from what Sir Fred Clarke long ago castigated as 'telephone numbers' (Clarke, 1929). This is a topic that has figured in studies themselves covering a considerable time-span and are linked with estimates of young children's capacity to 'understand the past', about which there is now less scepticism than formerly (Joan Blyth, 1988). However, there are very few widely accepted procedures for finding out how well children at different age-levels, or, more likely, different experiential levels, are able to handle the time-scale.

THINKING SKILLS

Educationally speaking, thinking skills are more important than skills of representation. Among these, three are relatively distinctive to humanities; the evaluation of diverse evidence; the capacity to decide the more probable explanations of events where certainty is unattainable; and the exercise of empathy. The study of evidential skills has been particularly related to historical understanding, partly through the *'Clues, clues, clues'* unit from the Schools Council Project *Place, time and society 8–13*, devised by Waplington (1976) and through the work on '*Evidence*' developed later in the bet-ter-known *Schools Council History Project* which, though designed for older secondary pupils, drew public attention generally to the importance of the weighing of evidence as a skill to be fostered in schools. Similar develop-ments have taken place in relation to geographical, economic and social data which, being mainly located in the present, are at least partially open to empirical supplementation but which remain qualitatively different from the kinds of data considered elsewhere in the curriculum. The capacity to learn how to evaluate evidence is, of course, closely related to general in-tellectual acuity and to language development, but depends also on the kinds of educational experience that arise uniquely in humanities.

The ability to develop probabilistic thinking – that is, to come to terms with social uncertainty and to look for the most likely explanations – is in-herently more difficult to assess. For the capacity to cope with uncertainty can only be assessed in situations that themselves allow on an indetermi-nate range of possible outcomes whose value can be judged only in terms of adequacy of thought, not of correctness of answer; and this, too, re-quires the kind of holistic appraisal already mentioned in relation to the APU language testing programme.

Empathetic thinking, the third of these higher-order intellectual skills, might be defined as the capacity to imagine accurately the ways in which specific other people feel and think. It involves trying to understand other ages, places and cultures, as far as possible, from the point of view of the people who inhabit or inhabited those life-spaces, and it has a cognitive as well as an affective basis. Of the three kinds of specific thinking skills, this is probably the most difficult to assess; this sensitive and quite sophisticated skill can so easily be trivialized through tasks that provoke speculation di-vorced from detail rather than accurate imagination. Empathetic thinking is more likely to be detected through a chance insight or observation made by a child in oral or written work, and is thus generally open to appraisal rather than assessment.

Indeed, in all aspects of skill acquisition, it is evident that global estimates of development, based on appraisal through disussions and on the monitor-ing of topic books and other outcomes of children's regular work, are more revealing than formal tests. Any strategy of assessment must take this into account.

Assessing Concepts in Primary Humanities

Concepts are more difficult to discuss than skills. They are also more diffi-cult to define. Much attention has been paid to concept formation and at-tainment (Langford, 1987) as they affect primary education, but with few exceptions (for example, Taba, 1962; Bruner, 1966; see also Elliott, 1976) little direct attention has been paid to concepts in primary humanities. That does not, and should not, prevent teachers and others from discussing con-cept formation. In such discussions it is becoming quite usual to distinguish between two kinds of concept; substantive (general ideas used in the or-ganization of content and knowledge) and methodological (ways of hand-ling and analysing content and knowledge). This distinction was used in *Place, Time and Society 8–13*, in which the substantive concepts chosen where communication, power, values and beliefs, and consensus/conflict, while similarity/difference, continuity/change and causes and consequences figured as the methodological element (Blyth et al., 1976). It is also possible to specify two categorical concepts, namely space and time (in Kant's sense) without which organized knowledge and experience themselves lack coherence. The relation of these concepts to skills is quite complex, since concept formation is itself a skill, while the acquisition of skills depends in part on the ability to use methodological and categorical concepts. For example, children's progressive understanding of the conventional time-scale is closely bound up with their comprehension of continuity/change.

This being so, it is difficult and perhaps unnecessary to try to appraise or assess methodological and categorical concepts in isolation from particular applications, especially since they figure to some extent elsewhere in the curriculum and notably in primary science, as well as in tests of general intellectual capacity. Yet they deserve inclusion among the issues to be discussed in assessing primary humanities.

With substantive concepts the case is different. The humanities component in the primary curriculum involves the gradual building up, by individual children, of personal frameworks of concepts. There is no one sequence in which these concepts should be acquired; yet there exists a broad pattern from which individuals are unlikely to deviate totally. That broad pattern is a part of the professional knowledge about children, derived from a wide range of research and experience, which teachers need to take into account when monitoring children's concept acquisition (Dearden, 1979). A repertoire of concepts considered important can be used to guide both learning and assessment. Groups of teachers around the country are busy developing a repertoire of this kind, bearing in mind general guidence such as that afforded by Her Majesty's Inspectorate in their subject guides (HMI, 1985, 1986; others will follow). This approach enables appraisal and assessment to extend from simple recall to the more demanding processes of cognate and general transfer, as I have attempted to show in the case of primary industry education (Blyth, 1988). Questions about a labour force in one place can lead on to contrasts with other specific workplaces and thence to the notion of employment, and unemployment, in general. Similarly, questions about a particular castle can give way to reasoning about other castles built or modified at about the same time, and then to similar structures built in other times, and finally to the concept of physical defensive strategies in general.

For such purposes, one of the most fruitful approaches is by way of the Gunning–Wilson concept ladder (Gunning, Gunning and Wilson, 1981; see also Gunning, Marsh and Wilson, 1984), by which teachers map out a probable sequence of concept formation and then try to find out how far individuals have succeeded in climbing the 'ladder'. This is an approach worth refining; perhaps it could be tried out with skills too. Other quite promising techiques include sentence-completion starters (oral or written), 'absurdities' derived from the Terman-Merrill tradition ('I bought this for £1.50 in the United States...') and the insertion of data on computer software, a useful step towards self-assessment. As with assessing skills, the most useful approach of all is the everyday monitoring of children's work, supplemented by taped conversations with small groups for subsequent analysis, however rudimentary, provided that all the children have taken an adequate part. All such methods must be tailored to the actual learning experiences that the children have undergone, rather than being derived from some external agency. Even in a national curriculum, the nearest approach to standardization that can reasonably be expected in concept appraisal or assessment is the general framework of professional understanding already mentioned, supplemented by systematic exchange of experience between schools as is indeed likely to be required (TGAT, 1988).

Assessing Attitudes and Values in Primary Humanities

Although attitude formation is rightly included among the aims of primary humanities, there are formidable problems in introducing appraisal, let alone, assessment, in an area so fraught with technical difficulties and ethical sensitivities. The Task Group on Assessment and Testing (TGAT, 1988) decided not to attempt the extension of its brief to attitudes. Had they been more concerned with primary humanities than they apparently were, their misgivings might have been still greater, for this is a part of the curriculum in which children are not only at grips with other people's attitudes, but are also busy developing their own.

Some of those attitudes are a part of general personal development, relating closely to outcomes of moral and religious education; these are relatively resistant to assessment by other people. But there are other attitudes more open to observation, especially those concerned with the value of objectivity in study, or those based on an extension of direct experience, such as a visit to a farm or an inner-city district, which may have changed and enriched perspectives. It is also possible to monitor changes in attitudes to forms of study, for example the sharing of tasks so that individuals can make effective contributions from their strengths (or on the contrary can find ways of evading making more than token contributions), an issue that lies at the interface between attitudes and social skills. For such purposes it is yet again wise to base appraisal on informal conversations with children, taped for subsequent analysis. In the process, children may reveal changing attitudes towards necessary tedium and difficulty in the work itself, as well as (perhaps) towards individuals and groups previously viewed with condescension. Of course, some people consider that even this kind of procedure exceeds what should be ethically permissible, but that is a view that I do not share, provided that any resulting records contain only positive comments on individuals.

Assessing Task Procedures in Primary Humanities

A word should be added about children's understanding of task procedures. By these I mean the capacity to mobilize particular skills and perhaps concepts in order to set about solving a problem or presenting an argument or a display. Linked with that capacity is the attitude of willingness and readiness to undertake the task. Clearly it would be difficult to prescribe a formula for appraising or assessing this complex capacity, but it is important, because it embodies the ability to synthesize and generalize the various kinds of learning involved in primary humanities. Perhaps the best way of approaching this issue is through sensitive written or oral work of a summative nature, for example an account by an individual of how a scheme of work has been undertaken, alone or in a class or a group, together with suggestions for transfer to another similar but not identical activity. Unlike the monitoring of specific skills, concepts or attitudes, this style of appraisal belongs mainly to the upper junior years, when synoptic planning of this nature becomes more practicable. The procedures previously discussed have their place across the junior school and to some extent in the infant years too.

Assessing Content in Primary Humanities

Although content is not the first priority in a process curriculum, it is still important as the means by which skills, concepts, attitudes and task procedures are learned. It also has intrinsic importance in so far as it relates to children's immediate experience, as in the case of family life in human societies, or of the local environment, both of which have some, if not uniform, significance for most children. In any event, content is a part of the collective achievement that any scheme of work represents, and must figure in the dramatic climax at its conclusion, when summative assessment becomes involved. Content also figures, as was indicated earlier, in the gradual building up of the major historical epochs and the distribution of continents and oceans that become a part of everyone's necessary (but not always secure) frame of reference. Appraisal of content is most readily achieved by what can now be seen as the basic procedure to be used in assessing primary humanities, that of inspection of topic books or their equivalents, reinforced by oral questioning to facilitate accurate recall. As children grow older, assessment of content by rapid and humorous oral and written testing, or by games and computer software, becomes more practicable, and can itself facilitate further learning. Moreover, the practice of accurate specific learning in one context is itself a cognitive skill that can and should be transferred.

Yet, just because each class's own work is rooted in particular experiences, there could be no useful standardized tests of this kind of content. There might be standard questions about localities, but there could be no standard answers. And if a National Curriculum were to require young children to learn about particular events or situations, because these were deemed important on grounds other than their relation to development or experience (for example, because they are archetypal stories or patriotic landmarks or valuable as moral examples) then their introduction and assessment would need to be justified on other grounds, including the onus of proof that these, rather than any other situations or events, should be voted into the national programme. Pride of place, even in the assessment of content, should be given to material selected for its capacity to enable children's skills, concepts, attitudes and values to develop fully and healthily; and for this purpose it is, as has been repeatedly emphasized, the individual teachers' holistic appraisals, matured through interactions with other teachers, that should carry the most weight.

The foregoing suggestions are intended to apply within any curricular structure found in primary schools, though they may be easier to develop where a process or enabling curriculum is under way and where teachers are keen, confident, and aware of the need to depend on something more than general impressions and fallible memories. In any case, the emerging patterns of procedure in the National Curriculum will require the maintenance of some kind of consistent records, to be coordinated and moderated, according to the TGAT proposals (TGAT, 1988), across schools. So the whole question of record keeping (Hicks, 1987) requires some attention, though space will not permit the consideration that it really deserves.

First, it is difficult to devise any format that can do justice to all age-levels and all aspects of curriculum; within existing patterns, humanities has often received scant attention (Clift et al., 1981), apart from Cooper's useful introductory booklet (Cooper, 1976). Second, it is equally hard to find a level of sophistication in recording that is neither too trivial to be worth using, nor too complex for busy teachers to consider adopting. I have been experimenting with a system that requires nothing more than the noting, for each child, of anything unusual or unexpected about their progress or interests; and this does seem to present a practicable minimum outcome that does not rely solely on teachers' longer-term memories. Finally, there is the danger that any record keeping as such may be viewed with suspicion, though here, as previously indicated, it should be possible to allay worries by insisting on only positive comments.

This last issue exemplifies the wider problems that emerge when assessment is seen in its social and political context (Broadfoot, 1984; see also some of her other writings and the chapter by Murphy in the present volume). Expectations of appraisal and assessment are notoriously diverse – the procedures suggested in this chapter are based on the assumption that the emphasis in assessment should be on diagnosis and the enabling of potential, rather than on testing and the ranking of children in an apparent order of attainment. Parents, administrators, employers, politicians (of all persuasions), the community at large, and even some of the children, might take different views. So might some teachers and the circumstances of a National Curriculum might widen the gap between those teachers and others. All of them will need informed support if they are to act in a manner worthy of a mature, reflective and principled profession, capable of tolerating and adjusting to a measure of diversity within its ranks. Without that support, they may see little alternative to bowing before what they perceive as the most insistent of the pressures bearing upon them under the management structures now to be established. Those pressures could bode ill for the assessment, or even the survival, of humanities in the primary curriculum. If that were to happen, I believe that a vital, enabling element in the education of young children would be imperilled. That is what I, and many others, have been working to prevent. My views are now more fully present elsewhere, and in an extended form in a recent book (Blyth, 1990).

References

Assessment of Performance Unit (1982). *Language Performance in Schools. 1982 Primary Survey Report.* Windsor: NFER-NELSON.

Bale, J. (1987). *Geographical Work in Primary Schools.* London: Routledge and Kegan Paul.

Blyth, J.E. (1989). *History in Primary Schools.* (revised Edn). Milton Keynes: Open University Enterprises.

Blyth, W.A.L. et al. (1976). *Place, Time, and Society 8–13: Curriculum Planning in History, Geography and Social Science*. Glasgow/Bristol: Collins/ESL Bristol.

Blyth, W.A.L. (1984). *Development, Experience and Curriculum in Primary Education*. London: Croom Helm.

Blyth, W.A.L. (1988). Appraising and assessing young children's understanding of industry. In: Smith D. (Ed.) *Industry in the Primary School Curriculum*. Lewes: Falmer Press.

Blyth, W.A.L. (1989). *Making the Grade: Assessing Humanities in Primary Schools*. Milton Keynes: Open University Enterprises.

Blyth, W.A.L. (1990). *Making the Grade for Primary Humanities*. Milton Keynes: Open University Press.

Brimer, A. (1969). *Bristol Achievement Tests*. Windsor: NFER-NELSON.

Broadfoot, P. (1984). *Selection, Certification and Control: Social Issues in Education Assessment*. Lewes: Falmer Press.

Boardman, D.J. (1983). *Graphicacy and Geography Teaching*. London: Croom Helm.

Bruner, J.S. (1966). *Towards a Theory of Instruction*. Cambridge, MA: Belknap Press.

Catling, S. (1979). Maps and cognitive maps: the young child's perception. *Geography, 64*, 4, 288–94.

Catling, S. (1980). For the junior and middle school: map use and objectives for map learning. *Teaching Geography, 5*, 15–17.

Clarke, Sir Fred. (1929). *Foundations of History Teaching*. London: Oxford University Press.

Clift, P.S. et al. (1981). *Record Keeping in Primary Schools*. Schools Council Research Series. London: Macmillan Education.

Cooper, K.R. (1976). *Evaluation, Assessment and Record Keeping in History, Geography and Social Science*. Glasgow/Bristol: Collins/ESL Bristol.

Dearden, R.F. (1979). The assessment of learning. *British Journal of Educational Studies, 27*, 2, 111–24.

Elliott, G. (1976). *Teaching for Concepts*. Glasgow/Bristol: Collins/ESL Bristol.

France, N. and Fraser, I. (1975). *Richmond Tests of Basic Skills*. Windsor: NFER-NELSON.

Great Britain. Department of Education and Science and Welsh Office (1988). *A Report*. National Curriculum Task Group on Assessment and Testing (TGAT). London: HMSO.

Gunning, D., Gunning, S. & Wilson, J. (1981). *Topic Teaching in the Primary School*. London: Croom Helm.

Gunning, D., Marsh, C. and Wilson, J. (1984). Concept ladders in primary school topic work. Trent Papers in Education. Nottingham: Trent Polytechnic.

Her Majesty's Inspectors of Schools (1985). *History in the Primary and Secondary Years*. London: HMSO.

Her Majesty's Inspectors of Schools (1986). *Geography from 5 to 16*. Curriculum Matters Series. London: HMSO.

Hicks, J. (1987). Record keeping in infant and junior schools. *Evaluation and Research in Education, 1*, 9–18.

Langford, P. (1987). *Concept Development in the Primary School*. London: Croom Helm.

Levy, P. & Goldstein, H. (1986). *Tests in Education*. London: Academic Press.

Taba, H. (1962). *Curriculum Development: Theory and Practice*. New York: Harcourt Brace and World.

Waplington, A. (1976). *Clues, Clues, Clues*. Glasgow/Bristol: Collins/ESL Bristol.

The Assessment of Social Adjustment and Social Skills

8

Sue Spence

Before the issue of the assessment of social adjustment and social skills can be tackled, it is important to clarify how these terms are to be defined. Throughout this chapter, social adjustment will be taken as synonymous with social competence and social adequacy. These terms all represent evaluative judgements about the quality of an individual's performance in a given social situation (McFall, 1982). Social skills, on the other hand, can be defined as the specific abilities which enable people to obtain positive judgements from others regarding their performance in a social situation.

One of the major points to be made in this chapter is that there are many reasons why a child may be judged as socially competent by others. The judgemental process brings into play many variables, only some of which refer to the characteristics of the child and his or her social skills. Many others concern the characteristics of the person making the judgement and the social situations with which the child must deal. It is important that each of these areas is explored during assessment in order to understand fully why a child is judged by others to be socially maladjusted. Only then can intervention programmes be designed to rectify matters.

The consequences of social maladjustment can be far reaching, with many studies demonstrating the adverse effects on short- and long-term psychological well-being. Social problems in childhood are reported to be associated with later juvenile delinquency, school drop-out and adult mental health problems (Green and Forehand, 1980). Given the importance of being able to interact appropriately with others it is surprising that relatively little attention has been paid to social development from an educational perspective. Although many teachers will claim, quite rightly, that social enhancement has always been an aim within the education system, it is only relatively recently that attempts have been made to programme social adjustment education formally within the school curriculum. Some schools have made such education available to all children taking a preventative line (for example, Spivack and Shure, 1978). Others have tried to identify children for whom problems of social inadequacy exist with the aim of remediation (Mannarino et al., 1982). The aim of this chapter is to identify the major determinants of social functioning and outline those methods which may facilitate the assessment of social adjustment and social skills within the educational setting. The information obtained can then be used to design individually tailored social enhancement programmes.

Assessing Social Adjustment

The most obvious first question which an assessor must ask is whether a problem of social maladjustment exists? This precedes issues such as where is there a problem, with whom, how often, in what social situation and why? The initial questioning represents a screening phase in which the evaluative judgements of others are considered. Relevant information can be obtained from teachers, peers and, of course, the child him or herself.

The initial screening process to identify children judged to experience social problems is not a particularly easy task. Not only must the different perspectives of the child and relevant others be taken into account, but there are many different ways in which social problems may be manifest. In some instances the child may handle situations in an aggressive manner, demonstrating overt, acting-out behaviours. In others, children may avoid social situations or deal with them in a more submissive or passive way. Children may also differ considerably in the type of situation in which they have problems, the type of person with whom problems occur and the frequency with which they happen. The initial screening process must try to cover an extensive range of interpersonal problems which children may experience. A wide variation in interpersonal difficulties may be evident with a school setting, as demonstrated in the case examples in Box 8.1. It is clear from these brief case descriptions that the nature of interpersonal problems may differ considerably. The child's behaviour may present a problem to different people, such as the teacher, the peer group or to the child him or herself. For some children, the problem concerns a lack of a particular behaviour, such as a low rate of conversations with or approaches to peers. For others, the problem concerns some behavioural excess such as verbal abuse or physical aggression. The initial screening process needs to cover this range of options.

Screening Out Children with Interpersonal Problems

It is difficult in the early stages of assessment to separate out children whose social problems are related to some social skills deficit from those whose difficulties are not. The first stage therefore merely identifies children who have difficulty getting on with others and does not try to explain why this might be the case.

Various screening methods are available which are designed to complete the first stage of assessment, namely identifying children who have difficulty in certain social situations. These methods concern information produced by teachers, peers or the children themselves. This chapter will consider each data source in turn and is limited to social behaviour within the school setting. Obviously, it would be naïve to assume that social problems at school should be considered in isolation from interpersonal difficulties at home but the main emphasis here is on assessment within the school environment.

SCREENING METHODS FOR COMPLETION BY TEACHERS

A child's teacher holds much valuable information to assist in the assessment process which can be obtained either from interview or questionnaire format. In the screening phase of assessment the aim is generally to scan

---

Box 8.1

Illustration of the wide variation in interpersonal difficulties

Tom
Tom is nine years old. He is a small, overweight boy who is competent at his school work but poor at sports activities. Throughout primary school years he has failed to develop friendships and is generally disliked by his male peers. He is frequently teased and bullied by his classmates and tends to be picked on by a group of older boys within the school. His response to teasing and bullying is typically one of overt distress, crying and seeking the protection of a teacher. He currently avoids peer interactions, preferring solitary activities, particularly in the vicinity of a teacher.

Mandy
Mandy is seven years old and is judged by her teachers to be an attractive child. After two years at school she has failed to form friendships and rarely interacts with other children. Instead, she tends to hover on the side-lines of peer activities. She rarely approaches other children and they typically ignore her presence. Mandy is an only child and has had little experience of other children's company. Both her teacher and her parents feel that Mandy is unhappy at school. She has recently been complaining of frequent stomach aches, headaches and nausea for which no medical cause can be found.

Pat
Pat is six years old and has recently been transferred to a special class which deals with behaviour problems within the classroom. Pat talks excessively in class, interrupting the teachers frequently during lessons. Attempts to reprimand her tend to result in violent temper tantrums in which Pat shouts abuse at the teacher and storms out of the classroom. She has no close friendships and has been involved in several fights with other children at school following incidents of teasing and criticism from peers.

---

the classroom to identify those children with interpersonal difficulties who may benefit from a social enhancement programme. Various questionnaires are available for this purpose, with the majority covering a wide range of problem behaviours, of which social functioning is just one aspect. The *Walker Problem Behaviour Identification Checklist (WPBIC)* (Walker, 1983) is particularly useful here. The WPBIC yields five subscales, namely acting out, withdrawal, distractibility disturbed peer relationships and immaturity. High scores on the acting out, withdrawal and disturbed peer relationship reflect difficulties in interpersonal relationships which warrant further investigation.

Numerous other teacher-completed questionnaires are available to assist in the screening process. Examples are the Teacher Report Form of the Achenbach and Edelbrock (1983) *Child Behaviour Checklist*, the *Conners Teachers' Rating Scale* (Conners, 1969) and the *Pittsburgh Adjustment Survey Scales* (Reardon et al., 1979). Alternatively, teachers may rank or rate all children in their class on criteria such as popularity among peers, time spent alone, frequency of peer conflicts or aggressive outbursts. Informal methods of this type are very useful in identifying socially maladjusted children but the reliability and validity of such techniques is questionable. This problem can be reduced by using informal screening methods in conjuction with information from other data sources to confirm the accuracy of the findings.

USING PEERS FOR SCREENING PURPOSES

The peer group has been used frequently as a means of identifying children with interpersonal problems. Most commonly, sociometric methods have been applied in which the peer group are asked to nominate or rate their peers in terms of specific criteria. Two major types of sociometry have been developed, namely peer nomination and roster or rating systems. Peer nomination requires each child in the class to specify a certain number of children with whom they would most like/dislike to take part in a particular activity, such as play or a constructional task (see Box 8.2). In the rating method, each child rates each class-mate on a scale of like–dislike in relation to participation in particular activities.

Box 8.2 illustrates a nomination method used in a study reported by Tiffen and Spence (1986). Numerous variations of sociometric methods exist and the interested reader is referred to Kane and Lawler (1978) or Asher and Hymel (1981) for useful summaries. Studies have now shown that various subgroups of children can be identified from sociometric methods. These include rejected children who tend to receive a large number of negative votes from their peers, popular children who tend to receive many positive votes, neglected children who receive few votes of any type and various residual categories of less interest here (Coie et al., 1982). The va-

---

Box 8.2

'Keep private: choosing other people'

Name:
The teachers are arranging some school activities and, to help, we would like to know which children you would like to be with. Look at the list of children in your class and decide which ones you would like to do each activity with and which ones you would prefer not to be with. You can't choose someone from another class but it is alright to pick someone who is away from school today. You can pick boys or girls. Please fill in every space and then keep your writing to yourself. As it is private, please do not talk about your choices.

For each choice, write the person's first name and initial of their last name (for example, Jimmy S.).

A. I would choose to *play* with these children:
1. _____ 2. _____
B. I would choose to *work* with these children:
1. _____ 2. _____
C. I would choose *not to play* with these chidlren:
1. _____ 2. _____
D. I would choose *not to work* with these children:
1. _____ 2. _____

lidity of these distinct categories of rejected, popular and neglected children has been established in several studies (Dodge, 1983). Generally, rejected children are found to show higher rates of acting out and aggressive behaviour. Neglected children on the other hand tend to spend more time alone and converse less with their peers. Such findings support the use of sociometric methods as a means of identifying children who are likely to experience interpersonal problems. The short term test–retest reliability of most sociometric methods is found to be acceptable, further supporting their use in the classroom (Busk et al., 1973).

The information produced by sociometry provides little indication as to the specific problem behaviours shown by individual children. Such information can be elicited from the peer group using alternative methods. For example, Coie et al. (1982) describe the use of the peer group to identify those elementary school children who tend to show specific positive and negative social behaviours. The method used presented a short behaviour description such a 'this person starts fights. He or she says mean things to other kids and pushes them and hits them' (p. 559). Children were asked to identify classmates who most closely fitted the description.

SELF REPORT SCREENING MEASURES

There are various ways in which children can experience interpersonal problems. Some children may feel a desire for certain events to happen more or less often, such as desire for more friends or less bullying from peers. Others may experience negative emotions such as fear, anxiety or anger in particular social situations. During the screening process, children can be asked to state whether they experience interpersonal problems either in terms of a desire for different social outcomes or in terms of negative emotions. Furthermore, they can provide information about how they would be likely to respond in a range of social situations and these responses can be assessed as to their social acceptability.

A useful means of assessing a child's overall view of his or her social abilities is the Perceived Competence Scale for Children (Harter, 1982). This scale measures perceived competence in cognitive, social and physical domains and in relation to general self-worth among nine to 12 year olds. A more specific measure of social problems experienced by children and adolescents was developed by Spence (1980).

The area of assertive behaviour has received particular attention and it is worth noting two assessment instruments which focus on assertion and have been extensively researched. The Children's Action Tendency Scale (CATS; Deluty, 1979, 1984) and the Children's Assertive Behaviour Scale (CABS; Michelson and Wood, 1982) provide a measure of passive, aggressive and assertive responding and are useful in identifying children who tend to respond inappropriately to social dilemmas which require an assertive response.

Assessing the Determinants of Social Competence

During the second stage of assessment the aim is two-fold. First, the assessor needs to clarify the interpersonal problem by investigating exactly what the child tends to do or not to do that is judged to be a problem – where, when, who with, how often and on what social task. Second, the assessor should explore the likely determinants of social competence, using a hypothesis-testing approach to work out why the child is judged to be lacking in social competence in certain situations. The following sections discuss how these goals may be achieved and this necessitates an outline of the major factors which determine social competence. Problems in any one or more of these aetiological areas may result in a child being judged as socially maladjusted. The major areas to be considered are outlined in Table 8.1.

Table 8.1: Social-cognitive skills involved in the determination of social competence

---

Social perception (and empathy)
- attending to social information from others and social environment;
- interpreting social information;
- taking the perspective of others;
- knowledge of social rules.

Social problem solving
- identifying and defining the social task;
- generating alternative solutions;
- predicting consequences (long- and short-term);
- matching predicted outcomes against desired outcome;
- selecting appropriate strategy (cognitive plan).

Performance of selected strategy
- appropriate level and use of micro-skills;
- coordination of micro-skills;
- initiate selected strategy;
- monitor performance;
- match performance against cognitive plan;
- monitor response of others/outcome;
- compare outcome with anticipated outcome.

SOCIAL-COGNITIVE AND BEHAVIOURAL SKILLS

There are many reasons why a child behaves inappropriately in social interactions. In some cases the child may not have the skills to enable him or her to behave more appropriately. In others, the child may be competent in all social skill areas and yet for some reason select a course of action that is judged to be socially unacceptable. It has been proposed that skills may be inhibited if excessive anxiety is present or if a child's attitude regarding the situation inhibits the selection of appropriate responses. An example of the latter point could be the pupil who holds strong anti-authoritarian beliefs and whose dislike of teachers in general leads him or her to be verbally abusive to staff when approached regarding a homework task. The child may be capable of behaving in a much more prosocial manner and yet may elect to respond in an antisocial fashion. The possibility of maladaptive beliefs and attitudes should be considered, along with the role of anxiety and social skills deficits, when assessing interpersonal problems.

The ability to select an appropriate course of action and carry it out in a way that others judge to be competent involves a long and complex sequence of cognitive and motor skills. Evidence is gradually accumulating to support the importance of both cognitive and overt performance skills during assessment and remediation, rather than focusing on either area alone. Let us look first at the social-cognitive skill domain.

Numerous authors have described the complex series of cognitive skills that are involved in social information processing and which are proposed to determine how a person behaves in a given social interaction (for example, Dodge, 1986; McFall, 1982). These stages can be summarized as involving social perception, social problem solving and enactment processes.

Social perception.
Social perception refers to the ability to recieve, perceive and interpret correctly social information from the outside world. This includes information regarding the social context and other people's non-verbal cues such as facial expression, tone of voice, posture and gestures. Children who have attentional or sensory deficits are particularly at risk, and failure to interpret correctly important social information may lead a child to select an inappropriate course of action. Take the hypothetical example of Tim, who had a long history of aggression at school. Assessment revealed that Tim tended to interpret incorrectly most social cues as indicating aggressive intent on the part of others. Tim reacted to this by responding aggressively to approaches of others, even if their intent was friendly. On social perception tests, Tim interpreted a wide range of facial expressions and tones of voice incorrectly, tending to label most as conveying anger, or aggression. Not surprisingly, people tended to respond to his aggressive behaviour in a negative way, hence confirming his initial theories about their aggressive intent.

Numerous methods are available to assess the different aspects of social perception, although few have been demonstrated to have satisfactory psychometric properties. The area of empathy has probably received the most attention, with tests such as *Feshback and Roe Affective Situation Test for Empathy* (Feshback and Roe, 1968) and the *Index of Empathy for Children* (Bryant, 1982). Role-taking ability has been assessed for example by the *Borke Test* (Borke, 1971) which is useful in practice but there appears to be a lack of research into its psychometric properties. Various measures have also been developed to assess the child's ability to correctly interpret the non-verbal cues of others. For example, Spence (1980) presented a practical method for assessing children's ability to label correctly the cues of posture, gesture, facial expression and tone of voice.

Social problem solving.
Social problem solving skills represent the next sequence of social-cognitive abilities which are important in determining social competence. Social problem solving requires a person to be able to identify the occurrence and characteristics of an interpersonal dilemma, to generate a range of alternative possible responses, to predict the likely consequences of each alternative and then to select the best course of action by matching likely

consequences with the desired outcome. There is a need here to be able to consider short- and long-term gains in selecting the most socially competent strategy for solving an interpersonal dilemma. Children whose intellectual abilities limit their skill in social problem solving are likely to find it difficult to complete these stages satisfactorily. Certain children may also have specific difficulties in the social problem solving domain. An example here could be Jenny, aged eight years, who has very few ideas about how to approach her classmates in order to join in a game of 'chase'. Her only suggestion is to wait until she is asked and she hovers around the edge of the playground. Her peers tend to perceive her as a loner who prefers her own company and they consequently neglect to invite her to join in.

Very few methods of assessing social problem solving skills have been researched to establish their reliability and validity. The measures developed by Spivack, Shure and colleagues have received the most attention in the literature. The *Preschool Interpersonal Problem Solving Test* (*PIPS*; Spivack and Shure, 1974) evaluates the ability to generate alternative solutions to interpersonal problems among three to five year olds and has been found to be useful with children up to eight years. The test involves two sets of age-relevant problems, one dealing with a peer conflict and the other concerning a conflict with a parent, to which children are asked to produce possible solutions without regard to the social acceptability of these responses. An adaptation of the *PIPS* test is reported by Rubin et al. (1984), which takes into account the quality of solutions offered rather than just the quantity. In addition to the *PIPS*, Spivack and Shure (1974) also describe the *What Happens Next Game* which is designed to assess children's ability to predict the consequences of behaviour. Platt and Spivack (1975) developed the *Means-Ends Problem Solving Test* (*MEPS*) to assess the child's ability to produce step-by-step methods for reaching solutions to interpersonal problems. Each story presents a beginning and an end to an interpersonal problem and the child is asked to fill in the middle to indicate various ways in which the problem may have been solved.

Performance of selected strategy.
Even if a child is competent in the social-cognitive skills outlined so far, he or she must then be able to perform the strategy selected in a way that is judged as socially adequate by others. It is the performance aspect of social skills that seems to have received most attention in remediation programmes. Children must be able to integrate an enormous number of responses, in particular the non-verbal components of behaviour, in order to successfully perform the course of action that they have selected. For example, Jenny goes out into the playground and a group of classmates are playing hopscotch. She assesses the situation carefully, plans out alternative responses, predicts consequences, and selects a course of action. She proposes to wait for the next child to complete her turn and then walk up and say 'may I have a turn please when you've all had your go?' Even though Jenny has selected an appropriate response strategy, she must still be able to integrate numerous non-verbal responses such as her tone of voice, posture, facial expression, latency of response or rate of speech, to mention just a few. These non-verbal responses make up the micro-skills that are frequently the focus of social skills training programmes. Gradually, it has

become accepted that assessment and intervention must consider both cognitive and overt behavioural skills in order to improve social competence.

Even if a child's performance is adequate in terms of micro-skill usage, there are still further stages of social cognition to consider. Children need to be able to monitor their own behaviour to ensure that they stick to the social plan they have made, to monitor the response of others and adjust their behaviour as required. This brings us full circle back to the process of social perception.

As mentioned already, much attention has been paid to the micro-skill usage aspect of the enactment process. Considerable evidence has been produced to confirm how important many micro-skills are in determining the impression that a child makes on others. For example Spence (1981) demonstrated that, with juvenile offenders, responses of eye contact, verbal initiations, smiling, fluency of speech and amount spoken influenced adults' judgements regarding indices of social competence. Table 8.2 provides some indication of the wide range of micro-skills that should be considered during assessment.

Table 8.2: Micro-skills to consider during assessment

Non-verbal	Quality of speech	General
eye contact	tone	amount spoken
facial expression	fluency	content of speech
smiling and laughter	volume	(relevance, interest, appropriateness)
social distance	pitch	turn taking
latency of response	clarity	meshing
orientation of body to others	rate	initiating interactions
gestures		
posture		
head movements		

An interview with the child can elicit information and provide a structured setting in which the assessor can observe the child's micro-skill usage. It must be remembered, however, that the interview situation is considerably different from most situations with which the child must deal, and his or her behaviour during interview may not necessarily be representative of usual behaviour.

Self report methods such as questionnaries and rating scales may have some use in behavioural social skill assessment but are dependent on the child's awareness of his or her behaviour and willingness to report this honestly. This difficulty may be reduced if self report information is crosschecked with information from other sources to confirm its validity. The Matson Evaluation of Social Skills with Youngsters (MESSY; Matson et al., 1983) is a useful measure which covers a wide range of social situations. The emphasis on positive and negative ways of dealing with various social interactions rather than micro-skill use. It is a valuable method for clarifying the type of situations children find difficult and has been widely used with children up to 18 years of age. The *MESSY* is also available in a teacher rating form which provides a useful comparison with the self reported information.

The assessment of micro-skill use is probably best achieved from observation of the child in controlled or naturalistic settings. Naturalistic situations provide the best indication of how a person usually behaves, assuming the observer's presence does not cause a change in behaviour. Several methods of observing and coding child behaviour in naturalistic settings have been developed (for example, Furman and Masters, 1980; Scarlett, 1980). These methods typically require considerable training and practice on the part of the observer before adequate levels of inter-observer reliability can be achieved. Many teachers or psychologists may prefer to use rating scales in which they rate performance on specific micro-skills based on their subjective judgement of adequacy such as that outlined by Spence (1980). Other assessors have contrived situations such as roleplays or simulated play situations to make observation an easier task (Bornstein et al., 1977; Tiffen and Spence, 1986). Unfortunately, some studies have suggested that roleplay behaviour is not necessarily representative of real life behaviour (Van Hasselt et al., 1981), hence roleplay assessment data should preferably be checked against other sources of information.

THE ROLE OF MALADAPTIVE COGNITIONS AND AFFECT

Although social-cognitive and performance skills are important in determining behaviour in a particular social situation, a child may have an adequate skill repertoire and yet behave inappropriately with others. A variety of maladaptive cognitive and emotional processes may interfere in the selection of response strategies causing the child to behave in a way that is judged to be socially maladjusted. The most common competing cognitive and affective processes concern anxiety, anger and depression. If a child is very anxious in certain social situations, he or she is likely to rehearse a range of worrying thoughts such as, 'I can't do it, what's the point in trying, no-one will want to play with me. They will all laugh at me and think I'm stupid.' A range of anxious physiological responses may also occur such as sweating or shaking, and inhibition of certain skills such as eye contact is likely. Furthermore, the child may avoid entering the feared situation if possible and experience an aversive feeling of discomfort when having to deal with the situation. Given such symptoms of anxiety, a child is unlikely to perform in a particularly competent manner in anxiety-provoking social situations even if an adequate repertoire of social skills exists.

Depression is another factor which needs to be considered given evidence of a close relationship between depressive symptoms and social functioning among children (Puig-Antich et al., 1985). Children who are classed as experiencing problems of depression tend to exhibit poor social relationships and these are found to improve as the depressive symptoms are reduced. It is likely, however, that a circular cause–effect relationship exists between social skills and problems of social anxiety, anger control and depression. The presence of skill deficits may lead to problems in relationships with others which, in turn, produces negative emotional states which inhibit skill usage, further producing problems in relationships with others.

There are obviously many ways in which problems of affect, cognition and physiological control influence the way in which children behave in social situations. Such possibilities need to be considered during assessment so that intervention programmes can tackle these areas. There would be little point in spending many hours teaching social-cognitive and performance skills if maladaptive cognitions and affect are still acting to prevent the use of the skills being taught. For some children intervention would be much better geared towards methods such as cognitive restructuring, or relaxation training rather than interpersonal-skills training.

The assessment of social anxiety, anger control and childhood depression is complex and it would be foolhardy to attempt a brief summary here. Interested readers should find the work of Novaco (1975) helpful in the area of anger control. An extensive discussion of the assessment of childhood depression is provided by Kovacs (1981) and Reynolds et al. (1985). In the area of social anxiety, Warren et al. (1984) report the use of the Watson and Friend (1969) *Social Anxiety and Distress Scale (SADS)* and the *Fear of Negative Evaluation (FNE)* with junior high school students as a means of assessing certain components of social anxiety.

Various other maladaptive attitudes and belief systems may also be considered. For example, the child's general self esteem may be relevant and can be assessed using measures such as the *Piers–Harris* (Piers and Harris, 1969). Attitudes to authority figures may also be worthy of assessment, particularly with the youth offender group.

Additional Factors to Consider During Assessment

The main emphasis so far has been on the importance of factors which determine how a child behaves in a particular social situation. Whether a person is judged as socially competent or not, however, is determined by a multiplicity of variables. As mentioned earlier, it is not so much what a person does or says in a situation that determines social success, but whether his or her behaviour is interpreted by others as competent. This judgement process is influenced by the characteristics of the performer, the social task and the person making the judgement, in addition to how the performer behaves.

There is considerable evidence that personal characteristics, such as physical attractiveness, cleanliness, grooming, style of dress, physique, sporting prowess, school attainment and presence of physical handicaps, may influence whether a child is judged to be socially competent (Rathjen, 1980). During assessment it is therefore important to consider whether a child's social problems may be influenced by their personal characteristics. For example, if a child is unpopular in the classroom and rejected by classmates, this may be due partly to some personal characteristic to which other children react in a negative way. Intervention may then involve changing the attitudes and behaviour of the peer group, rather than focusing on the target child. It should be considered whether unrealistic expectations on the part of the teacher, or excessively difficult social tasks for which the child is developmentally unable to cope, may explain the difficulties experienced by the child. Again, intervention would need to tackle these aspects.

All social interaction involves a degree of reciprocity in which one person's behaviour is influenced by that of another. Social behaviour, as with any other form of behaviour, is highly influenced by environmental events. Certain antecedent events may trigger off particular behaviours, for example, provocation by peers may trigger off aggressive outbursts from the provoked child. The consequences of behaviour will also determine how a child responds in the future. Hence, if the peer group rewards a child with attention and giggling when he or she is rude to the teacher, that child may be more likely to be abusive to the teacher in future. A careful analysis of antecedents and consequences of the problem behaviour is therefore needed.

Finally, there are two further points that are worth mentioning in relation to the child's environment. The first concerns social opportunities and support networks. Children differ in terms of their social opportunities, having varying chances to interact with family members, extended families, neighbourhood children and activity groups outside school. Children who have few opprtunities to interact with others outside of school may be limited in their chances to develop their repertoire of social skills. This point needs to be explored during assessment. The second point concerns cultural influences within the school context. Different requirements for competent social behaviour exist within different cultures (Argyle, 1972) and problems may occur when a child from one culture is required to interact with children and/or adults from other cultures. These children must learn to discriminate the rules for social behaviour across different cultures so that they can adjust their behaviours according to the requirements of the setting. Most children make this transition successfully but, as many classrooms are multicultural in the mix between children and/or children and their teachers, the possibility of cultural influences in judgements of social competence should be considered.

Special Populations

The need to consider problems of social competence has particular significance for children with sensory, intellectual and physical handicaps. Given the restrictions that may be produced on the cognitive and performance aspects of social skills as the result of specific handicaps, it is perhaps not surprising to find that many disabled children experience difficulty in their interactions with others. The type of interference in social functioning that results is likely to be determined by the nature of the child's handicap.

VISUALLY AND HEARING IMPAIRED CHILDREN

Children who have sensory disabilities such as visual or hearing limitation are restricted in the amount of social information that they receive from others. Accurate social perception therefore becomes difficult if information from auditory or visual channels is absent. Obviously, children may compensate to some extent by the use of unaffected sensory channels, but where sensory deficits are severe or multiple, children are likely to have considerable difficulty with skills such as the decoding of non-verbal messages or in the receipt of social contextual information. It would not be surprising therefore to find that children with severe sensory handicaps are more likely to respond inappropriately with others than their nonhandicapped peers. Evidence does indeed suggest that, in general, children with visual or hearing disabilities tend to be judged less favorably by their nonhandicapped peers and to show some evidence of social skills deficits (Van Hasselt et al., 1985; Matson et al., 1986). Research into the nature of such social skills deficits is sparce and much more attention needs to be paid to the identification of specific social skills deficits experienced by sensory impaired children. Hearing handicapped children have also been shown to experience interpersonal problems in comparison with their nonhandicapped peers (Macklin and Matson, 1985; Matson et al., 1985) although again the exact nature of such deficits remains unclear.

The assessment of social competence amongst children with sensory impairments has received relatively little attention. To a large extent methods such as direct observation, teacher report and self report remain applicable, although consideration must be given to issues of reliability and validity when measures are developed for use with nonhandicapped children and then adapted for use with special populations. Matson and his colleagues have carried out considerable research into the use of the *MESSY* self-report and teacher report questionnaires for the assessment of social skills amongst hearing and visually impaired children. The *MESSY* has been found to have acceptable psychometric properties and to provide valuable information in the assessment of social responding with special populations such as these. Adaptations have involved audiotaped presentation of questions and braille answer sheets for visually impaired children. To date, the *MESSY* probably represents the most useful and appropriate system of assessing social skills amongst hearing and visually impaired children.

CHILDREN WITH INTELLECTUAL DISABILITIES

Children with intellectual handicaps are also likely to have interpersonal problems particularly with areas such as social problem solving, knowledge of social rules and interpretation of social cues. It has been demonstrated repeatedly that children with mental handicaps are less popular amongst their nonhandicapped peers than are their nonhandicapped counterparts (Gresham, 1981). This has been suggested to result partially from the deficits in cognitive processes which are necessary for appropriate social responding. As with children with other forms of handicap, intellectually disabled children are likely to experience a restricted range of social experiences and a reduced number of appropriate social models. Such limitations in opportunity for the learning of appropriate social skills may contribute to deficits in social competence.

The severity of interpersonal difficulty tends to increase as the level of cognitive impairment increases. Even children with relatively mild levels of intellectual disability have been found to show some evidence of inappropriate social responding and to show problems in the understanding of nonverbal communication patterns (Bryan, 1978). The approach to assessment of social competence and its subsequent remediation with mildly intellectually handicapped children closely mirrors that outlined for nonhandicapped children. The nature of interpersonal skills deficits and the focus of assessment obviously changes when the degree of cognitive impairment becomes more severe. Many profoundly handicapped children have minimal speech and communication ability and the focus of assessment emphasizes the very basic elements of interpersonal communication. Skills such as orientation of gaze, basic communication gestures, attention and listening responses become primary foci during assessment. Measures such as the *Vineland Social Maturity Scale* may be valuable in the assessment of social competence amongst severely intellectually handicapped children whereas the *MESSY* has been used sucessfully with mildly mentally handicapped children (Matson et al., 1980).

Summary

This chapter outlines an approach to the assessment of social adjustment and social skills. The approach begins with a general screening phase in which children who experience social problems of any type and for whatever reason are identified within the school setting. The second phase of assessment then attempts to clarify the nature of the social difficulty and identify the determinants of social competence which are operating. This process therefore provides considerable information about why each child is experiencing social problems and enables an individually tailored intervention programme to be designed.

The information used is collected from a wide range of data sources, including teachers, peers and the children themselves. In selecting assessment methods, consideration needs to be given to the reliability and validity of the measures used. To date, there has been a failure to consider psychometric properties during the development of many assessment methods in the area of social competence. This position needs to be rectified in relation to new measures and those already in common usage.

References

Achenbach, T.M. & Edelbrock, C. (1983). *Manual for the Child Behaviour Checklist and Revised Child Behaviour Profile*. Vermont: University of Vermont.

Argyle, M. (1972). *Psychology of Interpersonal Behaviour*. London: Penguin.

Asher, S.R. & Hymel, S. (1981). Children' social competence in peer relations: Sociometric and behavioral assessment. In: Wine, J.D. and Smye, M.D. (Eds). *Social Competence*. New York: The Guildford Press.

Borke, A. (1971). Interpersonal perception of young children. *Developmental Psychology, 5*, 263–9.

Bornstein, M.R., Bellack, A.S. & Hensen, M. (1977). Social skills training for unassertive children: A multiple-baseline analysis. *Journal of Applied Behaviour Analysis, 10*, 183–95.

Bryan, T.S. (1978). Social relationships and verbal interactions of learning disabled children. *Journal of Learning Disabilities, 11*, 107–15.

Bryant, B.K. (1982). An index of empathy for children and adolescents. *Child Development, 53*, 413–25.

Busk, P.L., Ford, R.C. & Schulman, J.L. (1973). Stability of sociometric responses in classrooms. *The Journal of Genetic Psychology, 123*, 69–84.

Coie, J.D., Dodge, K.A. & Coppotelli, H. (1982). Dimensions and types of social status: A cross age perspective. *Developmental Psychology, 18*, 557–70.

Conners, C.K. (1969). A Teacher's rating scale for use with drug studies with children. *American Journal of Psychiatry, 126*, 6, 884–8.

Deluty, R.H. (1979). Children's Action Tendency Scale: A self report measure of aggressiveness, assertiveness and submissiveness in children. *Journal of Consulting and Clinical Psychology, 47*, 1061–71.

Deluty, R.H. (1984). Behavioural validation of the Children's Action Tendency Scale. *Journal of Behavioural Assessment, 6*, 115–30.

Dodge, K.A. (1983). Behavioural antecedents of peer social status. *Child Development, 54*, 1386–99.

Dodge, K.A. (1986). A social information processing model of social competence in children. In: Perlmutter, M. (Ed.) *Cognitive Perspectives on Children's Social and Behavioural Development. The Minnesota Symposia on Child Psychology, Vol. 18.* Hillsdale, NJ: Lawrence Erlbaum.

Feshbach, N.D. & Roe, K. (1968). Empathy in six and seven year olds. *Child Development, 39*, 133–45.

Furman, W. & Masters, J.C. (1980). Peer interactions, sociometric status, and resistance to deviation in young children. *Developmental Psychology, 16*, 226–36.

Green, K.D. & Forehand, R. (1980). Assessment of children's social skills: A review of methods. *Journal of Behavioural Assessment, 2*, 143–59.

Gresham, F.M. (1981). Social skills training with handicapped children: A review. *Review of Educational Research, 51*, 139–76.

Harter, S. (1982). The Perceived Competence Scale of Children. *Child Development, 53*, 87–97.

Hops, H., Fleishman, D.H., Guild, J., Paine, S., Street, A., Walker, H.M. & Greenwood, C.R. (1978). *Programme for Establishing Effective Relationships Skills (PEERS). Consultant Manual.* Eugene, OR: University of Oregon, Centre at Oregon for Research in the Behavioural Education of the Handicapped.

Kane, J.S. & Lawler, E.E. (1978). Methods of peer assessment. *Psychological Bulletin, 85*, 555–86.

Kovans, M. (1981). Rating scales to assess depression in school-aged children. *Acta Paedopsychiatrica, 46*, 305–15.

Macklin, G.F. & Matson, J.L. (1985). A comparison of social behaviours among nonhandicapped and hearing impaired children. *Behavioural Disorders, 11*, 60–5.

Mannarino, A.P., Christy, M., Durlak, J.A. & Magnusen, M.G. (1982). Evaluation of social competence training in the schools. *Journal of School Psychology, 20.*

Matson, J.L., Kazdin, A. & Esveldt-Dawson, K. (1980). Training interpersonal skills among mentally retarded and socially dysfunctional children. *Behaviour Research and Therapy, 18*, 419–27.

Matson, J.L., Rotatori, A. & Helsel, W.J. (1983). Development of a rating scale to measure social skills in children: The Matson Evaluation of Social Skills with Youngsters (MESSY). *Behavioural Research and Therapy, 21*, 335–40.

Matson, J.L., Macklin, G.F. & Helsel, W.J. (1985). Psychometric properties of the Matson Evaluation of Social Skills with Youngsters (MESSY) with emotional problems and self concept in deaf children. *Journal Behaviour Therapy and Experimental Psychiatry, 16*, 117–23.

Matson, J.L., Heinze, A., Hebel, W.J., Kapperman, G. & Rotatori, A. (1986). Assessing social behaviours in the visually handicapped: The Matson Evaluation of Social Skills with Youngsters (MESSY). *Journal of Clinical Child Psychology, 15*, 78–87.

Michelson, L. & Wood, R. (1982). Development and psychometric properties of the Children's Assertive Behaviour Scale. *Journal of Behavioural Assessment, 4*, 3–13.

McFall, R.M. (1982). A review and reformulation of the concept of social skills. *Behavioural Assessment, 4*, 1–33.

Novaco, R.W. (1975). *Anger Control: The Development and Evaluation of an Experimental Treatment.* Mass: Lexington Books.

Piers, E. & Harris, D. (1969). *The Piers–Harris Children's Self Concept Scale.* Nashville, TN: Counselor Recordings and Tests.

Platt, J.J. & Spivack, G. (1975). *Manual for the Means–Ends Problem-solving Procedures (MEPS)*. Philadelphia: D.M.H.S.

Puig-Antich, J., Lukens, E., Davies, M., Goetz, D., Brennan-Quattrock, J. & Todak, G. (1985). Psychosocial functioning in prepubertal major depressive disorders. 1. Interpersonal relationships during the depressive episode. *Archives of General Psychiatry, 42*, 500–7.

Rathjen, D.P. (1980). An overview of social competence. In: Rathjen, D.P. and Foreyt, J.P. (Eds). *Social Competence: Interventions for Children and Adults*. New York: Pergamon Press.

Reardon, R.C, Hersen, M., Bellack, A.S. and Foley, J.M. (1979). Measuring social skill in grade school boys. *Journal of Behavioural Assessment, 1*, 87–105.

Reynolds, W.M., Anderson, G. & Bartell, N. (1985). Measuring depression in children: A multimethod assessment investigation. *Journal of Abnormal Child Psychology, 13*, 513–26.

Rubin, K.H., Daniels-Beirness, T. & Bream, L. (1984). Social isolation and social problem solving: A longitudinal study. *Journal of Consulting and Clinical Psychology, 52*, 17–25.

Scarlett, W.G. (1980). Social isolation from agemates among nursery school children. *Journal Child Psychology and Psychiatry, 21*, 231–40.

Spence, S.H. (1980). *Social Skills Training With Children and Adolescents: A Counsellor's Manual*. Windsor: NFER-NELSON.

Spence, S.H. (1981). Validation of social skills of adolescent males in an interview conversation with a previously unknown adult. *Journal of Applied Behaviour Analysis, 14*, 159–68.

Spivack, G. & Shure, M.B. (1974). *Social Adjustment of Young Children*. San Francisco, CA: Jossey-Bass.

Spivack, G. & Shure, M.B. (1978). *Problem Solving Techniques in Child Rearing*. New York: Jossey-Bass.

Tiffen, K. & Spence, S.H. (1986). Responsiveness of isolated versus rejected children to social skills training. *Journal of children Psychology and Psychiatry, 27*, 343–55.

Van Hasselt, V.B., Kazdin, A.E. & Harsen, M. (1985). A behavioural–analytic model for assessing social skills in blind adolescents. *Behaviour Research and Therapy, 23*, 395–405.

Van Hasselt, V.B., Hersen, M. & Bellack, A.S. (1981). The validity of roleplay tests for assessing social skills in children. *Behaviour Therapy, 12*, 202–16.

Walker, H.M. (1983). *Walker Problem Behaviour Identification Checklist: Manual*. Los Angeles, CA: Western Psychological Services.

Warren, R., Good, G. & Velten, E. (1984). Measurement of social-evaluative anxiety in junior high school students. *Adolescence, 19*, 642–8.

Watson, D. & Friend, R. (1969). Measurement of social evaluative anxiety. *Journal of Consulting and Clinical Psychology, 33*, 448–57.

The Assessment of Children with Sensory and Motor Difficulties

9

The assessment of children who are visually impaired

Mike Tobin

Most blind children and all partially sighted children can see. The classification of children as visually imparied in the UK is based primarily upon the strength of their distance vision or visual acuity (see Box 9.1). However, the ability to make sense of near and distant objects is not dependent solely upon the measured acuities. For this reason, teachers and psychologists working with visually impaired children have a responsibility to try to assess what the children can see in classroom situations. In addition, the effects of chronological age and age of onset of the impairment are likely to be significant factors in determining how effectively the children may be able to use their residual vision. Even with the totally blind child, age of onset can be of importance, since the possession of some sight, if only for a year or two, can have beneficial consequences, especially in the development of orientation and mobility skills.

Assessors must constantly ask themselves whether they are conveying their intentions clearly. Otherwise there is a danger that the task confronting the child is different from that which is intended; for example, verbal reasoning and perceptual discrimination items may be transformed into tests of short-term memory by failure to repeat, perhaps *sotto voce*, the instructions. A task is a function both of its content and its mode of presentation; a sighted assessor of a visually handicapped child must not forget this.

Measuring Functional Vision for Classroom Purposes

With children in nursery classes, much useful information on visual functioning can be obtained informally by direct observation of their approach to and handling of conventional pegboard equipment, toys, light emitting sources such as pocket torches, and light reflecting materials such as silver paper and mirrors. Infants who can do no more than make an orienting re-

---

Box 9.1

Classification of visual measurement

Acuity
The eye's ability to resolve fine detail and thus to register difference. Normal adult acuity is usually attained by about three years of age. Levels of illumination markedly affect acuity.

Distance vision
Conventionally and formally measured by means of the Snellen chart, on which are printed rows of letters, each row having letters designed to subtend specified angles upon the retina at specified distances. A resulting index of, for example, 3/60 indicates that the subject identified at three metres those letters identified by normally sighted subjects at 60 metres. People with distance vision between 3/60 and 6/60 are registrable as partially sighted.

Near vision
Conventionally but informally measured by means of such tests as the N Print Test, which consists of a series of cards on which are printed letters of a specified size, successive cards being printed with letters of decreasing size. The subject is allowed to choose and vary the distances and angles at which the cards are held. Near vision is then recorded as the size of the smallest print, e.g. N6, read by the subject at his preferred distance – an important measure, relevant for all close tasks in the classroom, such as reading writing, drawing, and needlework.

Visual functioning and visual efficiency
Subjects having the same measured distance and near vision acuities may nevertheless differ greatly in their use of any residual vision; intelligence, previous experience, learning, ease, comfort, and general motivation all contribute to their ability to extract meaning from the stimuli reaching the retina. It is claimed that functioning and efficiency can be improved by appropriate training and encouragement.

---

sponse to light from a torch or reflected from silver foil may be demonstrating that this residual vision could be useful for basic mobility and independence. Children who can place wooden rods into holes by visually monitoring their attempts at a distance of three or four inches is demonstrating a much higher level of functioning even if it may never be good enough for reading printed texts.

With young school-age children, much information about functional vision can be garnered in the course of administering standardized tests that are being used for some other purpose. For example, the *British Picture Vocabulary Scale* (Dunn et al., 1982) is described as a test of receptive vocabulary. What it can do, in addition to providing a 'receptive vocabulary' score, is to show how willing children are to use their remaining sight, how successfully they use it, at what distance from the material they prefer to work and how willing they are to suspend their judgement until they have scanned all four pictures.

Other instruments that can be informative about children's ability and willingness to use their sight are the *Barraga Visual Efficiency Scale* (Barraga, 1964, 1970) and the Schools' Council *Look and Think Checklist* (Tobin et al., 1979).

The *Barraga Scale* contains four sub-scales designed to evaluate the child's ability to respond to items of increasing complexity in size, detail, and interpretation. Also for children in the age range five to 11 years, the *Look and Think Checklist* is an inventory for use by teachers of the visually handicapped, tabulating what the experienced teacher notes over an extended period of classroom observation. Like the Barraga, it is linked to a set of teaching activities. Its value to the educational psychologist may reside in its attempt at comprehensiveness and in its flexibility. The *Barraga* and the *Look and Think* instruments will, as tests of visual perception, yield something more than merely an understanding of what the five or six year old can see. They will, for example, indicate whether he or she can use verbal labels related to size and space and to a variety of relational concepts. With this information, the tester will be in a better position to judge whether anything is likely to be gained from the administration of more familiar tests.

Measuring Intelligence

The *Williams Intelligence Test* (Williams, 1956) is the only British test that has been standardized for use with visually handicapped children over the whole school age-range. The test is for individual administration, and is predominantly verbal, with only a few 'performance-type' items. The main processes tapped are reasoning, short-term memory, spatial imagery, and retrieval and application of knowledge.

Some psychologists are now using sections of the revised *British Ability Scales* (Elliott et al., 1983), especially with partially sighted children, and many of the sub-scales can be used without any alteration. Among these are those involving verbal reasoning (similarities and social reasoning), short-term memory (recall of digits), and retrieval and application of knowledge (word definitions and verbal fluency). Clearly, the sections where the principle stimulus mode is visual, for example, Matrices, Block Design, and Recall of Designs, would be entirely inappropriate. There is some justification, however, for using the Speed of Information Processing sub-scale with the partially sighted (*vide* Mason and Tobin, 1986), since it may also reveal useful information about near-vision skills. Some very competent children have achieved scores placing them as high as the 80th centile, and would be able to cope quite adequately in a fully integrated classroom. Those at the opposite end of the scale, however intelligent they may be, would have considerable difficulties in keeping up with their fully-sighted peers in academic subjects requiring extensive reading.

Assessment of Reading

For the partially sighted pupil, the standard print of the *Neale Analysis of Reading Ability* (Neale, 1958, 1989) is useable. Typeface and typesize make the first two passages easily decipherable by most children if they are allowed to bring the page as close as they wish. The later passages are acceptable to most pupils despite the reduction in print size, provided the prescribed spectacles or low-vision aids are used. The *Neale* sub-scales (Accuracy, Speed, and Comprehension) are not completely independent of one another, with performance on the Accuracy sub-scale determining when the test is to be terminated. This can lead to an underestimate of a partially sighted child's comprehension ability. What also must be expected are much lower reading speeds than those obtained by fully sighted readers of the same age.

There are three tests available for use with braille readers. These are *Tooze Braille Speech Test* (Tooze, 1962), the *Lorimer Braille Recognition Test* (Lorimer, 1962), and a standardized, braille version of the *Neale Analysis of Reading Ability* (Lorimer, 1977). Lorimer has modified the *Neale* test by replacing the introductory pictorial 'cues' with a short oral description of the setting that helps to orient the blind reader, and by extending the 'pause before correction' to allow the child more time to identify and 'unpack' the contracted forms. The restandardizing of the test on blind pupils now makes it possible, where desired, to compare a blind reader with both blind and sighted peers. More importantly, its diagnostic potential is now available to those teachers and psychologists working with blind children.

The Blind Learning Aptitude Test

A potentially extremely useful instrument is the *Blind Learning Aptitude Test* (Newland, 1971), which was designed to throw light on aspects of blind children's aptitudes and potential that were not being illuminated by existing tests of intelligence and achievement. The test now published makes use of abstract symbols, rather larger than the conventional braille cell. There are, however, some drawbacks to the instrument, some of these the deviser has himself acknowledged in the Manual. He sees it a 'constituting only the first stage in the development of a measure of the learning aptitude of blind children' and states that 'much work is needed to refine it'.

Despite the reservations, this test could be most useful to educators and psychologists working with blind children in all English-speaking countries. It has the advantage of a relatively low verbal content, and therefore very few changes would have to made in the instructions to be given to the children. It is the only standardized instrument of its kind that consists entirely of tactile symbols. It is 'culture fair' and thus does not discriminate in favour of or against specific groups of children, and this in itself is of some significance for the many blind pupils coming into schools from immigrant families. The fact that it is sufficiently different from existing tests of intelligence, aptitude, or achievement is also a point in its favour. It may therefore be a useful complement to them, giving teachers and psychologists a more rounded or complete assessment of a child's potential.

Conclusion

The dearth of tests standardized on a population of visually handicapped children makes assessment difficult, especially in the subject domains of mathematics and social and adaptive behaviour. Poor or no vision can restrict the range of experiences available to a child, thus making transfer and generalization less certain. Nevertheless, testers would be well advised to use instruments and procedures with which they are familiar, even if there is no 'visual handicap' standardization data to hand. While extra time, ingenuity in modifying materials, and caution in drawing inferences may all be necessary, there remains the fact that these pupils have much in common with their fully sighted peers.

The assessment of children who are hearing impaired

Alec Webster

Introduction

Hearing-impaired children do not form a homogenous group, since deafness interacts in an unpredictable way with all other factors which contribute to individual differences, such as family background, school experience, personality, motivation, together with potential for learning. Deafness may be mild and transitory, or profound and permanent. A hearing loss which is congenital, but not discovered until three or four years of age, will have a different impact from deafness acquired after the child had begun to talk, but which is recognized quickly and appropriate management given. A few children appear to be greatly impeded in their learning by the recurrence of a mild conductive hearing loss, often associated with catarrh and infections of the middle ear (otitis media). Some, but by no means all, children overcome many of the obstacles which a severe sensori-neural hearing loss presents to development, and achieve sophisticated levels of language and literacy. It is this apparent diversity of cause and effect which has helped to fuel arguments about the best teaching approach to hearing-impaired children, for example, sign language versus oral methods, or mainstream versus special school settings. (For further discussion, see Webster, 1986.)

The case notes in Boxes 9.2 and 9.3 give a small sample of the complex range of individual needs, educational practice and developmental progress associated with different kinds and degrees of hearing loss. The ordinary class teacher, without any specialist training or experience, is in a good position to detect children who may have a hearing loss (see Table 9.1), and may be asked to shoulder the major teaching responsibility for a child with a known hearing loss in an integrated setting. Teachers can make an important contribution to the planning, implementation and evaluation of a programme for a hearing-impaired child. In many local education authorities a team approach is adopted to planning and decision-making, involving family medical officers, psychologists, audiologists, speech therapists, specialist and non-specialist teachers, who meet together regularly to review a child's

---

Box 9.2

Example of hearing loss which was slow to show

Robert, for example, was thought to be 'lazy' and 'dull' because he daydreamed, always asked for instructions to be repeated or forgot what he had to do, had very little attention span and was a poor reader. At eight years of age, Robert's speech showed immature pronunciation, with both limited vocabulary and sentence structure. His difficulties were noticeably greater in listening and language work, such as 'phonics', than in practical activities. Although he had passed a school hearing test Robert was later discovered to have an intermittent conductive deafness. A peripatetic teacher of the deaf was able to advise on seating arrangements to lessen noise and distraction, suggest activities to help listening and auditory skills, whilst careful liaison was kept with home so that medical help could be sought whenever Robert's hearing appeared to worsen.

Box 9.3

Example of hearing loss from an early age

Sarah was diagnosed as having a severe sensori-neural loss at the age of two years, which could not be 'treated', except in the sense that hearing aids were provided and advice given to the family. Through her primary years Sarah attended an ordinary school which was resourced to meet the needs of hearing-impaired children, such as smaller teaching groups, sound-proofing and carpetted areas to improve listening conditions, additional classroom help and regular in-service programmes for staff. At ten years Sarah was not a confident child socially and she needed a lot of help and explanation to participate in ordinary class settings. However, her speech was usually understood by others where the context was clear, progress was being made in all basic skills, and she was felt to be happy and well-adjusted.

---

progress. (For a fuller discussion of how such a team operates, see Webster et al., 1985.)

As part of the ongoing process of teaching and appraisal of hearing-impaired children, information is usually collated on the child's intelligence, language and communication, school attainments, social skills and emotional maturity. Test results may inform school placement, teaching objectives and the monitoring of progress over time. In the section that follows, a brief survey is made of formal test material devised for, or used with, hearing-impaired children. Because of a number of pitfalls in traditional approaches to cognitive, language and attainment testing of deaf children, many professionals have turned to informal approaches, such as skill-profiling. More recently, in the light of research which has uncovered secondary learning difficulties in hearing-impaired children, to do with patterns of adult–child

Table 9.1: Warning signs of a possible hearing loss

- Medical records or siblings show a history of ear infections or failed screening tests, especially in winter.
- Complains of earache, popping ears, catarrh, discharging ears, mouthbreathing or snoring.
- Frequent absences from school with coughs and colds.
- Daydreams, distractible, poor concentration, often asks for repetition and help, can't listen to stories, slow to follow instructions.
- Watches others to see what they do, doesn't answer to name, needs to sit nearer TV or have volume turned up.
- Immature speech, vocabulary and sentence structure.
- Appears to respond better in quiet conditions, when speaker's face is visible or in small groups.
- Irritable, listless, poor motivation, stress signs such as nail-biting, more frequent upsets in school, easily tired, difficult to reach.
- Difficulties in language-related work, confused by phonics, reading delay, maybe much better in practical subjects.
- Periodic falling away of learning and increased demands for individual help.

---

interaction, attention has also been focused on methods of assessing the learning and teaching environment.

COGNITIVE ABILITIES

The aim of intelligence testing is to determine a child's potential for learning. Tests which rely on good rapport, verbal instructions or responses for administration, tasks which are timed, or material which draws directly or indirectly on the child's linguistic facility, will tend to reveal more about the child's (or examiner's) communication skills, rather than logical reasoning or problem solving. It is for these reasons that formal tests are usually restricted in their use to trained psychologists. Many so-called 'non-verbal' tests use visual, coloured or shaped materials for sorting, sequencing or jig-saw-type tasks, but depend on the comprehension of oral instructions and tap underlying language concepts. However, a number of Performance scales have been specially constructed, re-standardized or evaluated for use with the deaf. The Hiskey–Nebraska and Snijders–Oomen tests have norms for both hearing and hearing-impaired children, but require considerable practice to carry out. The Leiter, Raven's Matrices, and the Columbia Mental Maturity Scales have been extensively used with deaf groups, giving normal distributions of scores, but slightly lower means (Kyle, 1980). The British Ability Scales has several sub-tests which can be used with deaf children, although lower scores may be expected (Galbraith, 1984).

The IQ test most widely used with the deaf is the Performance scale of the WISC-R. Although the mean IQ score of a sample of American deaf children was found to be lower than for hearing groups (Anderson and Sisco, 1977), most researchers would agree that any differences in performance abilities between deaf and hearing children are likely to be due to communication factors rather than non-verbal intelligence. Psychologists can confidently use selected items from scales such as Griffiths, McCarthy and Piagetian-based tests where there are clear developmental criteria, so long as reservations about task-comprehension are borne in mind. Whilst language difficulties associated with deafness do not preclude problem solving or logical inference, Verbal IQ tests may highlight large discrepancies in experience, range of concepts and linguistic reasoning. With deaf children, particularly, standardized tests are limited in their predictive value, and give scant information on individual strengths and needs. For teachers planning a programme, a much more fruitful approach to assessment is skill-focused, where an informal observation framework is used to identify whether a child has acquired a specified range of educationally relevant skills in important behaviour domains.

COMMUNICATION SKILLS, SPEECH AND LANGUAGE

There is a very wide range of test materials available for the formal assessment of language and communication in deaf children, and this is obviously an important area associated with successful integration in mainstream schools, academic achievement and social adjustment. Again, care must be exercised that tests of vocabulary or concepts do not simply reflect a child's grasp of instructions. Three main areas can be considered briefly, with more detailed discussion available in Webster and McConnell (1987).

Speech intelligibility and lip-reading
Tests of sound articulation are of more value to the speech therapist and require knowledge in phonetic transcription and interpretation. Speech therapists can make a valuable contribution to the multi-agency team described earlier, both in interpreting specialized diagnostic tests, and in drawing out the practical implications when the overall management of a child's programme is planned. The *Edinburgh Articulation Test* analyses the child's pronunciation of consonant sounds based on research in normal development. Other researchers, such as Conrad (1979), have produced rating scales which give a percentage measure of how well understood a child's speech may be by unfamiliar adults out of context. Conrad (op cit.) also includes a measure of the child's ability to lip-read the speech of others.

Receptive language
Although not devised for hearing-impaired children, the *Peabody* and *British Picture Vocabulary Scales* give some idea of the child's comprehension of vocabulary items. The *Reynell* test has been extensively used with the deaf and includes a receptive scale with increasingly complex spoken instructions involving the manipulation of the toy materials. The *Test of Syntactic Abilities* (Quigley et al., 1978) is an American procedure using a written format, which assesses the deaf individual's ability to recognize a wide range of English grammatical structures, with distractor items drawn from errors which deaf individuals have made.

Expressive language
A number of profiles have been developed for analysing the grammar of children's spoken language. *LARSP* tabulates each instance of particular grammatical features, such as determiners, copula, aspects of phrase and clause structure, within a developmental framework and highlighting

strengths and weaknesses. There are several experimental tests which examine communicative function, rather than English grammar, which are more appropriate to children whose language includes aspects of sign, such as the *Bristol Syntax-free Scales*.

EDUCATIONAL ATTAINMENTS

Obviously, a test which requires the deaf child to read aloud will assess ability in speaking rather than reading. Consequently, teachers and psychologists have turned to silent reading comprehension measures, such as the *Southgate*, *Widespan* or *Picture Assisted Reading Test*. Detailed studies have been published (Webster *et al.*, 1981; Wood *et al.*, 1981) which examine the use of such tests with deaf children. There are some pitfalls in using standardized reading tests with non-standard groups. Evidence suggests that the patterns of right answers and errors made by deaf and hearing groups are different, although reading ages may be nominally the same. Questions of validity arise since deaf children appear to use a different set of strategies in tackling such materials. However, there can be greater confidence in assessing basic mathematical operations, using tests such as the *Vernon–Miller Graded Arithmetic Test*, which makes minimal demands on reading and appears to tap similar processes in deaf and hearing children (Wood *et al.*, 1983).

SKILL PROFILES

In view of the hazards associated with formal testing of deaf children, professionals are turning increasingly to skill profiles as a basis for structuring observations in order to set teaching objectives and monitor progress. In terms of planning and evaluation, teachers can use profiles to inform their own teaching approach, whilst the evidence derived from the classroom context will make an important contribution to the multi-professional review described earlier. Profiles can be constructed in any behaviour domain and involve the setting out of a developmental sequence of clearly observable skills which reflects the teaching curriculum, and which it is hoped the child will acquire. Along the continuum of 'listening', for example, early target skills would include: 'turns head to loud sound', and 'responds to tone of voice indicating No'; whilst later skills might include: 'takes a message through hearing only, such as over the telephone'. On a literacy continuum, early items on the skill profile might include: 'writes own name by copying a model', or 'uses picture clues to guess a word'; whilst more mature skills include: 'ties sentences together in free-writing using connectives such as so, but, then, next'. Social maturity could be assessed along a dimension including items such as: 'invited by hearing children to join in playground games', or 'independent in organizing books, materials and homework'. Examples of skill profiles which have been designed specifically to reflect the likely areas of concern with regard to deaf children's development are given in Webster (1986) and Webster and Ellwood (1985).

ASSESSMENT OF THE TEACHING AND LEARNING CONTEXT

A recent direction in the assessment of deaf children is the analysis of variables within the language and teaching context. Evidence shows that the strategies which adults use as they interact with children has a significant effect on development, particularly language. In the first extract in Table 9.2, the adult appears to negotiate the child's intended meaning, using strategies such as handing conversation back to the child and allowing time for reply; interpreting, restating and expanding what the child says; giving comments from personal experience and phatic responses (Ooh, that's nice) to sustain the dialogue. There is no attempt to control the dialogue, correct errors or pronunciation, as the adult helps the child by trying to share something of her social world.

Deaf children may be exposed to adult styles of behaviour which are more managerial and controlling, with a concern to teach language through questionning, modelling and repetition. The second sample in Table 9.2, taken from a textbook on the teaching of deaf children, illustrates how a focus on the correct form of language, as opposed to sharing meaning, can result in disruption of the conversational flow. This kind of linguistic encounter has been shown to be very inhibiting to children. Although such styles may characterize adult/child interactions in many educational contexts, children with special needs may have further obstacles to surmount as a result. A major justification for testing children is to facilitate teaching and learning. Since some of the learning difficulties associated with deafness are located within the teaching milieu, rather than the child, it is important to take account of these factors in any comprehensive assessment. (For further discussion and techniques for observing interaction see Wood et al., 1986, or Webster and Wood, 1989.)

The assessment of children who are motor impaired

Sheila Henderson

So far in this chapter we have dealt with the assessment of sensory impairment in children. We now turn to motor impairment which is rather different from the previous deficits in that it takes so many different forms and has so many different causes. Three examples must suffice to illustrate this diversity and the implications for assessment.

First, there are children who suffer specific physical impairments, which may be severe in themselves, but are unrelated to other aspects of their

Table 9.2: Samples of conversational interaction
(adult intentions are glossed in brackets)

Sample 1 (Source: Wells, 1986, page 98)

Child (Rosie)	Teacher	Gloss
Carol got a bed and Kelvin...and Carol		
	Um hum. What about Donna?	(Signals interest invites Rosie to extend)
Donna – we're sharing it		
	You're sharing with Donna are you?	(Rephrases, invites confirmation)
(nods emphatically)		
	Do you have a cuddle at night?	(Invites extension)
Yeh an I – When I gets up I creeps in Mummy's bed		
	For another cuddle?	(Extends, invites confirmation)
(Rosie nods)		
	Ooh that's nice It's nice in the morning when you cuddle	(Adds social oil, personal experience)

Sample 2 (Source: Van Uden, 1977, page 265)

Child	Teacher	Gloss
	Why do you like nice weather?	(Request for talk)
Because...because father and mother...father and mother, brother and I go swim		
	Say it better	(Requests restatement)
Because father and mother, brother...		
	Brothersss...	(Interrupts/models)
Brothers and I go for a swim		
	That is right	(Confirms correct grammar)

development (for example, postural defects such as scoliosis, childhood arthritis, polio). Such children may be unable to perform many of the tasks their peers perform with ease, may be deprived of full involvement in the physical activity of the classroom and spend long periods of their lives in hospital. These problems may indirectly affect a child's schoolwork but need not do so. There is often no need for assessment other than by the medical profession.

Our second example, cerebral palsy, is actually not a single condition but a variety of conditions. Cerebral palsy is caused by damage to the central nervous system around the time of birth. Such damage is rarely confined to the parts of the brain which control movement. Consequently, although all children who bear this diagnosis have movement difficulties, many have other handicaps. Perceptual and intellectual impairments are frequent. Emotional problems may also be present. Assessment of these children is, therefore extremely complex and usually involves different professions.

Our third example is chosen to remind the reader that motor impairment does not necessarily imply overt physical handicap. Among children who are bright, articulate and apparently physically normal are a small group who experience considerable difficulty in acquiring everyday motor skills. Sometimes labelled 'clumsy', these children constitute a neglected group. Yet, their difficulties in school are often severe and merit intervention.

In view of the variety of motor impairment illustrated so briefly above, it seems essential to devote all the space available here to a discussion of motor assessment. However, it must always be borne in mind that in many children other problems occur which have implications for their educational progress (for a more comprehensive review see Henderson, 1986a, b). In what follows, three different approaches that have been taken to the assessment of *motor* impairment in children will be briefly described. In the first, assessment is focused on action at a functional level; in the second, concern moves to the description of the movements comprising actions and in the third, the analysis of the component elements of actions is undertaken.

(1) FUNCTIONAL ASSESSMENT

The tests described in this section focus on movement at a level sometimes described as 'functional'. This means they assess the performance of everyday purposeful actions, providing a record of *what* a child can or cannot do. The instruments range from simple check-lists to more complex batteries for which special equipment and instructions are provided. In content they differ considerably. For example, tests designed for use with the more severely handicapped child often focus on self-help skills. The tester is concerned with whether the child can hold a spoon, use a toothbrush, go to the toilet and so on (for example, Whitehouse, 1983). In contrast, tests which assess more moderate degrees of impairment tend to examine the child's ability to use a pen, handle a ball, hop and jump, and so on (for example Bruininks, 1978; Stott, Moyes and Henderson, 1984). An example is given in Table 9.3.

Another distinction which exists within this class of tests concerns the way the tests are scored. Some are *criterion-referenced*, others are *norm-referenced*, while other tests are directed towards the identification of only those children experiencing difficulties and are best regarded as screening instruments.

Over the last decade, various criticisms of functional tests have been expressed. Two are of practical importance. The first concerns the usefulness of tests, standardized on populations of normal children, for the assessment of handicapped children. If a test is designed to encompass the entire range of performance in a particular area of development then the resolution of the test has to be so coarse that it will not register small differences be-

Table 9.3: Some items from the Henderson Revision of the Test of Motor Impairment in the norm-referenced component

Task	Recorded
Completing a peg board, (first with right hand then left)	Time taken
Bouncing and catching a ball	Number of catches out of 10
Walking heel to toe (on a one-inch wide line)	Number of correct steps

tween impaired children. For the same reason, such tests may not identify small changes in performance resulting from intervention. The second criticism is that such tests rarely offer guidance to the individual assigned the task of trying to help the child with difficulties.

In spite of the criticisms these tests nevertheless serve some useful functions. For example, at a preliminary stage of assessment it is necessary to determine whether the 'clumsiness' noted by a teacher stems essentially from motor incoordination and is not the result of other problems. This, of course, only applies to children who do not exhibit an overt physical handicap. Functional tests also provide a starting point from which to determine future courses of action. To do this, it is better to ignore composite scores and examine the profile of the child's performance across tasks.

(2) DOCUMENTING HOW ACTIONS ARE PERFORMED

The assessments considered in this section have one critical feature in common. They focus on the characterization of *how* we move as opposed to what is achieved in the performance of a particular action. Without exception, they take as their point of departure the fact that there is noticeable regularity in the way human beings perform actions like walking, running, throwing or manipulating objects. The two approaches described below illustrate contrasting means towards this end.

Verbal description
The main feature of the instruments grouped under this heading is that they require an observer to watch *how* a child performs a particular task and check their observations against verbal descriptions of components of the movement pattern (for example, McClenaghan and Gallahue, 1978; Ulrich, 1984). The actions required in these tests are often identical to those in tests described as 'functional' (for example, throwing, catching, hopping). What differs is what the tester records (see Table 9.4). The criteria against which performance is judged are derived either from what is considered to be a mature or efficient pattern of movement or from documentation of specific stages within a developmental sequence leading to maturity. More usually they describe common faults characteristic of poor performance (Stott, Moyes and Henderson, 1984).

Table 9.4: Two items from Ulrich's (1984) Battery, which assesses how children perform some everyday tasks

Task	Recorded
Horizontal Jump: (as *long* as possible).	(1) Preparatory movement including flexion of both knees with arms extended behind the body. (2) Arms extend forcefully forward and upward, reaching full extension above head. (3) Take off and land on both feet simultaniously. (4) Arms are brought downwards during landing.
Overhand Throw: (as *far* as possible).	(1) A downward arc of the the throwing arm initiates the windup. (2) Rotation of hip and shoulder to a point where the nondominant side faces an imaginary target. (3) Weight is transferred by stepping with the foot opposite the throwing hand. (4) Following-through beyond ball release diagonally across body toward side opposite throwing arm.

These instruments, too, have limitations. In particular, they are not instruments which can be easily used without considerable experience in observing movement. Physical education teachers or therapists usually find them straightforward to use, whereas psychologists, often assigned the job of assessment, may find them more difficult.

Biomechanical analysis
This type of movement analysis lies at the other end of the spectrum of technical sophistication from the qualitative approach we have just dealt with. Here the view of the human body as a machine is most evident. What is of interest is the quantification of the spatial properties of the body parts as they change over time. The location of key parts, the angles of joints and the time relations between movement in one joint and movement in another can all be recorded. In addition to these measures, collectively called 'kinematic', others are often taken simultaneously. These include measurement of the forces exerted during an action and recording of the electrical activity of the muscles involved (EMG). Neuheuser (1975) provides a review of this approach. At the moment, this particular method of assessment is confined to clinical settings where special equipment is available. However, as newly qualified teachers and therapists emerge, able to use film and video analysis, the prospect of more widespread use becomes closer.

THE IMPORTANCE OF COMBINING APPROACHES (1) AND (2)

When the complete range of techiques which focus on the movements comprising an action are considered, there is no doubt that they add to what we learn from the 'functional' tests described in the first section. Nevertheless, it is important to note that one is not a substitute for the other. The relationship between the outcome of an action and the movements that comprise the action is a complex one, not yet well understood. Also in the case of impairment there are factors which have to be taken into account that differ from those normally operating. For example, if a child who had experienced difficulty learning to walk does so in a way that seems inefficient and tiring, then it is useful to consider ways of helping him to change the way he walks. However, it is not always possible for this to be achieved and the inefficiency may have to be tolerated because of the general importance of locomotion. In children with less severe difficulties an example of the same dilemma can be found in handwriting problems. Many children hold the writing implement in an odd way. Sometimes the grip can be changed to good effect, at other times it becomes apparent that the attempt is having a negative rather than positive effect. In sum, it is necessary to examine the outcome of the action and the way it is performed in conjunction. The approaches are, therefore, complementary rather than exclusive alternatives.

(3) ANALYSING COMPONENT PROCESSES

Over the last decade, approaches to the assessment of children with problems have diversified considerably. One strand of this diversification has arisen out of the development of closer links between cognitive and clinical psychology. The effect that cognitive psychology has had on the study of atypical behaviour is to focus attention on the analysis of the processes which underlie performance rather than measuring attainment in a blindly empirical fashion. This approach is often called the 'information processing' approach.

In numerous areas of educational practice the influence of this way of thinking about behaviour is increasingly evident. In the perceptuo-motor domain various authors have drawn attention to its value (for example, Connolly, 1984; Wedell, 1973) but its adoption by practitioners still seems to be limited.

Within the range of more formally presented test batteries there are two which exhibit the influence of the information processing approach (Stott, Moyes and Henderson, 1984; Laszlo and Bairstow, 1985). In the case of my own test (Stott, Moyes and Henderson, 1984) the approach provides a framework for the check-lists that accompany each item. The battery of Laszlo and Bairstow (1985) is based on their own information processing model of motor performance and contains a series of tests each designed to evaluate one or more of the processes they believe to be relevant to motor skill acquisition. The battery is designed on a rather grand scale and is intended to be used as a permanent fixture in a clinical setting and not for the preliminary stages of assessment.

Although, strictly speaking, task analysis is not a method of assessment, it would be impossible to discuss assessment without mentioning it. Also, though not necessarily linked to the information processing model of behaviour there are many who do view the approach in that way.

Breaking down a task into its component parts and designing sequences for teaching the components often involves inferences about the processes involved. For example, teaching a child how to catch a ball may include a stage of stopping a rolling ball. By implication, it is assumed that the processes involved in the latter task are less complex than the former. If this type of assessment could be successfully combined with the two types mentioned earlier then we may eventually attain a satisfactorly methodology.

SUMMARY

As we have considered a wide range of tests designed for different purposes it is difficult to make many general points about their efficacy in assessing motor impairment. However, the following observation may serve as an overview of the current 'state of the art' in this area. For administrative purposes it can be cautiously concluded that the psychometrically sound instruments are as satisfactory as their counterparts in other domains. We can reliably identify children at the severe end of the continuum but we commit too many errors when subtle problems are at issue. Within the realm of intervention, however, strong criticism of the failure of the tests to register small improvements which take place over an extended period of time are expressed. Another problem which is particularly acute in the motor domain is the relationship between levels of measurement. Intuitively, we are all aware that there is no one-to-one relationship between change measured by a physiotherapist, say, and that noted by the classroom teacher. Yet, empirically, we know very little about the variables which intervene to affect these relationships. This problem becomes ever more frustrating when we ask about the most appropriate remedial strategies, the most appropriate outcome variables to measure, what constitutes effective intervention and so on. What is singularly lacking is a comprehensive instrument with a sound theoretical rationale which cuts across levels and permits us to evaluate systematically the relationships between them.

References

REFERENCES ON THE ASSESSMENT OF CHILDREN WHO ARE VISUALLY IMPAIRED

Barraga, N.C. (1964). *Increased Visual Behaviour in Low Vision Children*. New York: American Foundation for the Blind.

Barraga, N.C. (1970). *Teacher's Guide for Development of Visual Learning Abilities and Utilization of Low Vision*. Louisville: American Printing House for the Blind.

Dunn, Lloyd, M., Dunn, Leota, M., Whetton, C. & Pintilie, D. (1982). *British Picture Vocabulary Scale*. Windsor: NFER-NELSON.

Elliott, C.D. (1983). *British Ability Scale*. Windsor: NFER-NELSON.

Lorimer, J. (1962). *The Lorimer Braille Recognition Test*. Bristol: College of Teachers of the Blind (now available from the Association for the Education and Welfare of the Visually Handicapped).

Lorimer, J. (1977). *Neale Analysis of Reading Ability Adapted for use with Blind Children. Manual and Directions and Norms*. Slough: National Foundaton for Educational Research.

Mason, H., & Tobin, M.J. (1986). Speed of information processing and the visually handicapped child. *British Journal of Special Education*, 13, 69–70.

Neale, M.D. (1958). *Neale Analysis of Reading Ability. Manual of Directions and Norms.* London: Macmillan (2nd Edn, 1966).

Neale, M.D. (1989). *Neale Analysis of Reading Ability: Revised British Edition.* Windsor: NFER-NELSON.

Newland, T.E (1971). *The Blind Learning Aptitude Test.* Champaign, IL: University of Illinois Press.

Tobin, M.J., Tooze, F.H.G., Chapman, E.K. & Moss, S. (1979). *Look and Think: A Handbook on Visual Perception Training for Severely Visually Handicapped Children.* London: Schools Council/RNIB.

Tooze, F.H.G. (1962). *The Tooze Braille Speed Test.* Bristol: College of Teachers of the Blind (now available from the Association for the Education and Welfare of the Visually Handicapped).

Williams, M. (1956). *Williams Intelligence Test for Children with Defective Vision.* Windsor: NFER-NELSON.

REFERENCES ON THE ASSESSMENT OF CHILDREN WHO ARE HEARING IMPAIRED

Anderson, R.J. & Sisco, F.H. (1977). *Standardization of the WISC-R Performance Scale for Deaf Children.* Washington DC: Office of Demographic Studies, Gallaudet College.

Conrad, R. (1979). *The Deaf School Child.* London: Harper Row.

Galbraith, D. (1984). Psychological assessment of deaf children. *Journal of the Association of Educational Psychologists*, 6, 19–27.

Kyle, J.G. (1980). Measuring the intelligence of deaf children. *Bulletin of the British Psychological Society*, 33, 54–7.

Quigley, S.P., Steinkamp, M.W., Power, D.J. & Jones, B.W. (1978). *The Test of Syntactic Abilities.* Beaverton, OR: Dormac.

Van Uden, A. (1977). *A World of Language for Deaf Children, Part 1: Basic Principles; a Maternal Reflective Method.* Lisse, The Netherlands: Swets and Zeitlinger.

Webster, A. (1986). *Deafness, Development and Literacy.* London: Methuen.

Webster, A. & Ellwood, J. (1985). *The Hearing Impaired Child in the Ordinary School.* Beckenham: Croom Helm.

Webster, A. & McConnell, C. (1987). *Children with Speech and Language Difficulties.* London: Cassell.

Webster, A., Scanlon, P. & Bown, E. (1985). Meeting the needs of hearing-impaired children within a local education authority. *Journal of the Association of Educational Psychologists*, supplement to 6, 5, 2-10.

Webster, A. & Wood, D.J. (1989). *Children with Hearing Difficulties.* London: Cassell.

Webster, A., Wood, D.J. & Griffiths, A.I. (1981). Reading retardation or linguistic deficit? I. Interpreting reading test peformances of hearing-impaired adolescents. *Journal of Research in Reading*, 4, 2, 136–47.

Wells, G. (1986). *The Meaning Makers: Children Learning Language and Using Language to Learn.* London: Hodder and Stoughton.

Wood, D.J., Griffiths, A.I. & Webster, A. (1981). Reading retardation or linguistic deficit? II. Test-answering strategies in hearing and hearing-impaired school children. *Journal of Research in Reading*, 4, 2, 148–57.

Wood, D.J., Wood, H.A., Griffiths, A.I. & Howarth, I. (1986). *Teaching and Talking with Deaf Children.* Chichester: John Wiley.

Wood, D.J., Wood, H.A. & Howarth, S.P. (1983). Mathematical abilities in deaf school-leavers. *British Journal of Developmental Psychology*, 1, 1, 67–74.

REFERENCES ON THE ASSESSMENT OF CHILDREN WHO ARE MOTOR IMPAIRED

Bruininks, R.H. (1978). *Bruininks–Oseretsky Test of Motor Proficiency.* Minnesota, Windsor: American Guidance Service NFER-NELSON.

Connolly, K.J. (1984). The assessment of motor performance in children. In: Brozek, J. & Schurch, B. (Eds). *Malnutrition and Behaviour: Critical Assessment of Key Issues.* Lausanne: Nestlé Foundation.

Henderson, S.E. (1986a). Problems of motor development; some theoretical issues. In: Keogh, B.J. (Ed.) *Advances in Special Education.* Greenwich CT: JAI Press Inc.

Henderson, S.E. (1986b). Problems of motor development; some practical issues. In: Keogh, B.J. (Ed.) *Advances in Special Education,* Vol 5. Greenwich, CT: JAI Press Inc.

Laszlo, J.I. & Bairstow, P.J. (1985). *Perceptual-motor Behaviour: Developmental Assessment and Therapy.* Eastbourne: Holt Saunders.

McClenaghan, B.A. & Gallahue, D.C. (1978). *Fundamental Movement: A Developmental and Remedial Approach.* Philadelphia, PA: W.B. Saunders.

Neuhauser, G. (1975). Methods of assessing and recording motor skills and movement patterns. *Development Medicine and Child Neurology, 17,* 369–86.

Stott, D.H., Moyes, F.A. & Henderson, S.E. (1984). The *Henderson Revision of the Test of Motor Impairment.* San Antonio, USA Footscray, UK: Psychological Corporation.

Ulrich, D.A. (1984). Test of gross motor development. Austin, TX: Pro-Ed. Inc.

Whitehouse, J. (1983). *Mossford Assessment Chart for the Physically Handicapped.* Windsor: NFER-NELSON.

The Law Relating to Assessment

Lynda Eaton

10

This chapter provides a background to the law in relation to education, which has produced many significant changes over the last 40–50 years including the introduction of compulsory education. The Education Act 1944 imposed on every Local Education Authority a duty to ascertain which children in their area required special educational treatment and prescribed formal procedures for discovering and placing handicapped pupils. The assessment and education of children with special educational needs is now provided for by the Education Act 1981, which was the response to the Warnock Report 'Special Educational Needs', the Report of the Committee of Enquiry into the education of handicapped children and young people (HMSO 1978, Cmnd 7212). This, together with the Education (Special Educational Needs) Regulations 1983 establishes the code of practice for the assessment of special educational needs in children under 19 years of age, the special educational provision to be made for such children in ordinary or special schools and the rules of procedure. The Act came fully into force on 1st April 1983 and contains provisions as to identifying and assessing children with special educational needs, children being defined in the Act to include any person who has not yet reached the age of 19 years and is registered as a pupil at a school. The main section of the Act is contained in Box. 10.1.

The purpose of an assessment under these provisions is to get as much information as possible about the child's needs to enable a decision to be taken about the type of special provision to be made, if required. It may involve any of the professional staff concerned with the child and will always, where the child attends school, involve consultation with the teacher who knows the child, one of the Authority's educational psychologists and a school doctor. Parents should be fully consulted and have every opportunity of making their views known during any assessment process. A child has special educational needs if he or she has a learning difficulty which calls for special educational provision to be made for him or her and a child is defined under the Act as having a learning difficulty if (a) he or she has a significantly greater difficulty in learning than the majority of children of the same age or (b) he or she has a disability which either prevents or hinders him or her from making use of the educational facilities of a kind generally provided in school in his or her area or (c) he or she is under the age of five years and is or would be, if special educational provision was not made

---

Box 10.1

The main section of the Act referring to special educational needs

Section 5, Education Act 1981.
(i) Where in the case of a child for whom a Local Education Authority is responsible, the Authority are of the opinion:

   (a)   that he has special educational needs which call for the Authority to determind the special educational provision that should be made for him; or

   (b)   that he probably has such special educational needs; they shall make an assessment of his educational needs under this Section...

(iii) If a Local Education Authority propose to make an assessment of the educational needs of a child under this Section they shall before doing so serve notice on the child's parent informing him:

   (a)   that they propose to make an assessment;

   (b)   of the procedure to be followed in making it;

   (c)   of the name of the officer of the Authority from whom further information may be obtained; and

   (d)   of his right to make representations and submit written evidence to the Authority within such period (which shall not be less than 29 days beginning with the date on which the Notice is served) as may be specified in the Notice.

(iv) When a Local Education Authority have served a Notice under Sub-Section 3 above and the period specified in the Notice in accordance with paragraph (d) has expired the Authority shall, if they consider it appropriate after taking into account any representations made and any evidence submitted to them in response to the Notice, assess the educational needs of the child concerned.

---

for him or her, likely to fall within either of the preceding cases (Section 1 (1), 1981 Act).

In relation to a child who has reached the age of two years, special educational provision is defined as being educational provision additional to or otherwise different from provision made generally for children of this age in schools maintained by the Local Education Authority concerned, and in relation to any child under that age it means educational provision of *any* kind. (See Box 10.2.) A child is not to be taken as having a learning difficulty purely because the language in which he or she is or will be taught is different from the language which is at any time spoken in his or her home. A statement is not required if, in the opinion of the Local Education Authority, the child's needs can be dealt with in a remedial class in an ordinary school. Formal procedures are not required where ordinary schools provide special educational provision from their own resources in the form of additional tuition and remedial provision, or in normal circumstances where the child attends a reading centre or a unit for disruptive pupils. No formal procedures are required when there is a need for extra help of short duration.

Section 5 of the 1981 Education Act refers to a notice to be served by the Authority in a specified form and gives the name of an officer from

---

Box 10.2

The section of the Act referring to the statementing of children

Section 7, Education Act 1981.
(i) Where an assessment has been made in respect of a child under Section 5, the Local Education Authority who are responsible for the child shall, if they are of the opinion that they should determine the special educational provision that should be made for him, make a statement of his special educational needs and maintain that statement in accordance with the following provisions of this Act.
(iii) Before making such a statement a Local Education Authority shall serve on the parent of the child concerned:
   (a)   a copy of the proposed statement; and
   (b)   a written explanation of the effect of Sub-Sections (4) to (7) below.
(iv) If the parent upon whom a copy of the proposed statement has been served under Sub-Section 3(a) above disagrees with any part of the proposed statement, he may before the expiry of the appropriate period:
   (a)   make representations (or further representations) to the Authority about the content of the proposed statement;
   (b)   require the Authority to arrange a meeting between him and an officer of the Authority at which the proposed statement can be discussed.
(ix) On making a statement under this Section a Local Education Authority shall serve upon the parent of the child concerned:
   (a)   a copy of the statement;
   (b)   notice in writing of his right under Section 8(i) of this Act to appeal against the special educational provision specified in the statement; and
   (c)   notice in writing of the name of the person to whom he may apply for information and advice about the child's special educational needs.

---

whom further information can be obtained, and will give a statement of the parent's rights to make representation and submit written evidence to the Local Authority about the assessment within a minimum of 29 days. After taking into account comments made and information submitted by the parents, the Authority will generally decide whether or not to proceed with the assessment. Sections 4 to 10 inclusive of the 1981 Act are the sections which contain provisions as to the identification and assessment of such children, for example, Section 4 refers to children under age two and Section 7 refers to the statementing of children (see Box 10.2). If the Authority decides full assessment is not necessary, the parents are informed in writing and have a right of appeal against that decision if they wish.

The making of an assessment at the request of parents. In the case of R. versus Hereford and Worcestershire County Council, *ex parte* Lashford (1986) (*The Times*, 10th November) it was held not to imply that education at a special school might be necessary and an application (as in that case by parents) to quash the decision of the Education Authority not to make a statement under Section 7 of the Act, was dismissed. It was indicated in that case that the 1981 Act made it clear that children of special educational needs were placed in two categories, the majority for whom no statement would be made and a small proportion for whom a determination and a statement was necessary. It was only if a child probably would need educational provision outside an ordinary school that a Local Education Authority would require to make a statement under Section 5, which would then lead to a statement under Section 7.

If a decision is made to proceed with an assessment, the parents are informed in writing and given reasons why the Authority proposes to do so. They may, at that stage, put forward their views on their child's special educational needs either by putting them in writing or discussing them during the assessment with the professionals concerned. The assessment will normally include an examination by a doctor or an interview with an educational psychologist, unless they have already recently been carried out, and the parents have a right to attend such interview. If the parents fail, without reasonable excuse, to comply with a notice served under Schedule 1, Paragraph 2 of the 1981 Act, requiring the attendance of the child for examination, then they are guilty of an offence and liable to a fine. An assessment is basically made in such manner as the Authority considers proper and appropriate and, after making such assessment, the Authority will normally make a draft statement of the child's special educational needs and the provision it proposes to make in the light of the information and advice received (Section 7). The parents will be sent a copy of the draft, which should include any comments already made by the parents, either in writing or in discussion, and they will be invited to comment further on it to the Authority and at that stage can require an interview with an officer of the Authority to discuss the proposed statement and can also ask, if it proves necessary, to meet any of the professionals to discuss the advice given to the Authority, if there are points on which they disagree. After further comments and representation are considered, the Authority will either make the final statement, in either the proposed or modified form, or decide not to make a statement. There are again rights of appeal by the parents and the notice indicating the right of appeal should give the name of the person to whom the parents may apply for information and advice about the child's special educational needs. The 1983 Regulations prescribe the frequency with which assessments should be repeated in respect of children for whom statements are maintained under Section 7 of the 1981 Act.

With regard to the Children Act 1989 for England and Wales, Schedule 12 paragraph 36 relating to children with special needs is operative and a new section is to be inserted after Section 3 in the Education Act 1981. This new section, 3A, allows a local authority to make arrangements for a child for whom they maintain a statement under Section 7 to attend an establishment, such as the Peto Institute in Hungary, outside England and Wales. Arrangements can also be made as to subsistence costs, fees and travelling expenses.

Where parents appeal against a statement made under the 1981 Act, they may appeal to an Appeals Committee in accordance with arrangements made by the Local Education Authority under Section 81 of the 1981 Act (see Box 10.3). The Appeal Committee can only consider whether the special educational provision specified in the statement is proper, after formal assessment has been made. If the Local Authority does

---

Box 10.3

The section of the Act referring to the appeals procedure

Section 8, Education Act 1981.
(i) Every Education Authority shall make arrangements for enabling the parent of the child for whom they maintain the statement under Section 7 to appeal, following the first or any subsequent assessment of the child's educational needs under Section 5, against the special educational provision specified in the statement.
(ii) Any appeal by virtue of this Section shall be to an Appeal Committee constituted in accordance with paragraph 1 or part 1 of Schedule 2 to the Education Act 1980.
(iv) An Appeal Committee hearing an appeal by virtue of this Section, may:
   (a) Confirm the special educational provision specified in the statement; or
   (b) Remit the case to the Local Education Authority for reconsideration in the light of the Committee's observations.
(vi) In any case where:
   (a) an Appeal Committee confirm the decision of a Local Education Authority as to the special educational provision to be made for a child; or
   (b) a Local Education Authority inform an appellant of their decision in a case which has been remitted to them under Sub-Section 4(b) above;
the appellant may appeal in writing to the Secretary of State.

Box 10.4

The section of the Act referring to the parents' right to request reassessment

Section 9, Education Act 1981.
(i) If the parent of a child for whom a Local Education Authority are responsible, but for whom no statement is maintained by the Authority under Section 7, asks the Authority to arrange for an assessment to be made of the child's educational needs, the Authority should comply with the request unless it is in their opinion unreasonable.
(ii) If the parent of a child for whom a Local Education Authority maintain a statement under Section 7, asks the Authority to arrange an assessment of his educational needs under Section 5, and such an assessment has not been made within a period of six months ending with the date on which the request is made, the Authority should comply with the request unless they are satisfied that an assessment would be inappropriate.

---

not maintain or propose to maintain a formal statement, then no appeal to the Committee can be made, but there is a right of appeal to the Secretary of State against a decision not to determine special educational provision as was dealt with in the case of *R. v. Lashford* referred to above.

When a statement is maintained, parents can also request reassessment after a period of six months and the Authority should comply with that request, unless they are satisfied such assessment would be inappropriate (see Box 10.4).

A code of practice as to the constitution and procedure of appeals established under the Education Act 1980 and the Education Act 1981, was circulated in February 1985, intended for use as guidance upon which Local Education Authorities would want to base their own codes, and has no statutory force as such. It sets out the constitution and procedure of Appeals Committees and has generally been followed by most Local Authorities. The code under Paragraph 5 does suggest non-statutory discussions to avoid the need for an appeal, particularly in relation to appeals relating to special education and the emphasis in the procedures under the 1981 Act is on cooperation. Clearly Authorities generally would want to accommodate the wishes of the parents wherever possible. If an appeal is made under the 1981 Act, it has to be in writing, setting out the grounds on which it is made, and the Local Education Authority should, it is suggested, devise a *pro forma* including guidance for parents, which should be given to parents who express dissatisfaction with the formal statement, in accordance with Section 7 of the 1981 Act (see Paragraph 6 of the Code). Appeals under the 1981 Act often require calling more evidence than appeals under the Education Act 1980 (Section 7 of which gives parents the right to appeal against decisions on the schools their children should attend). There is an increased likelihood of parents seeking their own expert evidence in connection with appeals for special educational provision and the Code of Practice has to be adapted accordingly. An Appeal Committee can either confirm special provisions specified in the statement or readmit the case to the Local Authority for reconsideration, in the light of their observations, and parents should be informed of the Appeal Committee's decision in every case. Unlike appeals under the 1980 Act, any decision made by an Appeal Committee in respect of special educational provision, does not bind the Authority. If parents are then still dissatisfied with the decision of an Appeal Committee or an Authority after it has been requested to reconsider a case, they can appeal to the Secretary of State. Parents should be informed of the further right of appeal and the address to which they should write.

In Scotland, parents are under a duty to ensure that their children receive suitable education until they are 16 (Sections 30 to 31 Education (Scotland) Act, 1980). In order to fulfil the obligations imposed upon them, they are under a duty to ensure the child attends school and they again have a right to chose a child's education, but that has to be exercised in accordance with the welfare principle. Section 3(2) Law Reform (Parent and Child (Scotland) Act, 1986) provides that in any proceedings relating to parental rights the Court should regard the welfare of the child involved as the paramount consideration and should not make any order relating to parental rights unless it is satisfied that to do so will be in the interests of the child. In weighing up factors which determine what is in the best interests of the child, the Scottish courts have given considerable importance to ensuring the child obtains a religious upbringing. The Education (Scotland) Act 1981 amends the law relating to the special educational needs of children. It gives a border approach to the question of what are the special educational needs for children and assessment thereof, so that the abilities and potential should be recognized rather than disabilities and handicaps. Similar provisions to the law relating to the assessment of children with special educational needs as under the 1981 Act in England and Wales apply. There is also an appeals procedure which is to be followed and is set out in the legislation.

Northern Ireland's special education system has been different from that of the rest of the United Kingdom, mainly in the way in which children with mental handicaps were treated. However, in 1986 the Education (Northern Ireland) Order 1984 was implemented and set out a new basis for special education in the province which is similar to that of the Education Act 1981 in England and Wales. At that time the position of children who were mentally handicapped was not changed. That Order gave Education and Library Boards detailed responsibilities to assess and determine the needs of and provision for children with special needs, leading to a statement of special educational need which was legally binding on the Education and Library Board and parents have extensive rights to be involved in the process of preparing a statement. However, initially the rights and duties which were brought into force did not apply to children deemed unsuitable for education in school and children with mental handicaps were excluded. There was a campaign during 1983 and 1984 conducted by a group of parents of children with mental handicaps, involving a threat of going to the European Court of Human Rights and finally it was accepted that the education of children with mental handicaps was to be the legal responsibility of the Education and Library Boards.

References

Bookbinder, G., O'Hagan, F. & Swann, W. (1984). The new laws on special education. *Open University Supplementary Material*. Milton Keynes: Open University Press.

Dwyer, E. & Swann, W. (1987). Educational services for mentally handicapped children in Northern Ireland: A survey of provision. *European Journal of Special Needs Education, 2*, 25–44.

Education Act. (1981). London: HMSO.

Education (Scotland) Act. (1981). London: HMSO.

Education (Special Educational Needs) Regulations. (1983). London: HMSO.

Halsbury's Statutes. (1986). 4th edn, *15*, 306–26. London: Butterworths.

The Encyclopaedia of Forms and Precedents. (1987). 5th edn, *13*, 326–32, 529–72. London: Butterworths.

Thomson, J.M. (1987). *Family Law in Scotland*. London: Butterworths.

Warnock Report. Great Britain. Department of Education and Science. Report of the Committee of Enquiry into the Education of Handicapped Children and Young People (1978). *Special Educational Needs*. London: HMSO.

National Developments in Primary School Assessment

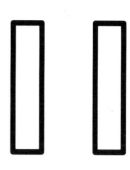

Roger Murphy

A range of factors, including the demise of the 11-plus examination in most parts of England and Wales, has led to the emergence of varied patterns of educational assessment in primary schools. The tests and assessment procedures reviewed throughout this volume are all used fairly extensively, but not in any particularly standard way. Prior to the proposals for National Curriculum assessments at seven and 11 years of age, LEAs might or might not have specified guidelines for pupil assessment in primary schools, and where they did have them they were likely to be fairly general, providing a framework rather than a straightjacket within which individual schools could operate. However Gipps et al. (1983) reported on the extensive introduction of LEA testing programmes in the 1970s, which in many cases appeared to be a somewhat confused attempt to respond to, or pre-empt calls for, greater accountability. In many cases such tests have little connection with the major objectives of the primary school curriculum, and as a result have done little to enhance the level of understanding of pupil achievement.

Thus in the 1970s and 1980s we have seen a general rise in the level of testing and assessment occurring in primary schools, but the variations in the procedures followed by individual schools have been enormous. A common tension around the country has nevertheless emerged in relation to some mistrust of commercially produced standardized tests as a basis for sensitively monitoring progress within the curriculum of any particular school. A consequence of this has been that where LEAs have gone in for large-scale blanket testing, using standardized tests, schools have continued to operate their own internal systems of pupil assessment and recording (Murphy, 1987a). Undoubtedly the approaches taken vary enormously, and there is a real danger of misrepresenting the full range of practice by attempting to describe it in summary form. It does, however, seem to be fairly typical for primary schools not to have an explicitly stated whole-school assessment policy. In many cases the philosophy is much more one of individual teachers adopting their own approach, informally in relation to their own class, with the recording and reporting of the findings of such assessments confined to a few brief notes or grades in a mark book. Clift et al. (1981) have provided an extensive review of the formal record-keeping systems that are used around the country, and in many cases these provide no more than a very modest view of the achievements that have occurred.

Where individual pupil record systems do exist there is widespread evidence that many teachers regard them as a chore to complete, and make very little use of them once they have been completed. This attitude towards keeping formal records of pupil assessments is often linked to the view that good primary school teachers can quickly form their own assessment of individual children when starting to teach them, and prefer to have a 'fresh start' rather than having their expectations coloured by formal records completed by other teachers.

Undoubtedly many primary school teachers are extremely gifted in terms of their ability to assess the potential, current skills and learning styles of individual pupils, and one can understand that brief, general statements on a record card may have little to offer them. Such a system does, however, demand a lot from each teacher, and may minimize the benefits that they can obtain from the insights of their colleagues about the children they are currently teaching.

The view that the educational process can benefit from teachers having a detailed understanding of the past achievements of the individual children they are currently teaching can be seen as an argument for the recording of such achievements in a form that can be passed from one teacher to another. Without such records the transfer of such information can only occur by word of mouth, and this introduces the related danger that where time is in short supply the message that is conveyed will be highly generalized, concerning the 'overall ability' of a child rather than more specific information about his or her particular strengths, weaknesses, talents or interests. Closely linked to this issue is the related concern of curriculum continuity, recognized as being very difficult to ensure for every child, particularly in primary education where many children are following what is in many respects an individual curriculum rather than a whole-class curriculum. Assessment and record keeping can be seen to have a vital role to play in assisting with the process of promoting curriculum continuity for all children.

Another major problem in relation to the prevalent informal approach to pupil assessment lies in the lack of specific information that it provides about a child's progress and achievements to other interested parties. Such information may be of interest to a wide range of individuals including curriculum consultants and other teachers with responsibility in the school, such as heads and deputy heads. Teachers within the school may be able to obtain the information that they need by occasional visits to the classroom, to teach or observe, and through discussions with the individual teacher when the need arises, but once again time may limit the extent to which this can occur.

More problematic are the needs of parents, governors, LEA officers and advisers, and other elected representatives with a responsibility for the provision of education in schools. There is widespread evidence that many such individuals feel frustrated by their lack of access to information about the achievements of primary school pupils. In some cases they will turn to such standardized test results as exist and are available to them, and may, as has already been noted, draw quite inappropriate conclusions from them.

In such a climate there is a fairly widespread support for attempts to develop pupil assessment systems in primary schools, so that they can more adequately satisfy the needs of the various interested parties mentioned. Approaches to this problem inevitably vary enormously and in each case the costs and benefits will need to be considered very carefully. For example, the resources required to develop and sustain any such new system need to be weighed against the potential benefits that may accrue from it. Shipman (1983), among others, has warned against the danger of spending much more time constructing such records than is ever spent consulting them. Nevertheless this is an area to which many primary schools are paying a great deal of attention. Some are involved in developments very similar to the profiling schemes that are being introduced in many secondary schools. These can involve pupils' personal records, negotiation, diaries and samples of work. In some cases these have been developed in liaison with the local secondary schools to which many of the pupils will move, as an attempt to aid the transfer process. Alongside this aim have been much broader aims related to the use of such information within the school as part of the teaching and learning process.

Such schemes may reveal a basis for developing pupil assessment in primary schools in a way that is both meaningful and manageable, and which produces results that reflect the achievements of individual children in relation to the curriculum they have followed. At present they are far from complete, or universally accepted, and if they are to develop they will need to be nurtured, resourced and protected from the demands of competing ideologies.

As this book is being completed development work relating to the proposed system of National Curriculum assessments is now well underway. All seven and 11 year olds being taught the National Curriculum will in due course be assessed against National Curriculum attainment targets. Their results on such assessments will be summarized and confirmed at the end of Years 2 and 6 of primary schooling. These assessments will be required by law, and schools will be required to publish the results at the end of Key Stage 2 (age 11) and have been strongly encouraged to publish their results at the end of Key Stage 1 (age seven).

The full implications of this return to compulsory pupil assessment within primary schools will only emerge fully once the system has begun to operate nationally for a few years. Piloting of the externally devised Standard Assessments Tasks (SATs) has already taken place, and as a result of the early trials a ministerial decision has been made to reduce the amount of assessment at the end of Key Stage 1. Teachers involved in the early trials of the Key Stage 1 SATs reported adversely on the tremendous workload that was associated with carrying out assessments across all of the Attainment Targets that are included in the core subjects and Key Stage 1.

The implications of this development for the future of pupil assessment in primary schools are enormous, and it is likely that substantial changes in practice will occur. Such changes are likely to lead to much greater uniformity of approach as all primary school teachers throughout England and Wales will be required to carry out assessments, throughout their teaching programmes, in relation to specified attainment targets for National Curriculum subjects.

The Proposed System of National Assessments

A system of national assessments, linked to the introduction of a National Curriculum, has been one of the key features, which has been stressed throughout the debate about the introduction of a National Curriculum. Since this was first mentioned in the Conservative Party's Manifesto prior to the 1987 general election. During the early part of 1987 these assessments were referred to by the Secretary of State as 'benchmark tests', but following the report of a special Task Group on Assessment and Testing (TGAT), later that year, a more comprehensive system of school-based and externally moderated assessments was proposed (DES, 1988).

The debate that has surrounded the proposals for national assessments has already been a turbulent one. It became front page news, for example, in the national newspapers during the spring of 1988, when a letter from the Prime Minister's office, which was critical of the complexity of the proposals contained within the TGAT report, was leaked. A key aspect of the debate, illustrated by the views expressed in the leaked letter, has been the conflict between a political interest in acquiring a simple index, which can be used to judge teachers, pupils and schools, and an educational concern over the potential damage that a narrowly conceived system of assessment could have on may aspects of education in schools (Murphy, 1987a and b, 1988a and b, 1990).

The TGAT report proposed a system of assessment which was far removed from the narrowly conceived idea of pass/fail tests administered to all seven, 11, 14 and 16 year olds. Their proposals were 'radical and evolutionary', and were based on a system that would give a central role to teachers in the assessment process, would attempt to assess and report achievement in relation to a wide range of attainment targets, and would attempt to describe each child's progress in each aspect of achievement in relation to a progression of ten levels.

In attempting to move away from a narrow system of pass/fail paper-and-pencil tests at each of the prescribed ages, the TGAT group recommended a much more ambitious system of assessment, which they hoped would more adequately reflect and support the diverse range of attainment targets contained within the National Curriculum. They also attempted to create guidelines for a system, which would allow different pupils to progress at different rates in relation to different aspects of the curriculum, and which could be administered and operated principally by classroom teachers.

One implication of the TGAT recommendations is that classroom teachers will need to be provided with considerable in-service training to prepare them for the role that will be required of them. Already most LEAs have run awareness-raising sessions, but before the system can become fully operational further training will need to be provided to support the development of criterion-referenced assessment procedures, new record keeping and information transfer systems, and procedures for groups of schools to operate cross-moderation procedures to ensure a uniformity of assessment standards throughout different regions.

All of this represents a fairly major culture shock for many primary school teachers for whom pupil assessment has in the past been a largely individual and low-key priority. Within a short space of time they have been moving into a nationally-controlled system, requiring them to produce detailed assessment information about the progress of all children in their classes in relation to a range of published attainment targets, select and administer a number of externally produced Standard Assessment Tasks at key stages, and liaise much more fully both within and between schools about assessment standards, moderation, record keeping, the transfer of assessment information, and the production of reports on individual pupil, year group, school and LEA assessment results.

Specific Concerns in Relation to National Assessment in Primary Schools

Considerable concerns have been expressed about the possible implications of national assessments for primary-school age pupils. Since the demise of the 11-plus examination, the primary school curriculum has, in the eyes of many, had the opportunity to take on a shape and form of development that can be severely hampered by the pressures brought about by externally imposed assessment systems. Individual pupils can be enabled to progress in different ways, and the curriculum experience offered can be viewed in a more holistic way than is possible when assessment has to be conducted in relation to subject areas within the overall curriculum.

Doubts have also been expressed about the wisdom of having too much assessment at this particular stage of a child's education, and an earlier proposal to make nine years a reporting age as well as seven, 11, 14 and 16 years was dropped as a consequence. Nevertheless assessments will need to be conducted throughout the period from five to 11 years of age, even though reporting and the requirement to complete several Standard Assessment Tasks will be mainly limited to the years in which pupils reach the ages of seven and 11. Thus, although teachers will be required to carry out their own in-class assessments throughout this time period, their use of the Standard Assessment Tasks will be limited to two particular years, and it was a firm recommendation of TGAT that the number of Standard Assessment Tasks should be limited.

Just what sort of impact all of this will have on primary schools, teachers and primary school pupils is difficult to ascertain. However, concern has been expressed about both the danger of the system leading to pupils being labelled, for example as being 'stuck at Level 1', in a way that hinders both their own development and their teachers' expectations for them, and of teaching being oriented much too narrowly onto those specific Attainment Targets and pupils that are regarded as being of prime concern in relation to raising a school's overall pattern of assessment results. Some pupils may be exempted from the assessment system, on the basis of special educational needs, but that in itself may lead to yet another type of labelling. Furthermore schools will not be legally required to publish their results for seven-year-old pupils (as they must at each of the other reporting ages) although they will be 'strongly encouraged to do so'. They will nevertheless have to provide parents with results for their children at this age, along with comparative data about the average levels of performance of children at that age both within the particular school and nationally.

A further concern in terms of interpreting results when a child is seven years of age has been the inability to gauge progress in relation to the achievement levels of children when they entered school. So, for example, schools that take in pupils who have been advantaged, for example by specific pre-school education, are likely to be assured of relatively impressive results at seven years of age, almost regardless of their provision from five to seven years of age. Such factors have led to concern over the impact of publishing results from primary schools, and about the way in which results may be misinterpreted by parents, the media and politicians. A likely but undesirable outcome will be that individual schools gain a reputation, and thus attract parents and pupils away from neighbouring schools, on the basis of what is thought to be a superior educational provision but which is really nothing more than an artefact arising from an unusually advantaged intake of pupils. In the context of the wider changes of the Education Reform Act, such as 'open-enrolment' and 'local financial management', such unwarranted shifts in the popularity of individual schools may have extremely damaging consequences on those schools whose results are interpreted less favourably, and who lose out as a consequence.

A final concern about the national assessment system relates in a more detailed way to the results that will be produced for each child and the extent to which they will be of use to the various interested parties. The national political concern seems to be to get results into the public arena where they can be used to judge the effectiveness of teachers, the curriculum and the schools (Murphy, 1990). This is all a long way removed from the day-to-day educational experience of each individual child, and the use of assessment to diagnose learning difficulties and/or to provide immediate feedback about progress, which can be effective in enhancing motivation and self-esteem. Although the TGAT report acknowledges the importance of these other functions of assessment, it seems that they will need to be carried out separately from the major national assessment procedures, which will be focused specifically on the fixed reporting ages.

The Impact of National Assessments on Primary School Assessments

All of these developments will undoubtedly have a major influence on primary school teachers throughout the UK. They will be required under the new system to apply certain assessment methods themselves, they will be trained to use some of them, and their whole thinking about assessment could be heavily influenced by the nationally declared attainment targets. However, it would be naive to consider that pupil assessment in primary schools under this new system will be limited to the procedures that will be enforced by the national assessment system at seven and 11 years of age. Even the TGAT report itself goes to great lengths to reinforce the view that effective pupil assessment goes well beyond the procedures that will be prescribed. Standardized tests will continue to have a role within the system. Indeed some of these may be used as one part of the procedure to determine the attainment levels of pupils in various curriculum areas at seven and 11 years. Others will be used for a wide range of purposes, such as screening, diagnosing, monitoring, selecting and setting, that are appropriate to their design, and have been discussed in this book.

National Curriculum assessments are likely to become a particular kind of response to a particular kind of political demand to make teachers, schools and LEAs more accountable. They also fit well with the drive towards giving parents the role of active consumers within an education system that attempts to provide choices about which school appears to offer the best prospects for the progress of their children. Inevitably the results of such assessment procedures will be kept simple, and the fact that they will only be revealed at two age points during the years of primary schooling will restrict their usefulness for teachers and pupils in terms of day-to-day progress within the classroom.

Apart from supplementing the prescribed National Curriculum assessment procedures with the additional use of certain standardized tests, many teachers will wish to continue to develop and improve their own continuous assessment and recording processes. Many primary schools have already been influenced by the move towards profile reporting in secondary schools and DES circulars heralding a national move towards producing records of achievement for all school pupils.

There has been an increasing interest in the potential for developing profiling and records of achievement approaches in primary schools. These approaches tend to be much more pupil-centred than other assessment approaches, and seek to create a running record of the major experiences and achievements of the individual pupil. These may be recorded and/or validated by a range of individuals including the child himself or herself. Generally where such systems have been operated (see Ryan, 1988) they have tended to become a dynamic influence on the whole teaching and learning process, and this has been widely reported by both teachers and pupils. A major feature in many profiling schemes already in existence is the self-assessment role which the pupil can adopt. Just how far this level of pupil involvement in the assessment process can be made in the early years of primary schooling remains to be seen, but it is nevertheless an enticing prospect. Again and again younger children have proved able to perform much more complex tasks than originally expected (Donaldson, 1978), and the exploration of different approaches to reporting on self-assessment could easily lead to similar developments in this area.

The Future of Pupil Assessment in Primary Schools

Pupil assessment can be seen as a vital dimension of the educational process experienced by each child. It has the potential to enlighten the learner about his or her own strengths and achievements, and can in turn be a vital element in attempting to enrich the experiences that are then embarked upon (Murphy and Torrance, 1988). Pupil assessment as such can suffer from becoming too formal and prescribed, because the results and procedures may become more and more remote from the day-to-day experience in the classroom. However the danger of informality is that pupil assessment may be assumed to be occurring as part of other routine classroom processes, but may in the event never be given the specific attention it requires.

Further attempts to define some of the major expected outcomes of primary schooling may help teachers in their own attempts to articulate and record the developments that they observe at regular intervals during their normal teaching activities. Assessment will still need to go well beyond the confines of the National Curriculum however, and it will still be necessary to create the broadest possible picture of educational progress for each child during the years of primary schooling.

We await the operational impact of the National Curriculum assessments and the records of achievement initiatives on primary schools, and much change is anticipated. It is hoped that individual schools will be able to use these initiatives as part of a general review of their own assessment practices and policies. The challenge here will be to produce a unified approach that makes sense in relation to the overall curriculum of the school, and the way in which it is being taught. When harnessed effectively to the taught curriculum, assessment can become a dynamic force for enriching and enhancing children's learning. Unfortunately, however, this is often not the case in practice, and assessment procedures can get in the way of good education rather than promote it.

The challenge that faces primary schools as they are forced to reconsider their approach to pupil assessment is a considerable one. Meeting that challenge will not be easy, but there is every reason to believe that it is a challenge that can in time be used to ensure a more central, and hopefully a more beneficial, role for assessment within primary school education.

References

Donaldson, M. (1978). *Children's Minds*. London: Fontana.

Clift, P., Weiner, G. & Wilson, E. (1977). *Record Keeping in Primary Schools*. London: Macmillan Educational Books/Schools Council.

Gipps, C., Steadman, S., Blackstone, T. & Stierer, B. (1983). *Testing Children: Standardised Testing in Local Education Authorities and Schools*. London: Heinemann Educational.

Great Britain. Department of Education and Science (1988). *National Curriculum Task Group on Assessment and Testing Report*. London: DES.

Murphy, R.J.L. (1987a). Pupil assessment in primary schools. *Forum, 30*, 1, 6–8.

Murphy, R.J.L. (1987b). Assessing a national curriculum. *Journal of Education Policy*, 2, 4, 317–32.

Murphy, R.J.L. (1988a). Great Education Reform Bill testing proposals. *Local Government Studies*, 14, 1, 39–45.

Murphy, R.J.L. (1988b). TGAT — a change of heart? In: Torrance, H. (Ed.) *National Assessment and Testing*. Edinburgh: BERA.

Murphy, R.J.L. (1990). National assessment proposals: analysing the debate. In: Flude, M. and Hammer, M. (Eds). *The Education Reform Act 1988*. Lewes: Falmer Press.

Murphy, R.J.L. and Torrance, H. (1988). *The Changing Face of Educational Assessment*. Milton Keynes: Open University Press.

Ryan, A.S. (1988). *Partnership in Assessment. Pupil-Centred Profiling in a Middle School*. University of Southampton, Department of Education, occasional publication.

Shipman, M. (1983). *Assessment in Primary and Middle Schools*. London: Croom Helm.

Curriculum Related Assessment: The Importance of Educationally Relevant Data

12

Robert Cameron

Although it may seem strange to have a topic like 'curriculum related assessment' appearing at the end of a book which has examined and evaluated many formal testing procedures, this chapter is not meant to be a quaint afterthought. Instead it is a timely reminder that the bulk of 'testing' which takes place in education does not use standardized and/or commercially available tests but arises naturally as a consequence of teaching. In short, as Cornwall (1981) reminded us 'the most important assessment techniques are not published at all, but proceeded by teachers for use in their own classrooms'.

In the past, there has been a tendency, especially among support professionals working outside the classroom, to devalue home-spun assessment procedures. Indeed, it is only relatively recently that the importance of curriculum-related assessment by teachers has been recognized (see Ainscow and Tweddle, 1979; Cameron, 1981; Cornwall, 1981). Yet there are several important differences between teacher-initiated assessment and standardized procedures. Not the least of these contrasting features concerns the usefulness of the data which are collected. One good 'test' of any test is whether the data generated lead to measurable improvements in the school, the class or at the teacher–pupil interface!

A Mis-match in Assessment?

The first LEA Educational Psychologist (Burt, 1921) argued that 'there is no standard of comparison that can surpass or supersede the considered estimate of an observant teacher working daily with individual children'. Despite this generally undisputed observation, for many decades, teachers and psychologists were encouraged to value a method of assessing pupil performance which had scarcely more than a fleeting relationship with what went on in the classroom. This approach consisted of using tests which attempted to measure endogenous or 'within-pupil' variables in the learning equation. Although such pupil-focused factors as intelligence, personality traits, laterality, specific abilities, attitudes and so on hold much fascination for people working outside the classroom, they the have common feature that they are only indirectly related to the teaching process and therefore have few direct implications to the teacher.

Although the within-pupil model of assessment was clearly only marginally related to the microcosm of life in the classroom, this drawback did not seem to effect its popularity and growth in the 1960s and 1970s educational scene. Nowhere was the gap between the psychologist's and the teacher's view of the world more apparent than in work with pupils who had special educational needs. Gibbs (1982), in a survey of tests used with children who had severe learning difficulties, was able to show that the vast majority of teachers favoured task or curriculum-related measures of pupil progress. Psychologists on the other hand seemed to prefer IQ and ability tests and, as Tyler and Miller (1986) pointed out, this within-pupil data was being used to aid educational decision-making, especially in 'selecting treatment goals, determining educational placement, planning educational programmes and the remediation of learning difficulties'. In other words, data which were only peripherally related to the teaching process were more highly valued than the more direct observations of the class or subject teacher. If the focus of assessment is on the task rather than the pupil, the problems in mathematics being experienced will be seen in curriculum terms and assessment procedures are likely to involve a close scrutiny of specific curriculum areas where difficulties are most evident. In the present circumstances, this could involve checking out the pupil's basic number skills (for example, numeration, computation, or operational processes) or it might mean examining an area of the mathematics curriculum where the pupil is experiencing particular difficulties. For example, in Box 12.1 the 'time' section of a mathematics curriculum is illustrated. Checking out the 'failing' pupil's performance on such a curriculum is likely to pinpoint certain objectives where the pupil needs practice of intensive teaching. With all forms of curriculum-related assessment, the purposes are twofold: to identify the pupil's current repertoire and to use this information to plan an individualized remediation programme for the pupil in question.

It is not the intention of this chapter to examine in detail the increasing criticism to which the 'within-pupil' approach has been subjected. An unwanted and apparently unavoidable outcome has been the problem which can arise as a result of using within-pupil data to label children (an excellent discussion of the phenomena of 'stigma' and 'spoiled identity' can be found in Scamble, 1984). However, the biggest deficit of tests of intelligence, personality, abilities and attitudes, was that they did not readily generate implications for changes in curriculum or classroom management. In other words, this type of data rarely yielded the information about a pupil's educational strengths or needs which could be used to adjust either the curriculum or teaching method. Indeed there was even the possibility that an exclusive focus on within-pupil variables could divert attention away from other features of the learning context which were more amenable to change for example, the quality of teaching, the choice of teaching materials, the section of appropriate curriculum objectives or the organization of classroom/school resources.

Box 12.1

One section of an agreed school curriculum in Basic Mathematics Skills

Section Topic: Time

	Class Teacher's Rating		
	Can do well	Needs practice	Cannot do
1. Differentiates 'day' and 'night'			
2. Differentiates 'morning', 'afternoon', 'night'			
3. Differentiates 'special days' e.g. Sunday/Monday			
4. Names days of week			
5. Understands 'yesterday', 'today', 'tomorrow'			
6. Names 'day after' and 'day before'			
7. Differentiates 'special times' e.g. getting up, bedtime, lunchtime etc.			
8. Tells time hours only			
9. Tells time $\frac{1}{2}$ hour & hours			
10. Tells time $\frac{1}{4}$ hours, $\frac{1}{2}$ hours & hours			
11. Names and sequences months			
12. Writes date correctly			
13. Uses calendar to plan ahead			
14. Uses calendar to review previous events			
15. Tells time (24 hour clock)			
16. Calculates journey times			
17. Calculates period elapsed between earlier historical events			
18. Understands 'time lines'			

Pupil Performance and Curriculum Objectives

Clearly there was a need to develop an educationally relevant alternative to 'within-pupil' measures. What was needed was an approach which allowed teachers to discuss in a more concrete way *how* teaching problems could be tackled, rather than providing an explanation of *why* each problem arose. In education, assessment began to shift away from 'the pupil' and concentrate more on 'the learning situation'. Bloom (1979) referred to this trend as an increasing concern with the 'alterable variables of teaching', two of the most important of these 'alterable variables' were what had been learned already and what needed to be taught in the future.

The need to develop appropriate curriculum-related assessment procedures had also been given a degree of urgency by educational legislation. The assessment of pupils' special educational needs required by the 1981 Education Act had been described as 'not an end in itself, but a means of arriving at a greater understanding of a child's learning difficulties for the practical purpose of providing a guide to his or her education and a basis against which to monitor his or her progress' (DES draft circular, 1982). Similarly, the Educational Reform Bill requirements on testing re-focused attention on educational rather than 'within-pupil' variables, with curriculum-related assessment of pupils progress recommended at ages seven, 11, 14, and 16 years.

Assessment in Perspective: Comparative, Diagnostic and Curriculum Related Procedures

If we take a broad view of educational assessment, then we can see that schools and local education authorities (LEAs) make use of a number of different assessment procedures. These fall into three main groups. The first consists of *comparative* tests used to discover 'where an individual pupil stands in relation to the group as a whole or other individuals' (Assessment of Performance Unit, 1978). Secondly, *diagnostic* tests are primarily concerned with identifying strengths and weaknesses of individual children (APU, op. cit.). The third group, *curriculum related* procedures are aimed at determining 'whether something that has been taught has been learned and/or mastered' (APU, op. cit.). These three types of assessment procedure will now be discussed in turn.

COMPARATIVE ASSESSMENT

Many of the attainment tests discussed in previous chapters fall into this particular category. Indeed there is no shortage of commercially produced tests (particularly in reading, spelling and basic number skills) which can be used for making comparisons between pupils, using norms obtained from a large UK-wide example of similar aged pupils. It is also hoped that the development of computer-stored test items banks could offer flexible forms of attainment testing which are more attuned to the needs of education authorities. The idea would be that an LEA would select relevant educational criteria in a particular topic area and use items standardized on national samples to develop their own tailor-made assessment procedures. Promising though such initiatives are, it is also important to consider the purpose of attainment testing. In a classroom setting, the results of attainment tests may be limited, especially since the data may tell the class teacher only a little more than was already known, namely that certain pupils may have special needs or problems in particular areas of learning. On the other hand, data from attainment tests can be of great value to LEAs, especially when allocating additional resources to pupils who have special educational needs.

One particularly interesting formula for allocating additional resources on a more rational and equitable basis has been employed by the Mid-

Hampshire Educational Psychology Service for the past two years. In Mid-Hants, under attaining pupils, initially identified by the school staff, can be tested on a comparative assessment procedure which is based on a national sample of school children (the *Salford Sentence Reading Test*) and an additional 30 minutes per day teacher-pupil contact time allotted to those pupils whose results fall below the fifth centile (15 minutes per day are available for pupils in the fifth to tenth centile range). It has been argued that this system does not require resources much in excess of present additional resources for special educational needs which are allocated on an *ad hoc* basis (Faupel, 1986).

DIAGNOSTIC ASSESSMENT

Once again there is no shortage of commercially produced materials in this area. Unfortunately for teachers, many of these diagnostic tests have been designed to measure 'within-pupil' variables, for example, IQ, abilities and so on. Such tests may be able to explain or suggest causes for some of the more intractable learning problems which pupils may exhibit. For example, the *Wechsler Intelligence Scale for Children* (WISC) might throw some light on the encoding, organizational or decoding processes of a poor reader. However, a better starting point for helping the pupil who is failing in reading would be to concentrate on those reading skills (for example, sound blending, word attack skills, scanning) that make up the reading task itself. Information of the latter kind can inform teachers about an appropriate teaching programme for the pupil with reading difficulties.

The increasing demand from teachers for core curriculum areas like reading, spelling, basic number skills and handwriting to be analysed into skill components and arranged if necessary in a hierarchial sequence which aids teaching, has led to a dramatic increase in commercially produced criterion-referenced assessment procedures. 'Criterion-referenced assessment describes what pupils know or can do in relation to curricular goals and without reference to the performance of others' (Drever, 1983). On a criterion-referenced check-list, each component skill becomes a carefully sequenced item on the check-list. (Component skills are often identified by classroom observation, or controlled research studies.) Assessment involves finding out what skills the individual has already acquired and this data can be used to plan an individualized curriculum for a future remediation programme.

The design of criterion-referenced measures is not without difficulties as Ingenkamp (1979) has pointed out. However, such skill-based procedures also have a number of advantages which can be summarized as follows:

1. A detailed picture of an individual's skill repertoire can be built up.
2. Unlike 'within-child' measures like the *WISC*, which are restricted to a small number of specially trained professionals, a criterion-referenced check-list usually requires little training to administer and can be completed by people in continuous contact with pupils over a period of time (see Wolfendale, 1988).
3. The data obtained from criterion-referenced procedures can be used to pinpoint important future teaching objectives.

CURRICULUM RELATED ASSESSMENT

Although the notion of specifying a curriculum in terms of proposed teaching objectives may have initially conflicted with the ideas of self development and discovery learning, which followed the publication of the Plowden Report (1967), the last decade has seen a considerable increase in the emergence of teacher-selected objectives which define specific curriculum content areas. The 'objectives' movement has gathered pace not only because of the integration of children with special needs into a mainstream setting but also because more 'teacher-friendly' models of curriculum planning have been developed (see especially, Lister and Cameron, 1986). Assessment by objectives seeks to measure pupil performance in any curriculum area against a list of pupil objectives which have been selected and agreed by teachers themselves. Although it implies an initial teacher time commitment of agreeing, clarifying and writing down the objectives which make up a particular content area, assessment by objectives has many advantages including the possibility of on-going (as opposed to once-off) assessment carried out by a person who can use the data most appropriately (that is, the class teacher). The information generated has direct relevance to the future curriculum and the teaching methods needed to guide the pupil more easily through the curriculum where difficulties are being experienced.

Although it is central to good teaching, assessment by objectives is not without its problems, chief of these being the possible narrowness of the curriculum objectives being measured. It is quite clear that the quality of pupil performance can vary considerably yet many curriculum-related assessment procedures have concentrated on the initial mastery of specific objectives. Only rarely have the more challenging features of learning, including the consolidation of learning and integration with the pupil's existing knowledge been considered. The problem has been summarized by Drever (1983) who highlighted the need for a reconciliation between 'higher' and 'basic' aspects of learning. Until such a *rapprochement* takes place 'a gap will remain between the teachers short term pedagogical concerns in the classroom and the long-term goals of the curriculum. The problem of narrow assessment measures was also highlighted in a Secondary Schools Examinations Council publication on *Policy and Practice in School-based Assessment* (1986). The Council argued that assessment and curriculum planning were linked and that there was an urgent need for 'process' assessment which included 'analysis enquiry and investigation, problem solving, research, selection and organization'.

A New Hierarchy of Learning

A number of exciting new possibilities have been opened up at the learning—teaching interface by work carried out at the University of Washington where Haring, Lovitt, Eaton and Hansen (1978) identified and described a new hierarchy of learning. This learning model is described in some detail in their pioneering text: 'The Fourth R: Research in the Classroom'. The starting point of Norris Haring and his colleagues was their belief that 'learning' was 'the ability to carry out skills in increasingly complex situations'. The learning hierarchy which emerged as a result of this longitudinal school-based research indicated five interlocking stages of learning: *acquiring* a new skill, performing it *fluently*, *maintaining* it over time and finally *generalizing* and *adapting* the skill in new problem situations. (See Box 12.2 for a summary of these steps.)

Box 12.2			
A new model of learning, adapted from White and Haring (1980)			
Level of learning	General description	General teaching objectives	Suggested assessment procedures
ACQUISITION	Emphasizing accuracy	To teach pupils correct new responses and help pupils to avoid/unlearn incorrect responses	Assessing levels of accuracy attained
FLUENCY	Combining speed and accuracy	To help pupils reach the required (or appropriate) level of mastery of the skill(s)	Assessing progress towards agreed levels of fluency
MAINTENANCE	Maintaining fluency	To help pupils to maintain a high level of fluency over a period of time	Assessing levels of skill retention and fluency over a period of time
GENERALIZATION	Changing materials or context for required skill	To help pupils performing skill(s) fluently to achieve mastery in different settings/contexts and with different materials	Assessing effect of: (a) using different teaching materials (differentiation) (b) Using different contexts (discrimination)
APPLICATION (OR ADAPTATION)	Adapting skill/ knowledge repertoire to new problem situations	To help pupils to discriminate key elements of new situations and provide appropriate responses	Assessing the level of adaptation e.g. using problem solving or simulation exercises

White and Haring (1980) went on to use this hierarchy as a model for developing methods of teaching which teachers would find most effective in helping pupils to proceed through these five different levels of learning. The possibility of using this five-stage model to examine links between early stages of learning (for example, acquisition) and the later, more complex stages involving the generalization and adaptation of acquired skills was suggested by Cameron, Owen and Tee (1986). They proposed that the Haring *et al.* (1978) hierarchy could be used as a framework for developing more flexible and sophisticated curriculum-related assessment procedures which could provide information on basic and/or higher order learning (see also Brown *et al.*, 1989). These five levels of learning will now be considered within the assessment context:

ACQUISITION

On the Haring et al. hierarchy, this is the earliest or most basic level of learning where emphasis needs to be on learning for accuracy. It is at the acquisition level that inappropriate as well as appropriate responses can be learnt. A good example of this is the person who learns to type using the inappropriate, and eventually limiting, strategy involving two fingers and a thumb and who is eventually overtaken and then outstripped by a colleage who acquires the more adaptable skills of touch-typing using all eight fingers and two thumbs. In much the same way, inappropriate sub-skills or incorrect responses can be acquired in the early stages of reading, handwriting, spelling and basic number skills and these 'bad habits' can cause major problems at later stages of learning. Hence the importance of the 'accuracy' component in the early stages of skill acquisition.

Many of the criterion-referenced check-lists referred to earlier are designed to measure pupil performance at the acquisition level. One particularly detailed example is the *Portage Early Education Checklist* (Bluma et al., 1976). Commercially available check-lists like these and the more common curricula, where objectives have been selected by teachers themselves (for example, Box 12.1) offer teachers a range of objectives which can be used as (a) an initial or ongoing assessment procedure and (b) a curriculum guide for future teaching. However, few guidelines about the quality of the learner's responses have been provided: the emphasis is on ensuring that these key skills are acquired in the first place.

FLUENCY

Fluency (or proficiency) can been seen as a combination of accuracy and speed. One frequently observed feature of pupils who have failed to make progress in a particular skill area (for example, reading) is that, although they may have acquired key reading skills, they are very slow at using these when compared with their 'good reader' counterparts. One set of assessment materials, in the *Daily Teaching Assessment – Primary Aged Children* programme (Ackerman et al., 1984) responded to research findings which indicated that fluency was an essential (and often neglected) stage of successful learning by providing accuracy and fluency for key objectives in handwriting, mathematics, reading and spelling. As a result of these assessment procedures, pupils, who had a history of underachievement in any of the core curriculum areas, could not only be receiving a DATA-PAC individualized teaching programme, but would also be expected to reach required levels of fluency in key objectives before proceeding to later objectives in the curriculum.

MAINTENANCE

Skills which are not practised or rehearsed from time to time tend to become redundant. It would be interesting to invite a group of teachers and psychologists to repeat the maths or history 'O' level papers which they sat when they were in the fifth form. Many people would probably be surprised at how rusty their 'O' level learning had become. For skills to remain functional, pupils need to be helped to maintain fluency over time.

There is little evidence of the use of school-based assessment procedures for measuring maintenance. One notable exception is the *Early Learning Skills Analysis* package where a column in the pupil progress record is entitled 'Check' and acts as a reminder to teachers that objectives which were previously mastered by pupils need to be checked systematically to ensure that even the best-taught skills are maintained at a reasonable fluency level (Ainscow and Tweddle, 1984).

GENERALIZATION

There are two essential features of generalization. The first is that pupils should be able to carry out the skill or skills which have been taught even if the context or the teaching materials change. Again there are a few examples of the assessment of pupil performance at this level of the learning hierarchy. Curtis (1983), who used roleplay situations to teach social skills to secondary pupils, highlighted the importance of generalization when he suggested that 'progress evaluation should be carried out by seeing how the learner can transfer these skills into a real life situation'. By 'real life situations' Curtis meant outside the teaching context, in real life social encounters, where events were less predictable and where help, in the form of prompts or advice from a friendly adult, was unlikely to be as freely available as it had been in the teaching context.

Generalization can also involve discrimination of subtle change in the teaching materials. In reference to learning basic number skills, for example, such discrimination may mean moving from the use of concrete aids (for example, counters or bricks) to semi-concrete aids (for example, tally marks) or moving from two-row addition to four-row addition. It may even mean helping pupils to discriminate between easily confused, early addition and subtraction processes. Despite the obvious importance of this stage of the learning hierarchy, once again there are very few published examples and equally few instances of teacher initiated assessment at the generalization level of learning.

ADAPTATION OR APPLICATION

In essence, the higher order learning processes of applying or adapting taught skills means 'problem solving'. Problem solving involves teasing out the key elements of a new or unfamiliar task and selecting appropriate responses, which would allow the new task to be satisfactorily completed. 'Skills are non functional unless they are usable in a modified form in response to new problems or new situations'. (Haring et al., op. cit.). Although this level of learning is the one which has always been declared to be of greatest interest to both teachers and support professionals in education, there are surprisingly few school-based examples of curriculum-related assessment at this level. In a crude sense, many 'A' level questions require pupils to adapt the scholastic skills they have acquired by asking questions which begin with the words 'discuss...'.

Computer programmes which give pupils the opportunity to problem solve in a simulated situation (for example, governing a 'banana republic', running a small business firm or even refighting the Battle of Britain) offer tremendous opportunities for assessment at the adaptation level. Carefully selected computer software programmes could be used to measure adaptation of previously acquired skills (see Palmer and Cameron, 1984).

Final Comments

Murphy (1986) discussed the need to explore new initiatives which include: employing a wider range of pupil achievement; providing meaningful and positive descriptions about what all pupils can do; promoting curriculum development; enhancing pupil motivation and teacher morale and encouraging a more harmonious relationship between assessment, curriculum design and teaching methods within individual schools. While curriculum-related procedures may not score high marks on all these criteria, it is hoped that some of these procedures described in this chapter may at least attain a reasonable grade for effort and intention.

Many of these current developments in curriculum-related assessment have been given an added urgency by the requirements of the great Education Reform Bill. Although much controversy and apprehension has surrounded the clauses which advocate national testing at seven, 11, 14, and 16 years, no one would deny that data of this nature will have major implications for teaching and resource allocation. Curriculum-related procedures offer the additional possibility for continuous assessment which spans a pupil's entire school career and which is of everyday relevance to the teacher in the classroom.

Already there is one aspect of curriculum-related assessment which is showing considerable promise. For many years, psychologists focusing on 'within-pupil' variables have used an esoteric vocabulary to attempt to share their findings with the class teacher. Similarly, both generalist and specialist advisers developed their own, but completely separate, jargon for conveying their point of view. Faced with advice of this sort, the understandable reaction of the class teacher was to give up and carry on what they were doing in the first place. Curriculum-related assessment has attempted to overcome these communication problems by offering a shared like language in education – a sort of educational Esperanto – which could allow everyone including teachers, parents, support professionals and policy makers to work more closely together for the benefit of all pupils within the educational system.

References

Ackerman, T., Gillett, D., Kenward, P., Leadbetter, P., Mason, L., Matthews, C., Tweddle, D. & Winteringham, D. (1984). *Daily Teaching and Assessment – Primary Aged Children*. University of Birmingham: Advanced Professional Training in Educational Psychology.

Ainscow, M. & Tweddle, D. (1979). *Preventing Classroom Failure: An Objectives Approach*. Chichester: Wiley.

Ainscow, M. & Tweddle, D. (1984). *Early Learning Skills Analysis*. Chichester: Wiley.

Assessment of Performance Unit. (1978). Assessing the Performance of Pupils. *DES Report on Education*, No. 93. London: HMSO.

Bloom, B. (1979). *Alterable Variables: The New Direction in Educational Research*. Edinburgh: Scottish Council for Research in Education.

Bluma, S., Shearer, M., Frohman, A. & Hilliard, J. (1976). *Portage Guide to Early Education*. Checklist. Windsor: NFER-NELSON.

Bookbinder, G.E.E. (1976). *Salford Sentence Reading Test Forms A, B and C.* Sevenoaks: Hodder and Stoughton.

Brown, M., Begley, J. & Cameron, R.J. (1989). Special needs: spelling. *Support for Learning.*

Burt, C. (1921). *Mental & Scholastic Tests.* London: Staples Press.

Cameron, R.J. (1981). Curriculum development: clarifying and planning curriculum objectives. *Remedial Education, 16, 4,* 163–70.

Cameron, R.J. Owen, A.J. and Tee, G. (1986). Curriculum management. Part 3. Assessment and education. *Educational Psychology in Practice, 2, 3,* 3–9.

Cornwall, K.F. (1981). Some trends in pupil evaluation: the growing importance of the teacher's role. *Remedial Education, 16, 4,* 157–61.

Curtis, M.A. (1983). Social skills training in the classroom. *Occasional Papers of the British Psychological Society Division of Educational and Child Psychology, 6, 3,* 22–31.

Drever, E. (1983). Curriculum objectives as assessment criteria: some problems of validity. *Programmed Learning and Educational Technology, 20, 1,* 54–9.

Great Britain. Department of Education and Science (1982). *Assessments and Statements of Special Needs.* Draft Circular. London: HMSO.

Faupel, E. (1986). *Learning Difficulties in Primary Schools* (Service Discussion Document). Winchester: Mid-Hampshire Educational Psychology Service.

Gibbs, T. (1982). Language Assessment of ESN(S) Children. *Special Education: Forward Trends, 9, 1,* 23–6.

Hampshire Advisory Teacher Educational Psychology Services. (1988). *Special Needs: Spelling.* Part 1: *Handbook;* Part 2. *High Frequency Words;* Part 3. *Phonically Regular Words;* Part 4. *Suffixing.* University of Southhampton: Continuing Professional Development in Educational Psychology.

Hansen, C.L. (1978). Writing Skills. In: Haring, N.G. *et al.* (Eds). *The 4th R: Research in the Classroom.* Columbus, OH: Merrill.

Haring, N.G., Lovitt, T.C., Eaton, M. & Hansen, C.L. (1978). *The 4th R: Research in the Classroom.* Columbus, OH: Merrill.

Ingenkamp, K.H. (1977). *Educational Assessment Series: European Trend Reports on Educational Research.* Slough: NFER.

Leach, D. (1980). Assessing children with learning difficulties. *Journal of the Association of Educational Psychologists, 5, 3,* 16–23.

Lister, T.A.J. & Cameron, R.J. (1986). Curriculum management (Part 1): Planning curriculum objectives. *Educational Psychology in Practice, 2, 1,* 6–14.

Murphy, R. (1986). A revolution in educational assessment, *Forum, 28, 2,* 41–43.

Palmer, C.C. & Cameron, R.J. (1984). Applied psychology and computer-assisted learning, In: Cameron, R.J. (Ed.) *The Psychologist and the Microcomputer.* Leicester: British Psychological Society.

Plowden Report. Great Britain. Department of Education and Science. Central Advisory Council for Education (England). (1967). *Children and their Primary Schools.* London: HMSO.

Secondary Schools Examinations Council (1986). *Policy and Practice in School-based Assessment.* Working Paper No. 3. London: SEC.

Scamble, G. (1984). Perceiving and copying with stigmatizing illness. In: Fitzpatrick, R. *et al.* (Eds). *The Experience of Illness.* London: Tavistock.

Tyler, B. & Miller, K. (1986). The use of tests by psychologists: Report on a survey of BPS members. *Bulletin of the British Psychological Society, 39,* 405–10.

Wechsler, D. (1949). *Wechsler Intelligence Scales for Children.* New York: The Psychological Corporation.

White, D.R. & Haring, N.G. (1980). *Exceptional Teaching.* Columbus, OH: Merrill.

Wolfendale, S. (1988). *The Parental Contribution to Assessment.* Developing Horizons No. 10. London: NCSE.

Test Reviews

As was mentioned in the Preface, we did not set out to produce exhaustive test review sections in these volumes. This would have defeated the object of providing readable introductions to an area, of a reasonable length. In any case, there are a number of encyclopaedic reference volumes produced regularly in which the interested reader can find basic factual information about the full spectrum of assessment materials published around the world.

Our aim has been less wide-ranging, but in some ways more difficult. We canvassed the views of many teachers, psychologists and academics and compiled a restricted list of assessments which fall into the following categories:

1. Tests which are widely used by teachers in schools.
2. Tests which are used by non-teachers such as psychologists in an educational context. Recent Education Acts and the growth of support services has ensured that the results from such tests impinge more and more on the lives of classroom teachers.
3. Newer tests with interesting features.
4. Some representative tests in areas where there is no tradition of large-scale assessment.

Reviewers were asked to write to a format – giving such basic information as the test's purpose, age, components, availability and technical properties. Finally, they were asked to evaluate whether – in their view – the test did what it claimed to do. Some of these opinions may be controversial, but we hope they will contribute to the arguments and discussions between test users, authors and publishers.

Given the introduction of national testing and the increased activity by test developers and growth of local testing initiatives we may produce a second edition of this book in the future. If you have a test that you would like to see reviewed in the next edition, please let us know.

Finally, any choice such as this will dissatisfy some users. If you have comments on our choice of tests, do let us know.

Assessment in Nursery Education

Test authors. M. Bate and M. Smith.

Purpose. This manual is intended for use by staff in nurseries to assess the development and performance of children, recording their progress during their attendance in nursery education provision.

Subject population. Children aged three to five years in nursery schools, classes and combined centres.

Administration time. The manual is designed for continuous use during play sessions, so the time taken will vary.

Materials. The items required for assessments include: the manual itself, record sheets, the pack of pictures, everyday nursery equipment.

Structure and administration. The manual is designed to assess performance in five key areas and each area is assessed through a number of related items. The groups of items are independent of each other and may therefore be used in any order. This manual is intended to be used in the normal classroom activities, so that a test situation is avoided, and flexibility in integrating the items in the play session is achieved through familiarity. Sections of the manual have been colour coded, so that the most appropriate tasks may be set for a child. The assessments include; social skills scales, social thinking, talking and listening, thinking and doing, and manual and tool skills.

Scoring and interpretation. The items are scored by ticking the box on the record sheet representing the descriptor which most accurately matches the child's response to the set task. Thus a glance at the record sheet will inform staff of the number of tasks attempted, and the levels of achievement. Such results may be used to decide on future activities for the child and it is anticipated that a child will be reassessed on a set of items after a six-month period so that progress can be noted.

Technical details

Standardization, reliability and validity. The manual is not intended to be used to compare the children's achievements with norms, and performance on items may be more dependent upon length of attendance at the nursery, rather than age or other factors. Standardization was based on observations involving trials of the materials with pilot groups, identified as exemplifying 'good practice', in different parts of the country. Detailed comments on the trial items were made by advisory groups which included teachers, advisers and lecturers. Inter–rater reliability was low at 54 per cent overall. The items are meant to be used in the nursery setting with familiar adults. In this case two psychologists were used. One wonders why staff teams were not used for this check. Bate *et al.* (1984) comment that validity will, in the end, be borne out in practical use in assessment manuals of this type. However, the manual is reported to have high validity on roughly half its items, when compared with five McCarthy scales on similar lines, and with teachers' ratings.

Evaluation. This manual proved somewhat over-facing to many teachers when it first emerged. With the colour codings it is intended to be more manageable but it would still require very frequent use to gain sufficient familiarity to be employed without constant referral to the text. The pictures supplied with the pack are unfortunately highly stereotyped and give the pack a dated look. To end on a positive note, however, the manual could offer the basis for staff discussions in the development of a school assessment record. This would be particularly important in schools where the pack might prove inappropriate, since there is no evidence of trials with bilingual children, nor awareness of cultural bias.

Country of origin. UK.

Publisher. NFER-NELSON.

Date of publication. 1978.

References.
Bate, M., Smith, M. & James, J. (1984). *Review of tests and assessments in early education (3–5 years)* (Revised). Windsor: NFER-NELSON.
Tyler, S.T. (1980). *Keele Pre-school Assessment Guide.* Windsor: NFER-NELSON.

Tricia David
University of Warwick

The Aston Index

Test Authors. Margaret Newton and Michael Thomson.

Purpose. The Aston Index is a screening test for use by classroom teachers. It is intended to identify children who are not 'maturationally ready' to learn basic literacy skills in reading and writing or who have unusual deficits which might hinder their early progress unless they are taken account of.

Subjects. The main group of subjects is children in the infant classes at primary school (that is, four to six year olds). It has also been used with older children and adults.

Administration Time. The administration time is up to 60 minutes in total but in the case of small children this would normally require to be spread over several sessions.

Materials. A score sheet is necessary for each child. The test materials consist of three sets of cards with symbols and pictures printed on them and four test booklets which contain pictorial material and instructions and material for various tests.

Structure and administration. There are 17 separate tests, four of which are only given to older children. The tests are relatively easy to administer, given a little practice. The teacher is required to give them, in most cases, to the individual child in a quiet setting away from distraction (hardly the average infant classroom!).

Scoring and interpretation. Scoring appears superficially to be straightforward and all teachers will be able to arrive at a final score and profile. However, reliable scoring of some of the tests is likely to be problematic (for example, the drawing tests).

Technical Details

Standardization. The standardization is based on two studies. One of these is a two-year follow-up of infants and the second is a study of good and poor readers at the older age levels. However, essential data missing include numbers in samples, ages of children, standard deviations of scores, sampling method and background of sample.

In some respects the *Index* is not strictly normative but more a criterion oriented test. It is not a device for which norms should be the main criterion of its worth, however at least a passing effort at fulfilling the basics of psychometric reporting might have been made.

Reliability. The standard tests used are highly reliable and for others, split-half reliability coefficients are quoted and are high. Inter-rater reliability is omitted, however.

Validity. Various correlations are quoted which show that there is some relation between the tests and literacy skills. It is also shown, unsurprisingly, that children at different levels of literacy achievement score at different levels on the tests. There are, however, other approaches to validity which could have been included.

Evaluation. The index gathers together in a compact and useful format a number of classroom techniques and tests which teachers should be familiar with and might find useful in certain situations. The overall presentation with 'norms' and 'profiles', overplays the realistic limits of the *Index* however.

Specific profile discrimination is claimed, which is unlikely, and as the general specific deficits approach to remediation is not particularly effective, the test is probably of limited use.

Country of origin. UK.

Publisher. Learning Development Aids.

Date of Publication. 1982.

Murray Porteous
University College Cork

Behaviour Assessment Battery

Test authors. Chris Kiernan and Malcolm C. Jones.

Purpose. A book of tests and check-lists for use by teachers and psychologists to assess children with severe and profound mental handicap, and to construct individual teaching targets and plans. It covers basic cognitive skills, play and social behaviour, communication and self-help skills. It gives a flexible and unique way of evaluating children functioning at a very low developmental level.

Subject population. Severely and profoundly mentally handicapped children. Some sections are also useful with physically, visually and auditory handicapped children.

Administration time. Depends upon the number of sections used. For the total battery not less than three hours.

Materials. The *Battery* is purely a book of tests; materials (including a tape recorder, toys and everyday objects) need to be assembled following directions given.

Structure and administration. The *Battery* has 13 sections each covering a major area of skill. Each has a series of items covering discrete skills, some of which (for example, Exploratory Play) are described in detail together with a method of presentation. For other items (for example, Communication), an interview schedule is given, to be administered to parents or care staff. Visual directions are given for the Sign Imitation Test.

Scoring and interpretation. The scoring sheets consist of 13 'lattice' diagrams, to be photocopied from the book. Items achieved by the child are scored out. Prompting and guidance are also recorded. The check-lists and interview schedules are not directly scored, but used as information for deciding whether a criterion behaviour is present and scoring it.

Technical Details

Standardization. Because this is a book of criterion-related rather than norm-related tests, no normative data is given. Details are included of the development sample of 174 mentally handicapped children gained from hospitals, nurseries and special schools.

Reliability. The authors quote test–retest reliabilities for nine sections involving direct testing, varying from 0.95 to 0.76. Percentage agreement between observers on these sections vary from 72 per cent to 92.86 per cent. For 11 sections, Guttman coefficients of reproducibility vary from 0.95 to 0.76 (1.00 being a perfect linear progression).

Validity. The main aim of the *Behaviour Assessment Battery* is producing individual teaching programmes. For this reason no validity information is given, although comparisons are made throughout with the *Uzgiris–Hunt*

Scales (Uzgiris and Hunt, 1975). No indication is given about its predictive value.

Evaluation. The quality and quantity of detail about a child given by using this *Battery* has to be weighed against its complexity in use, lack of test material and score-sheets and the length of time it takes to carry out. It is best considered as an item bank for use in the construction of intensive teaching programmes for individual children.

Country of origin. UK.

Publisher. NFER-NELSON.

Date of publication. 1977, revised 1982.

References
Dickens, P. & Stallard, A. (1987). *Assessing Mentally Handicapped People: A Guide for Care Staff.* Windsor: NFER-NELSON.
Kiernan, C.C. & Jones, M.C. (1980). The Behaviour Assessment Battery for use with the profoundly retarded. In: Hogg, J. & Mittler, P. (Eds). *Advances in Mental Handicap Research*, Vol. 1. London: John Wiley.
Uzgiris, I.C. & Hunt, J. McV. (1975). *Assessment in Infancy.* Urbana, IL: University of Illinois Press.

Paul Dickens
Forth Valley Health Board,
Stirling

Basic Mathematics Tests A, B, C, DE, FG

Test author. National Foundation for Educational Research.

Purpose. Tests in this series were first published between 1969 and 1971, and the stated purposes differ somewhat between them. They attempt to 'measure children's understanding of...fundamental relationships and processes', to provide measures of attainment, and to give some diagnostic information about individual strengths and weaknesses (not Test FG). Several Tests (B, C, DE, FG) attempt to 'eliminate...the effects of different teaching methods'. It is hard to imagine how this can be achieved, or indeed if it is possible.

Subject population. Children eight years 4 months to 15 years.

Administration time. About 50 minutes; scoring time five minutes.

Materials. Each test comprises a Manual and consumable booklets.

Structure and administration. Tests A and B are administered orally to groups or individuals; both can be given in two halves, split by the mid-morning break. Administrative details of both tests, and of Tests C and DE are clear and sensible. Little guidance on testing practice is offered for FG; there, the script for administration is sparse but adequate.

Tests A and B present items on equating; counting; adding; ordering; subtracting; classifying; multiplying and dividing. These operations are applied to the topics of size; shape; volume; fractional parts; the interpretation of bar charts and pictograms; place value; area; money; length; weight; and time.

Tests C and DE introduce reflection; order; use of number patterns and number bases. Topics covered include vulgar fractions; decimals and percentages; Venn diagrams; histograms; line graphs and 3-D drawings; set membership and set intersection; permutations, combinations and probability. In DE, most of the test items require a high level of reading competence, which is likely to adversely affect the scores of poor readers.

Test FG presents 55 items which cover choice of operations to satisfy number equations; calculation of volumes and areas; reading and interpreting tables; binary arithmetic; powers, series, inequalities; equivalent fractions; percentages and decimals; reflections and rotations.

Scoring and interpretation. Generally, the instructions for scoring are clear, and scoring keys are easy to use. Several manuals explain the meaning of standard scores clearly – C does not. On Tests A, B, and DE, and individual pupil's score is wisely reported as lying within a score band. Tests C and FG report single scores. On *no* test can the reader be sure that the standardizing sample is representative of the school population nationally.

On many Tests, test items can be classified to give scores on different topics and different operations. The diagnostic use of many tests are limited by the small number of items devoted to several of the topics. Test C fails to explain the diagnostic scoring scheme; FG has no diagnostic use at all.

Technical details

Standardization. Test A was standardized on 6000 pupils in the Midlands and a London borough; B on 7000 children in urban areas in West Yorkshire and the Midlands; C and DE on 8000 and 7000 children respectively in unspecified areas; EG provides three separate ill-defined standardizing samples! None of these samples can claim to be representative of the UK school population.

Reliability. The Manual reports the internal consistency (KR-20) for Test A to be 0.91, based on an ill-defined sample of 261 children; Test B reports KR-20 from an undefined sample of 362 children to be 0.91; on Test C, KR-20 was found to be 0.95 in an undefined sample of 297 children; on Test DE KR-20 was found to be 0.96; for Test FG one of the standardizing samples was used in its entirety (1579 children) to calculate KR-21 – a value of 0.96 was found. In all cases, the information about the sample composition is seriously deficient.

Validity. No validation studies have been conducted. Most of the tests provide a blueprint and detailed description of items which allow judgements to be made about content validity.

Evaluation. This series of tests is a considerable improvement on NFER's *Mathematics Attainment* series, which it seems to have been designed to replace. In many respects the series is inferior to *Mathematics 7–12* which seems to have been designed as its replacement.

Several of the Manuals in the *Basic Mathematics* series are clearly written and informative; test contents are usually interesting; test administration and scoring is usually well described and straightforward. The emphasis on a score band rather than a single score to report pupil attainment, used in many of these tests, is welcome. Also welcome is the effort to set out the rules for item construction. So too is the notion of using tests to diagnose pupil and class weaknesses as a basis for future remedial action, which is offered in most of the tests. No advice is offered about how to use the diagnostic information; no studies of the diagnostic uses of the tests are offered. There are problems with standardization, reliability and validity already mentioned.

Overall, *Basic Mathematics* is a patchy collection of tests – good in parts, but seriously deficient in others – too patchy to be used as a whole. *Mathematics 7–12* should be used instead.

Country of origin. UK.

Publisher. NFER-NELSON.

Date of publication. 1969 to 1971.

Jim Ridgway
University of Lancaster

British Ability Scales (BAS)

Test author. C. D. Elliott.

Purpose. The *BAS* is a battery of 23 tests for the individual assessment of cognitive abilities in children. It has developed from the British Psychological Society's support for a 'British Intelligence Scale' in the 1960s through an earlier version with L. Pearson and D. Murray as co-authors.

The *BAS* is a broadly diagnostic assessment, both to generate and test hypotheses of children's strengths and weaknesses as well as to identify or characterize learning difficulties. It provides data on sample-free ('criterion oriented') abilities as well as norm-referenced scores. The latter provide IQs of the traditional type, a General IQ, a Verbal IQ and a Visual IQ. The *BAS* includes two attainment tests. Further aims are to help define learning objectives, and to evaluate change in abilities over time.

Subject population. Children aged two and a half to 17 years. Some of the Scales apply only to the younger ages, and others to the older.

Administration time. Variable, depending on how many subtests are given. One subtest might take only five minutes. A realistic time for a Full-Scale IQ using ten scales would be at least an hour. Age and other characteristics of the child also affect time.

Materials. Four detailed, comprehensive manuals, and a small suitcase full of materials ranging from blocks, wooden toys and picture cards to written pro-forma.

Structure and administration. The *BAS* have a well-documented theortical background (see Manuals 1 and 2). The 23 'abilities' in the scales have been derived using the Rasch Model of psychometrics. The ability score is an absolute measure, and has the advantage of examining change independent of a norm. For example, the 'growth' of a child's Word Definition ability might be contrasted to his or her lack of growth in Word Reading Ability over a six-month period.

The *BAS* is theoretically based on a number of constructs and five processes: reasoning, spatial-imagery, perceptual-matching, short-term memory, and the retrieval and application of knowledge. Speed of processing is additional. The inclusion of verbal or visual stimulus modes and motor or verbal response modes provides a framework for the scales. A brief outline of each scale follows.

Speed.
Speed of information processing. Rows of numbers are crossed out under strict timing. Uses booklets.

Reasoning.
Similarities. Three words given orally, child to give linking concept.
Matrices. Booklets of designs with space to complete 'pattern'. Child draws it.

Formal operational thinking. Child looks at pictures of boy/girl with variously changed attributes, for instance hair. Has to state logical relationship. Based on Piagetian formal operational stage. (Time consuming!)

Social reasoning. Child is given 'mini-story' asked to comment on moral issues and comprehend social situations. Based on Kohlberg's moral development theories.

Spatial imagery.

Block design level. Blocks put together to copy a pattern shown on card. Timed.

Block design power. Same test as above but stricter timing to achieve score.

Rotation of letter-like forms. Child chooses a letter like shape to match one of six shown. Must imagine shape seen from different viewpoint.

Visualization of cubes. Cubes with different pictures on each face are shown. Child to choose which of four pictures of cubes represent the one held.

Perceptual matching.

Copying. Copying graded shapes.

Matching letter-like forms. As title!

Verbal-tactile matching. Picking items out of a bag that have been described by the tester, using touch only.

Short-term memory.

Immediate visual recall. Child verbally recalls, after study pictures that have been shown on one large card.

Delayed visual recall. As above but after 20–30 minutes delay.

Recall of designs. Child draws designs from memory after they are shown on card.

Recall of digits. Child repeats digits (increasing length), given orally at one per half second.

Retrieval and application of knowledge

Basic number skills. Mainly arithmetic items covering the four operations. Number concept for younger children.

Naming vocabulary. Naming objects pictures on cards.

Verbal comprehension. Following simple instructions with toy-like items.

Verbal fluency. Naming items under categories, for example things to eat.

Word definitions. A vocabulary scale.

Word reading. Individual reading of graded words.

The BAS is a test available only to those with appropriate training and qualification, and its administration requires a lot of practice and study. All the scales should never be given to one child. The selection of the appropriate test is a key feature of administration.

Scoring. The raw score for each scale is converted to an ability score. This measure is used as a basis for conversion to centiles and T-scores. These combinations along with z-scores enable the examination of changes in ability over time as well as comparing the child to a 'norm'. In addition there are useful discrepancy tables. One ability can be predicted from another. This enables reliable (5 per cent significance levels are given) evaluations of profiles. Individual variations, strengths and weaknesses in ability can be determined. Tables for calculating a general, verbal and visual IQ are given along with confidence limits.

Technical Details. A mass of technical information is provided with the BAS.

Standardization. Approximately three and a half thousand children in 75 LEAs across the UK from different geographical and social groups were involved (about 200 children for each year of norms). A US standardization is under way.

Reliability. Internal consistancies are given for all scales and all age ranges and for most there are around 0.7 to 0.9. Visual recall scales are the lowest at around 0.45 (depending on age). IQ reliabilities are between 0.9 and 0.95. Younger age groups gave rise to lower correlations on the whole. Confidence limits based on Standard error of measurement and score reliabilities are given.

Validity. A great deal of data is also given here. Considerably more than any comparable test (for example, the WISC). Construct validity and factorial validity, based on scale inter-correlation are presented. These support the verbal/visual dimensions of the scales. A number of other validity studies are summarized.

WISC (R). Correlations are full-scale/general 0.59, verbal/verbal 0.66, performance/visual 0.25.

WPPSI. Correlations full-scale/general 0.79, verbal/verbal 0.82, performance/visual 0.53.

Some significant correlations with 'O' levels, for example, English Literature 0.51 with Word Definitions; Mathematics 0.63 with Speed of Information Processing; Young Group Reading similar score to Word Reading. Research is also reported on special groups of children, for example, hearing impaired children are poorer on verbal items and better on some spatial imagery items. Children with specific written language difficulty (dyslexia) are poor on short-term memory items. There are characteristic profiles (see manuals for references to above).

Evaluation. The BAS is a comprehensive and up-to-date assessment of children's cognitive abilities. The detail given in terms of theoretical background and technical data is thorough. This positive information enables one to recommend the scales in psychometric terms. In addition there are many useful, practical features of the BAS, such as the ability scores, discrepancy tables, evaluation over time and items with good 'face validity'. These make the test useful for the applied psychologist. The scales can seem daunting: the very breadth of BAS can make it inaccessable unless one is prepared to devote a good deal of time to learning how to use the test. Experience in the use of the BAS is particularly required in choosing which of the various short tests for each scale to use for a given child. The BAS should be a key battery for the practitioner using regular formal cognitive assessments. For those preferring more informal assessment individual scales can be selected for use to provide more objective information.

Country of origin. UK.

Publisher. NFER-NELSON.

Date of publication. 1983.

References
Elliott, C.D. (1983). *The British Ability Scales Introductory Handbook*, NFER-NELSON.
Elliott, C.D. (1983). *The British Ability Scales Technical Handbook*, NFER-NELSON.

Michael E Thomson
East Court School,
Ramsgate.

British Picture Vocabulary Scale (BPVS)

Test authors. L.M. Dunn and C. Whetton.

Purpose. This is a test of a hearing vocabulary for standard English. It is also an achievement test in that it makes an assessment of the extent of vocabulary acquisition. This can be useful for a variety of groups: preschool children, early and general school use, foreign language students, clinical use with non-readers, autistic and even psychotic individuals. The subject should have no hearing difficulties.

Subject population. Two year olds to adults.

Administration time. My own experience with five and six year olds is a maximum of five minutes on the short form. Four year olds are more variable. Scoring time is under a minute.

Materials. There is a (verbose) manual including a large number of tables. There are booklets of pictures and record forms for the long and short forms and a plastic stand to present the pictures. The BPVS is contained in a convenient box.

Structure and administration. Those children under eight years are given training pictures, but I find that this is unnecessary even for most five years olds. The task is to point to one out of four pictures to indicate the word spoken by the examiner. The short form has a total of 32 items and the long form 150 items. As most teachers will use the short form only this will be described here. The object in testing is to find the critical range which provides maximum discrimination among those of similar ability. One begins at different points, depending on age, but moves further back if the items are too difficult. The basal point is where there are six consecutive correct responses and the ceiling is where out of six consecutive responses there are four errors.

Scoring and interpretation. As an example, suppose the last item administered for the ceiling was the 22nd item and the total number of errors was 6; these errors comprised of the four within the ceiling region and two within the region between the basal and ceiling regions. The raw score is 22 minus 6 which is 16. From the raw score the age-equivalents and percentiles can be looked up.

Technical Details

Standardization. The test was developed from the *American Peabody Picture Vocabulary Test*. A pool of 424 items (excluding American terms) were given to 1401 subjects ranging from two to 16 years, from which the short and long forms of the test were derived. The short form (mainly) was given to a representative sample of over 3000 children in the UK.

Reliability. Split-half reliabilities ranged from 0.75 to 0.86 for each year group from three to six years. But for 17 year olds reliability goes down to

0.41 on the short form, due to the small number of items. There are no measures of test–retest reliability.

Validity. The content validity is good in that there are 18 categories covered to ensure a breadth of vocabulary (for example, animals, actions). But no data are provided on direct tests of validity.

Evaluation. As pointed out in the manual, this is a test of hearing vocabulary by selecting pictures. It is not the same as the subject giving a definition of a word as in the *Stanford-Binet, Wechsler* and *BAS* scales. This is a distinction between measuring receptive language in the case of the *BPVS* and measuring expressive language as well. The test is well constructed to give a quick and efficient measure of current vocabulary level. Further research is needed to establish the connection between this test and intelligence tests. As other research has established strong connections between IQ and other vocabulary tests (including the *Peabody* from which the *BPVS* is derived), it is likely that a strong connection would be found. This does not mean that it should be treated as an IQ test, as testing vocabulary is only a limited aspect of cognitive abilities.

Country of origin. UK.

Publisher. NFER-NELSON.

Date of publication. 1982.

John R. Beech
University of Leicester

Bury Infant Check (BIC)

Test authors. L. Pearson and J. Quinn.

Purpose. To identify young children with learning difficulties during their first months in the infant/first school.

Subject population. Children about age five years.

Administration time. Approximately ten minutes per child (full form).

Scoring and interpretation. Each item in the five sub-scales (language, learning style, memory number and perceptual-motor skills) is scored 1 or 0, giving a possible overall total of 60 points. Suggested intervention scores are given for the language and number sub-scales and for the full *BIC*. The authors state that these are guidelines which may be raised or lowered by teachers in collaboration with colleagues. Standardization data indicate the percentages of children obtaining specific scores on the sub-scales and full *BIC*.

Technical Details

Standardization. An experimental version was produced in 1978. This was subsequently standardized on a sample of children (n = 1751) from one LEA reflecting a 'reasonably representative cross-section of the UK population'.

Reliability. Test–retest reliability was assessed with a small sample (N = 42) with a three-week interval between pre- and post-testing. Testing was carried out by M. Ed. students. It is not clear whether or not these students were also the children's usual class teachers. Total test–retest reliability was low (r = 0.67) but was higher for some sub-scales (for example, language r = 0.89) and for the quick check of teacher-rated items (r = 0.99).

Validity. Predictive validity was assessed for children (N = 255) from seven schools using the *Young's Group Reading Test (YGRT)* and *Young's Group Mathematics (YGMT)* as criteria. Few children obtaining poor scores on the criteria were 'missed' by the *BIC* two years earlier. The authors discuss the important point that manipulation of cut-off points influences the apparent predictive validity of the *BIC*.

Evaluation. The *BIC* is useful as a formal procedure for monitoring young children's progress if there is no effective school-based system. However, as the National Curriculum is gradually implemented, schools should be developing curriculum-based systems for monitoring learning. These will need to be supplemented with hearing and vision checks. The *BIC*, like the *Infant Rating Scales (IRS)*, provides a basis from which schools may develop monitoring of the National Curriculum.

Country of origin. UK.

Publisher. NFER-NELSON.

Date of publication. 1986.

References.
Pearson, L. & Lindsay, G. (1986) *Special Needs in the Ordinary School: Identification and Intervention.* Windsor: NFER-NELSON.

Ann Lewis and
Tricia David,
University of Warwick

The Children's Action Tendency Scale (CATS)

Test author. R. H. Deluty

Purpose. The CATS is a self-report inventory, designed to assess the tendency of children to respond in an aggressive or submissive manner to situations involving provocation, frustration, loss or conflict. It provides a means of identifying children who would be likely to benefit from assertion training.

Subject population. Children aged six to 12 years.

Administration time. Approximately 20 minutes plus 10 minutes scoring time.

Materials. Questionnaire booklet and scoring key.

Scoring and interpretation. The original version of the CATS contains 13 items, each of which describes a conflict situation to which children are asked to select the responses that they would be most likely to give. Each item provides three response alternatives in paired comparison format. Thus, for each conflict situation, all possible combinations of the three alternative response styles (aggressive, submissive and assertive) are presented and the opportunity to always select the socially desirable response is avoided. By comparing choices across these styles of responding, the relative tendency towards aggressive, submissive and assertive behaviour can be assessed, providing three separate scores on each dimension. An abbreviated form of the CATS is available (Deluty, 1979).

Technical Details. There appears to be a lack of large-scale standardization work in relation to the CATS and the normative data provided by Deluty (1979) are limited to small samples of US school children. The internal consistency of each of the aggressiveness, assertiveness and submissiveness subscales of the CATS is reported to be acceptable (Deluty, 1979) and test–retest correlations over four months were found to be moderate. The content validity of CATS items was given particular attention during the development of the questionnaire. The discriminant validity of the scale was supported by the finding of highly significant differences in CATS scores on the aggressiveness and assertiveness sub-scales between clinically aggressive children and regular school pupils (Deluty, 1979). The concurrent validity of the CATS has also been investigated (Deluty, 1984). This study demonstrated significant correlations between CATS scores and behavioural measures of aggressiveness, submissiveness and assertiveness taken over an eight-month period of direct behavioural observation.

Evaluation. The CATS is a useful measure of children's tendencies to engage in aggressive, submissive and assertive behaviour. Its main use is as a screening instrument as one means of identifying children with interpersonal problems. It provides minimal information as to specific social skills deficits or particular targets for intervention. Little consideration is given to those positive situations which require assertive responses, such as the giving of compliments or expression of affection. The lack of large-scale normative data also limits the clinical utility of the CATS.

Although the CATS is generally easy to administer, some children find it difficult to respond to forced choice pairs when they are unlikely to give either response (for example when the choice is between submissive or aggressive and the child's usual response would be assertive). This brings into question the validity of responses on forced choices for some of the CATS items.

Country of origin. USA.

Publisher. R.H. Deluty, Department of Psychology, University of Maryland Baltimore Country, Cantonsville, MD 21228, USA.

Date of publication. 1979.

References
Deluty, R.H. (1979). *Children's Action Tendency Scale*: A self report measure of aggressiveness, assertiveness and submissiveness in children. *Journal of Consulting and Clinical Psychology, 47,* 1061–71.
Deluty, R.H. (1984). Behavioural validation of the Children's Action Tendency Scale. *Journal of Behavioural Assessment, 6,* 115–30.

Susan Spence
University of Sydney
Australia

Children's Assertive Behaviour Scale (CABS)

Test authors. L. Michelson and R. Wood.

Purpose. The CABS is a behaviourally designed self-report instrument for children which measures general and specific social skills. It provides an indication of children's tendencies to engage in passive, aggressive or assertive behaviour.

Subject population. Five to 12 years. Fourth to sixth grade (US).

Administration time. 20 minutes, scoring time is 10 minutes.

Materials. Multiple choice response questionnaire and details regarding scoring are provided.

Scoring and interpretation. The CABS consists of 27 questions which ask children to select from five multiple choices the response which most closely describes how they would behave in a given situation. Each question describes a situation in which an assertive response is required. The five choices reflect a continuum from very passive to passive, assertive, aggressive and very aggressive. Three scores can be produced for the CABS; a passive score, an aggressive score and an overall assertiveness score.

Technical Details. The psychometric properties of the CABS are summarized by Michelson and Wood (1982) which cites two unpublished studies based on samples of 149 children and 90 children. The CABS is reported to have good test–retest reliability over four weeks and the internal consistency of the scale is also claimed to be good. The content validity of CABS response choices was assessed by requesting blind judges to assess the validity of the continuum of responses for each item, and inter-rater reliability among the six judges exceeded 89 per cent on all items. Factor analyses in two studies demonstrated a homogeneous factor structure. Scores on the CABS have been shown to be independent of sex, IQ and social desirability scores among fourth to sixth graders.

Attempts have been made to establish the concurrent validity of the CABS. Michelson and Wood (1982) report significant, albeit modest, correlations between CABS total scores and behavioural observation measures and teachers ratings of social skills. They also report evidence of discriminant validity for the CABS in that it was sensitive to the effects of social skills training and could distinguish children who had received eight hours of intervention from those who had received 16 hours.

Evaluation. The CABS is a useful method of assessing self-reported assertiveness. It is easy to administer and easy to score. The information provided allows identification of aggressive and submissive children but provides little data concerning the nature of any social skills deficits or causal factors. The relatively low correlation between CABS scores and direct behavioural observation brings into question the degree to which CABS scores are a true reflection of childrens' behaviour in real-life situations.

This aspect of the *CABS* warrants further exploration. There is also a need to investigate the use of the *CABS* with older age groups, as the age range is currently rather limited. Hopefully, more extensive normative data will also be produced to facilitate interpretation of scores.

Country of origin. USA.

Publisher. Michelson, L. & Wood, R.

Date of publication. 1982.

References

Michelson, L. & Wood, R. (1980). A group assertive training program for elementary school children. *Child Behaviour Therapy, 2,* 1–9.

Michelson, L. & Wood, R. (1982). Development and psychometric properties of the Children's Assertive Behaviour Scale. *Journal of Behavioral Assessment, 4,* 3–13.

Susan Spence
University of Syndney,
Australia

Matson Evaluation of Social Skills with Youngsters (MESSY)

Test author. Professor J.L. Matson.

Purpose. This test was designed to identify children who demonstrate deficiencies in social skills and to demonstrate the specific areas of skill deficit which may be selected as targets for intervention.

Subject population. Children four to 18 years, including various handicapped groups.

Administration time. Self report 15-25 minutes, scoring 10 minutes. Teacher report 15–25 minutes, scoring 10 minutes.

Materials. Materials include a self-rating form, a teacher-rating form and user guide.

Scoring and interpretation. The self-rating form of the MESSY involves 62 items, (the teacher form contains 64 items), concerning specific skill areas to which a response is made on a five-point scale. The self-report scale has been found to yield five main factors, namely (a) appropriate social skill, (b) inappropriate assertiveness, (c) impulsive/recalcitrant, (d) over-confident and (e) jealousy/withdrawal. The teacher rating form items fall into two main factors, namely inappropriate assertiveness/impulsive and appropriate social skills. Normative data for total scores and factor scores and exact details of scoring are provided by the author.

Technical Details. The normative data currently available was obtained from 442 non-handicapped children for the self-report form and 322 children on the teacher rating form. The normative sample was not carefully stratified and is restricted to US school children, which brings into question the applicability of the norms to other cultures. There is also a lack of breakdown of norms by age and sex. The internal reliability to teacher- and self-report forms is reported to be good for normal, deaf and visually handicapped children (Matson, et al., 1985, 1986). Information concerning test–retest reliability of the complete scales appears to be lacking, although items were only included in the questionnaires if test–retest correlations exceeded r 0.50.

The MESSY is claimed to have good content validity in that its items were derived from scales of psychopathology and social functioning, behaviours targeted in social skills training studies with children and clinical observations. There is strong agreement between teacher- and self-report evaluations of performance (Matson et al., 1983). Using the teacher-report form with deaf children, Matson, et al. (1985) demonstrated a high correlation between MESSY scores and ratings of emotional functioning, providing further support for the validity of the MESSY.

Evaluation. The MESSY represents a useful method of identifying children with poor social skills and provides some information as to the areas of skill deficit. Considerably more research is needed to provide data from a stratified normative sample for non-handicapped children and special populations. It is best used as an adjunct to the assessment process, rather than being used in isolation from interview and observational data. Its focus is primarily on the performance of specific social skill responses and the *MESSY* does not systematically explore the cognitive components of social skills.

Country of origin. USA.

Publisher. Professor J.L. Matson, Department of Psychology, Louisiana State University, Baton Rouge, LA 70803–5001. USA.

Date of publication. 1983.

References.

Matson, J.L., Rotatori, A. & Helsel, W.J. (1983). Development of a rating scale to measure social skills in children: The Matson Evaluation of Social Skills with Youngsters (MESSY). *Behaviour Research and Therapy, 21*, 335–40.

Matson, J.L., Macklin, G.F. & Helsel, W.J. (1985). Psychometric properties of the Matson Evaluation of Social Skills with Youngsters (MESSY) with emotional problems and self-concept in deaf children. *Journal Behaviour Therapy and Experimental Psychiatry, 16*, 117–23.

Matson, J.L., Heinze, A., Hebel, W.J., Kapperman, G. & Rotatori, A. (1986). Assessing social behaviours in the visually handicapped: The Matson Evaluation of Social Skills with Youngsters (MESSY). *Journal of Clinical Child Psychology, 15*, 78–87.

Susan Spence
University of Sydney,
Australia

Children's Behaviour Questionnaires

Test author. M. Rutter

Purpose. A short questionnaire to discriminate between children who show some behavioural or emotional disorder and those who do not, and to indicate the type of disorder shown.

Subject population. Children in the middle age range (approximately eight to 13 year olds). However, various studies report its use with children from the age of five years.

Administration time. Completed by parent or teacher in five to ten minutes. Scoring time two minutes.

Materials. There are two forms, – one for parents and one for teachers – and a short instruction leaflet. Details regarding standardization, reliability and validity are not given in this leaflet, but a list of references is given.

Structure and administration. The parent or teacher is asked to read and complete the questionnaire as it applies to the child in question. Clear written instructions are given at the beginning of each questionnaire.

Scoring. Each item is scored on a three-point basis, from 0 to 2 depending on the severity of the problem. This results in a total possible score of 62 for the 31-item parent's questionnaire and 52 for the 26-item teacher's questionnaire (most items in common). Children with a total score of 13 or more (9 for the teachers scale) are designated as showing some disorder. Certain items contribute to 'neurotic' score and others to an 'antisocial score'. The balance of these scores indicates the type of disorder shown by the child.

Technical details

Standardization. The original standardizations (1965–70) were based on 99 boys and 99 girls from the normal population (city of Aberdeen) and 72 boys and 45 girls from a clinic population (Maudsley Hospital). The questionnaire has been subsequently validated in other populations including 940 seven year olds in New Zealand (McGee et al., 1985).

Reliability. Retest reliability reported as 0.74 for 83 mothers rating 9 to 13 year olds with a two month interval. Interrater reliability between 35 mothers and fathers is given at 0.63.

Validity. The parents questionnaire correctly identified 77 per cent of antisocial children and between 55 per cent and 65 per cent of neurotic children (clinic population). There is an 80 per cent agreement between scale diagnosis and clinical diagnosis. General population studies give an incidence of 6 per cent in the normal population (Isle of Wight study, 1970).
    The items used in the subscores correctly discriminate between neurotic and antisocial children at the 5 per cent level of significance. Further factor

analysis indicates that there are three factors. The first two are broadly in agreement with Rutter's antisocial and neurotic groupings whereas the third factor relates to 'hyperactivity' (McGee et al., 1985, teachers questionnaire).

Evaluation. This questionnaire is a useful screening device for those involved with problem children. Because of its high reliability and validity it gives a good indication of the severity of the problem as well as more detailed information. The separate parent's and teacher's scales add to its validity and usefulness. It is a pity that an up-to-date manual giving technical information and a section on interpretation is not provided.

Country of origin. UK.

Date of publication. 1970.

Publisher. Institute of Psychiatry, DeCrespigny Park, Denmark Hill, London SE5 8AF.

References

Rutter, M., Tizard, J. & Whitmore, K. (1970). *Education, Health and Behaviour.* London: Longmans.

McGee, R., Williams, S., Bradshaw, J.L., Chapel, J.L., Robins, A. & Silva, P.A. (1985). The Rutter Scale for completion by teachers; Factor structure and relationships with cognitive abilities and family adversity for a sample of New Zealand children. *Journal of Child Psychology and Psychiatry, 26,* 727–39.

Leonora Harding
Royal Aberdeen Children's Hospital

Early Mathematics Diagnostic Kit (EMDK)

Test authors. D. Lumb and M. Lumb

Purpose. The kit helps teachers to diagnose early learning difficulties in mathematics. Diagnosis forms the basis for remedial action which is shown by re-evaluation and further action as appropriate.

Subject population. Children aged four to eight years and older children with learning difficulties.

Administration time. About 30 minutes; time for diagnosis and choice of remedial activities will vary a good deal, depending on the problems encountered.

Materials. The kit comprises a book of test items (including blocks of different weights and Unifix cubes, a handbook and disposable pupil record forms).

Structure and administration. 110 test items (not all of which are answered by every child) sample much of the content of early mathematics, including: number, length, money, shape, weight, time, representation, capacity, and foundation skills such as naming and matching.

Administration is easily achieved with the use of a short script/test item book and the kit can be presented as a whole, or in parts.

Scoring and interpretation. Correct answers are noted, and errors recorded. The kit is a diagnostic tool, and the tester's interest is focused on errors, rather than on total scores. Suggestions for follow-up activities are given and recommend a cycle of Do – Understand – Practise – Consolidate – Memorize. The general advice offered can serve as a useful reminder if the teaching skills already exist 'try...to develop a positive attitude towards mathematics'; but may be of little use otherwise. Suggestions begin with an introductory paragraph followed by page references to existing schemes of work where relevant activities can be found. Seven textbook series are referred to.

Teachers are encouraged to monitor their interventions by constucting their own check-list of key concepts, skills, practices and experiences, and to note the frequency with which the child meets each of these. A useful appendix provides a check-list of commonly used mathematical vocabulary; another provides suggestions for further reading.

Technical Details

Standardization. The kit is intended for diagnosis, and has not been standardized. Development began in Newcastle in 1977 and extension and improvement continued until 1983. Trials in more than 50 schools have involved over 100 teachers, advisers and educational psychologists.

Reliability. No reliability data are available.

Validity. No validity data are available. The Handbook claims 'Children with few or no problems at this stage of learning mathematics should achieve virtually 100% success on the items'. This claim is certain to be wrong for the age range four to eight years. It *might* be correct if the claim is restricted to able eight year olds. Only one study of test use is reported. Eighty first year juniors (mean age eight years two months, deviation 0.26) were selected on the basis that their class teachers judged them to have attained the objectives set in the kit. When two items were rejected, pupils made only two errors each, on average. The authors claim therefore that the items are accessible to 'the normal eight year old' and that poor performance indicates some learning problem which should be followed up. This evidence *doesn't* give information about 'normal' children. It might simply show that teachers can already spot children who don't need remedial activities without using this test. There are no reports of test use with either representative samples of pupils, or with pupils of low attainment. There are no reports of the effect on pupil attainment of following through the remedial programmes suggested.

Evaluation. This test aims to cover a set of skills encountered in early mathematics. Claims that all items will be accessible to normal children in the target range are certainly wrong, and apply only to older children (how many four year olds can tell the time to quarter hours, let alone twenty-five-to and ten-past the hour?). Its effectiveness as a diagnostic tool, and as the basis for remedial action cannot be judged, because no relevant information is provided. Nevertheless, the kit has merits. The choice of items reflects many of the topics encountered in mathematics in the early years; the basis for item design is made explicit, and some follow-up activities are suggested, along with references to a variety of published sources of ideas for ways to present and represent relevant mathematical experiences. The idea of monitoring one's teaching to examine the balance of topics is sound; the 'commonly used mathematical vocabulary' is useful. Mathematical learning is a complex, ill-understood business. The idea that 'learning difficulties' can be identified easily and can be put right by reference to existing textbooks seems somewhat doubtful.

   Nevertheless, the kit encourages teachers to observe systematically, experiment, evaluate, and reflect. I share the authors' sentiment: 'It is hoped that the use of *EMDK* will lead teachers to a greater understanding of the learning problems of children in mathematics'.

Country of origin. UK.

Publisher. NFER-NELSON

Date of publication. 1987.

Jim Ridgway
University of Lancaster

Edinburgh Reading Tests

Test authors. Godfrey Thomson Unit, University of Edinburgh (Stages 1, 2, 4 and *The Shortened Edinburgh Reading Test*) Moray House College of Education (Stage 3).

Purpose. The development of Stages 1–4 of this series of free-standing group reading comprehension tests for use by teachers was commissioned by the Educational Institute of Scotland and the Scottish Education Department. The tests were designed to fill the full range of possible school and classroom applications for standardized testing.

In addition a further test, *The Shortened Edinburgh Reading (SERT)* is published.

Subject population. Children, seven to nine (Stage 1) aged eight and a half to ten and a half (Stage 2), ten to 12½ (Stage 3), 12 to 16 (Stage 4) and ten to 11½ (*SERT*). Separate norms are provided for Scotland and England and Wales for Stages 1–4. National norms are provided for *SERT*.

Administration time. Stage 1 untimed (two 30-minute sessions). Stages 2–4 timed as follows: Stage 2, 105 minutes (two sessions); Stages 3, 110 minutes (two sessions); Stage 4, (60 minutes, two sessions. *SERT*, untimed (40 minutes). Separate practice test sessions are necessary for Stages 2 and 3.

Materials. A Manual of Instructions is published for each Stage. Items are presented in test booklets which are also used for recording answers and include a profile sheet. For Stages 1 and 3 there are two parallel forms of test (Forms A and B).

Structure and administration. The various subtests cover many areas of reading proficiency suitable to the particular reading stage (for example, vocabulary, syntax, use of context, comprehension, skimming, reading for facts).

With the exception of *SERT* the tests are generally longer than many other group reading comprehension tests. This makes the administration process relatively more demanding.

The directions for scoring and for converting raw scores to standardized scores or reading ages are straightforward.

Individual profile charts allow comparisons of performance across subtests. While no difficulty should arise in following the directions for first preparing these, their further interpretation is somewhat more complicated, as previous reviewers of the *Edinburgh Series* have noted (at least with intuitive understanding) is straightforward.

Technical details

Standardization. Stages 1–4 were each standardized on samples of well over 2000 children, drawn separately for Scotland and for England and Wales. It is worth bearing in mind (a) sampling explicitly excluded 'remedial' classes (not a usual practice in reading test standardization), (b) various regional and sex differences are manifested across the Series and (c) the original standardization date is from the early to mid-1970s, although Stage 3B was constructed somewhat later and standardized in 1982.

Reliability. KR-20 values (for full tests): Stage 1, 0.94; Stage 2, 0.97; Stage 3, 0.97; Stage 4, 0.96. KR-20 values reported for subtests range from 0.73 to 0.945 and many of these would be somewhat too low for scores to be regarded as free-standing estimates of reading ability.

Validity. No correlations with other tests or relevant educational criteria are reported. The high intercorrelation between subtests do not support the contention that these represent psychologically discrete dimensions of reading ability. The Manual for *SERT* which was published in 1986 contains a spirited riposte to this widely-voiced criticism of the Series – correlated processes are not necessarily identical processes. A long-promised statistical annexe has yet to appear.

Evaluation. The *Edinburgh Series* has been widely reviewed since its publication and its reviewers have tended to conclude with a favourable overall evaluation technical and conceptual flaws notwithstanding. *SERT* represents the way the Series can be further exploited as an item bank. It seems probable that even higher quality revised and updated norms will become available as the tests continue to be used in large-scale research surveys and Scottish national assessment programmes.

Conceptual evaluation is much more difficult. For, a test of reading attainment which pre-dates the publication of the National Curriculum runs the risk of being rendered obsolete. Whatever the outcome, the creation of this Series was a considerable advance in the field of reading test development in the UK. Certainly, Stage 4 remains one of the best reading tests for its age group, rivalled only by the reading tests produced by the DES Assessment of Performance Unit and *The English Language Skills Profile* (*TELS*) – also constructed by the Godfrey Thomson Unit.

Country of origin. UK.

Publisher. Hodder and Stoughton.

Other reviews of the tests:
Hewison, J. (1984). In Levy, P. & Goldstein, H. (Eds). *Tests in Education*. London: Academic Press.
Moseley, D.V. (1978). In *Journal of Research in Reading*, 4, 3, 152–155.
Nichols, R. (undated). A comparison of three group reading tests in surveying the attainment of first year secondary children (revised edn). University of Reading School of Education: Centre for the Teaching of Reading.
Pumfrey, P. (1985). *Reading: Tests and Assessment Techniques (2nd edn)*. Sevenoaks: Hodder and Stoughton Educational.
Vincent, D., Green, L., Francis, J. & Powney, J. (1983). *A Review of Reading Tests*. Windsor: NFER-NELSON.

Denis Vincent
North East London Polytechic

The Group Reading Test

Test author. D. Young.

Purpose. A reading test designed for easy application to a whole class.

Subject population. Ages six years five months to eight years ten months, and for older below average pupils up to 12 years ten months.

Administration time. Twenty minutes.

Materials. For parallel forms A and B, one test sheet per child, two scoring templates and manual.

Structure and administration. The test consists of 15 pictures (the child has to ring correct word from a choice of four) and 30 sentences (the child has to choose correct word to fit into sentence from a choice of five).

Marking ignores the division between these two sets and is quickly achieved by the use of templates. The total score is the number correct of a total of 45. Items correct after 10 failures are not counted (to control the chance factor). Raw scores are easily converted to reading age or quotient (mean 100, standard deviation 15). A useful table for converting Burt, Schonell, Vernon and Young scores to Salford and Young reading ages is also given. It should be noted that reading ages below five years four months are given for the Young Test only.

Technical details

Standardization. Restandardized between 1974 and 1979 on over 21,000 infants, 5000 first-year juniors and almost 2000 older pupils. There is a problem with a skewed distrubution apparent for the younger pupils.

Reliability. Correlation between the two forms is 0.945. Test–retest reliability is given in terms of differences between scores. For about 70 per cent of children the difference is three or less and for 90 per cent of children the difference is six or less (time interval not given). The reading age is reliable up to a reading age of eight years six months, but beyond this reliability declines. Internal consistencies (reported in terms of standard error of measurement) are high, but decline with age.

Validity. It might be argued that Young's test is largely a word recognition test (first part) and sentence completion test (second part) and that, as it does not test passage reading and comprehension, it is not a true reading test. However, as the author points out, reading tests which might be thought of as measuring different aspects of reading consistently correlate very highly. The picture items and easier sentences were constructed 'to minimize the demands on vocabulary, general knowledge and intelligence'. Distractors (wrong answers) were chosen with the aid of the Edwards and Gibbon word frequency test. Item analysis was used to select items with the most discriminating power and to eliminate sex bias.

Concurrent validity is high and was established by giving full classes of eight year olds (from four schools) the NFER Reading Test AD and the Young Test. Eighty children took a further two reading tests and the Non-readers Intelligence Test (see below).

	Correlation with Young's Test
Neale Analysis A (Accuracy)	0.884
Vernon's Graded Word Reading	0.884
NFER Test AD	0.878
Neale Analysis A (Comprehension)	0.735
Young's Intelligence	0.729
Teacher's order of merit	0.929

Evaluation. This test is a well-standardized test, which can be used with full classes of young children. As such it is of great practical value to teachers as a measure of class attainment and as a screening device for children, whose problems might then be further investigated. It is also a valuable measure for researchers (for example, Hannon, 1987).

Country of origin. UK.

Publisher. Hodder and Stoughton.

Date of publication. 1979.

Reference

Hannon, P. (1987). A study of the effects of parental involvement in the teaching of reading on children's reading test performance. *British Journal of Educational Psychology, 57*, 56–72.

Leonora Harding
Royal Aberdeen Children's Hospital

Infant Rating Scale (IRS)

Test author. G.A. Lindsay.

Purpose. An instrument to help teachers to identify young children's strengths and needs. (There are five scales; language, early learning, behaviour, social integration and general development.)

Subject population. Children aged five years (level 1) and aged seven years (level 2).

Administration time. Not given in manual.

Materials. A 24-page manual and two forms for each level; one gives criterion-referenced or normative levels of attainment. The second form provides a profile.

Scoring and interpretation. There is a straight-forward scoring system in which children are rated from 1 (low) to 5 (high) on each of a total of 25 items incorporated into the five scales (language, early learning behaviour, social integration and medical aspects). These scores can be combined to give (a) sub-scale scores (for example, for language), and (b) total scores (that is, for the five scales combined). Tables are provided in order to convert raw scores to a percentage reflecting the proportion of children in the age group expected to achieve at that level. Most, but not all, of the percentage tables reflect a normal distribution of scores in the population.

Technical details

Standardization. Level 1 has been standardized on a sample of children (N = 1324, mean age: five years and three months from one LEA. This sample explicitly excluded schools with a 'large proportion' of 'recent immigrants'. Level 2 was standardized on the children (N = 916) who had been given level 1 and were still available two years later.

Reliability. Inter-rater reliabilities were 'not feasible'; test–retest reliabilities (two-weeks interval) were good (r = 0.96 for total scores) although test–retest reliabilities for some individual items were as low as r = 0.65).

Validity. Predictive validity of level 1 was measured for sub-samples of children using as criteria level 2 and Young's Group Reading Test (YGRT) at age seven, and five other reading tests at age nine. Predictive validity of level 2 was assessed using the same reading tests, as for level 1. Predictive validities were generally good; level 1 with level 2, r = 0.61, level 1 with YGRT, r = 0.51. The language and early learning scales were the best predictors of later attainments in reading.

Procedures like the IRS which attempt to identify learning difficulties at an early stage have obvious problems in achieving predictive validity. Once the child's difficulty is identified, remedial action should follow with the hoped for result of the child's performance improving. Predictive validity can only be achieved by the absurdly unacceptable strategy of not proceeding with remedial interventions.

Evaluation. The *IRS* is a useful technique for monitoring young children's school progress. However, it lacks the specificity which is necessary when monitoring children's progress in the short term (for instance, over one term). The *IRS*, including important hearing and vision checks, provides a basis from which schools may develop their monitoring of children's learning in the National Curriculum.

Country of origin. UK.

Publisher. Hodder and Stoughton.

References
Pearson, L. & Lindsay, G. (1986). *Special Needs in the Ordinary School: Identification and Intervention.* Windsor: NFER-NELSON.

**Tricia David and
Ann Lewis**
University of Warwick

Keele Pre-School Assessment (KPAG)

Test author. S.T. Tyler

Purpose. This instrument is intended for use in preschool establishments to assist staff in:

* plotting a record of each child's progress,
* making a summative record to pass on to reception class,
* monitoring areas of individual need,
* stimulating staff discussion of the curriculum,
* articulating views of a child's development to parents and other professionals.

Subject population. Children aged three to five years.

Administration time. Time may vary but is usually a few minutes per day for two to three weeks at three- or four-monthly intervals.

Materials. The 31-page booklet, record sheets and normal play materials are all that is required.

Structure and administration. The KPAG is in two parts. Part I consists of a series of continua, each divided into a seven-point scale, representing different social attributes, for example, aggression–timidity. Staff are required to mark the point on the continua most appropriately representing their assessment of a child's observed behaviour. There are spare continua for staff to adapt the idea and record other social behaviour they consider it important to evaluate. The second section of the KPAG contains items grouped as: cognitive, language, physical skills and socialization. Each section is further divided into subsections, for example, the language category includes language use, vocabulary, speech and comprehension and there are five levels of difficulty in each set of tasks. The KPAG is intended to be used flexibly, with staff adapting or replacing items as they see fit and above all, administering the tasks as part of the normal play activities.

Scoring and interpretation. Staff mark the Part I items as described above. Part 2 items, if completed successfully, are scored by colouring the appropriate section on a circular grid, whose concentric rings denote levels of difficulty, and whose segments represents the different types of tasks. Thus, the more a child has been observed achieving competence at tasks, the greater the amount of colouring on the chart. This means there is no scoring as such, but adults will see at a glance the extent of the child's achievements as well as areas of omission or areas in need of extra encouragement.

Technical details

Standardization, reliability and validity. The items were piloted with a group of over 100 preschool children and discussed with staff in all types of preschool setting. However, the guide does not give details of statistical data, since the author's aim was to produce a working guide containing the most succinct material for practitioners. Those wishing to gain access to this information are advised to consult Tyler's (1980) unpublished thesis.

Evaluation. The original design included the notion of adaptability and flexibility, and linking with the curriculum found in many preschool groups. Consequently this guide remains a useful basic instrument, as Moore and Sylva (1980) state. It could now act also as a discussion document for those seeking to develop their assessment tools in anticipation of the requirements of the National Curriculum and the Standard Assessment Tasks. The author is currently working with a group of practitioners, to up-date and augment the KPAG. New items will include tasks to assess social knowledge, problem solving skills, rate of learning and additional linked items will focus on assisting staff in the assessment of bilingual children. Users of the guide may wish to refer back to the numerous stated aims of the KPAG to evaluate both the guide itself and their own practice.

Country of origin. UK.

Publisher. NFER-NELSON.

Date of publication. 1980.

References

Moore, E. & Sylva, K. (1986). *Assessment of Children under Five.* London: OMRP Updates.
Tyler, S.T. (1980). *The Evaluation of Children's Development in the Nursery.* Unpublished PhD. thesis. Keele: University of Keele.

Trica David and
Ann Lewis
University of Warwick

London Reading Test

Test author. A working party of the Inner London Education Authority.

Purpose. This is a group reading comprehension test specifically designed for screening of children with reading difficulty at transfer from junior to secondary school.

Subject population. Children ten years seven months to 12 years four months.

Administration time. Untimed (one hour is recommended).

Materials. Teacher's manual; practice test; test booklets (forms A and B).

Structure and administration. The test comes in equivalent forms (A and B), each consisting of two cloze procedure passages of 17 and 25 items respectively, followed by a 20-item prose passage comprehension test 'designed to tap the able reader's higher order comprehension skills'. The comprehension items are based on Barrett's (perhaps overrated) taxonomy and include objective, multiple choice formats and short written responses. The manual states that the test passages were written with the ILEA's 'urban multi-racial population in mind'.

Scoring and interpretation. Marking the cloze items is relatively straightforward: only words listed in a marking key, including recognizable misspellings, are scored as correct. The key also helpfully lists a number of common responses to be treated as incorrect. A greater degree of marker judgement is required for some of the comprehension items but this is an inevitable concomitant to testing comprehension beyond the realms of the trivial.

Clearly identified direction and tables are given converting raw scores to standardized scores. National and London norms are provided. The manual also gives some simple introductory advice on selection of children for further assessment, qualitative interpretation of cloze and comprehension scores, and on relating children's results to the readability of school textbooks. Some references to research in the text of this discussion are missing from the list of references.

Technical details

Standardization. The ILEA junior school norms are based on 1000 children per form, drawn from a stratified random sample of primary schools. The secondary norms are based on 1000 children and 20 schools per form. National norming was carried out by the NFER using samples of 5000 juniors and 5000 secondary pupils. Sub-samples of 1000 children also took Form B to provide calibrated norms for Form B. Although an 'economy measure' this would yield entirely adequate norms for Form B.

Reliability. KR21 0.95 (ILEA), 0.93 (National).

Validity. Substantial correlations with test scores on number of other reading tests are reported although these data do not appear to have been gathered very systematically. As far as the cloze component of the test is concerned there is plenty of research evidence to support its psychometric integrity a measure of reading comprehension. Inspection of the third comprehension passage gives rise to the question of whether such relatively short and bland texts can form a genuine basis for testing 'higher order' skills.

Evaluation. Readability, cloze procedure, and Barrett's taxonomy represent the reading technology of the early 1970s when they perhaps inspired greater professional faith and awe. As a normative screening test it was certainly superior in content and standards of construction to its (then) contemporaries. It remains a possible choice where innocuousness is the main criterion for selection and is greatly preferable to *any* sentence-completion test, however recent and technically excellent.

Country of origin. UK.

Publisher. NFER-NELSON.

Date of publication. 1978–80.

Denis Vincent
North East London Polytechnic

Macmillan Group Reading Test

Test author. The Macmillan Test Unit.

Purpose. This is a group test of sentence and word reading requiring the circling of chosen words on a printed form. A single administration of the test gives a standardized score and reading age for each child.

Subject population. Children with reading ability ranging from a reading age of six years three months to 13 years three months.

Administration time. The test will usually be completed in 30 minutes although it is untimed. Scoring will take 2–4 minutes.

Materials. There is a manual offering clear detail regarding the purposes for the test, administration, interpretation and standardization data. A record form is necessary for each child on each occasion tested.

Structure and administration. There are two parallel forms for the test. As two examples are given and the record form is crowded, there are likely to be difficulties in younger and learning disabled children fully understanding the tasks in a large group setting. There are five items where the child has to ring one of five words fitting a picture and 43 items where the child has to ring a word fitting a gap in a sentence.

Scoring and interpretation. Each correct answer is awarded one point towards a final score which can be converted to a standard score and (optional) reading age. A centile may be a simpler form for users to appraise individual performances and to compare with other measures such as ability, spelling or maths. It is suggested that a standard score below 85 requires further investigation. This limits consideration of children who may show underachievement or a mismatch in their reading as compared with ability, language or other circular measures.

Technical details

Standardization. The manual describes standardization on 7500 pupils from a variety of geographical/economic environments.

Reliability. The two parallel forms have correlation coefficients of between 0.35 and 0.94. Retesting on the alternative form seemed unlikely to produce significant increases in scores due to practice effects.

Validity. Validity, as assessed by comparing scores with teachers' estimates of their own pupils' reading abilities, ranges from 0.76 to 0.89. Six other reading tests have correlation coefficients ranging from 0.57 to 0.89 with this test. The precise skill tested with the *Macmillan Group Test* is not clear and individual children may well use different strategies to complete the task and consequently their scores may reflect different skills. A simple group test inevitably does not measure elements of reading such as fluency and comprehension which may require more individual or criterion-related measures.

Evaluation. This is an up-to-date, clearly presented, well-standardized test. It is likely to be quite successful in monitoring standards, assessing individual progress and offering information for school transfer. However, it will be quite expensive in record forms and will be under some competition from tests such as the NFER-NELSON *Primary Reading Test* and Hodder and Stoughton's *Group Reading Test* (Young). It is unlikely to be sensitive in screening for children with reading difficulties at infant levels and it is noted that reading scores above nine and a half years are liable to variation as each correct answer counts for nine months reading age.

Country of origin. UK.

Publishers. Macmillan Education.

Date of publication. 1985.

Margaret J. Snowling
The National Hospitals College of Speech Therapists

Peter Brooks
Hampshire County Council

Mathematics 7–12

Test author. Test Development Unit of the National Foundation for Educational Research, with Alan Brighouse, David Godber and Peter Patilla.

Purpose. This set of six tests is designed for use by teachers towards the end of academic year when pupils reach the age in the test title. Each test is intended to provide summative assessment of pupil attainment in the mathematics usually encountered in that school year. Tests can also provide information about strengths and needs of pupils (and classes) in particular areas, or on particular groups of tasks, and so has some diagnostic function. Content has been chosen so as to sample a wide range of topics appropriate to each school year; within these topics, items are designed to assess the ability to use a variety of concepts and skills.

Subject population. Children six years six months to 12 years 11 months.

Administration time. About 50 minutes; *Mathematics* 7 and 8 can be taken in two halves; scoring time five minutes.

Materials. *Mathematics 7–12* comprises six tests, each in the form of a disposable pupil booklet, a *Teachers' Guide* for *Mathematics* 7 and one which is used for *Mathematics* 8–12. Class record sheets are provided.

Structure and administration. Tests should be taken during the summer term, in the pupils' usual teaching room. Each test contains items relevant to number, measurement, shape, and pictorial representation with items appropriate to the ages of the target population. They are also subgrouped into items which examine recall, computation, application and understanding. Tests are untimed. A detailed (item by item) script is provided for *Mathematics* 7 and 8 enabling them to be orally administered. Details of test administration are exemplary.

Scoring and interpretation. Manuals provide marking keys, sectioned so as to correspond with each page in each test booklet. Page totals are summed and transferred to the front of the test booklet and converted to standard scores and percentiles, then transferred to a score line which shows how many points need to be added and subtracted to provide a 90 per cent confidence interval. This emphasis on the error inherent in all measurement, and the need to report a score band for a pupil rather than a single score is a welcome feature of the test. Test scores have three uses. The first is to compare each child's performance with data from a large sample of peers. The sheet also classifies each item in terms of the skill it demands, and shows the percentage of pupils in the standardization sample who got the question correct. This can help uncover weaknesses of the whole group. Diagnosis of individual problems is facilitated by the clear descriptions of item construction.

Technical details

Standardization. Tests were standardized with great care. Each test was standardized separately, using stratified random samples of schools, (over 20,000 pupils from over 500 schools). *Mathematics 7* has a marked ceiling effect, which will affect the standardized scores of older children. For example, to obtain a standard score of 100, a child aged seven years 11 months must answer 24 out of 28 items correctly. It is therefore more appropriate for testing pupils of low attainment, and younger children.

Reliability. Internal reliability is acceptably high (0.90 to 0.95 using KR-20, presumably on all the test data); so too is test–retest reliability, although the sample sizes are not given, surprisingly.

Validity. Tests are justified primarily in terms of content validity, and the blueprint of mathematical behaviours which underlies the choice of items. Some studies of concurrent validity compared test scores with teacher ratings, and scores on other tests. These studies are not very illuminating but show that test scores broadly reflect teacher ratings (some dramatically less so that others!) and scores on other tests. I find the content validity arguments more convincing than this supplementary evidence.

Evaluation. *Mathematics 7–12* sets out to provide a summative evaluation of mathematical attainment in each of six school years, together with some diagnostic help for individual pupils, and for whole classes. A strength of the series is that an effort has been made to describe the test designers' intentions, and the blueprint for test construction is provided, so that users can judge the suitablility of the tests for their purposes.

Users are encouraged to think about the skills assessed by particular items, and the way these skills can be encouraged in class – clearly a good thing. The recommendations for the remediation of poor performance are rather bland, however, and further references to work on diagnostic teaching might be a useful addition. Overall, this test series can be recommended to users who are satisfied by the balance of test contents.

Country of origin. UK.

Publisher. NFER-NELSON.

Date of publication. 1984 (*Mathematics 8–12*); 1987 (*Mathematics 7*).

Jim Ridgway
University of Lancaster

Neale Analysis of Reading Ability (Revised British Edition)

Test authors. Marie D. Neale (Australia). British adaptation standardized by Una Christophers and Chris Whetton.

Purpose. An individual oral test of reading ability for primary school children: structured diagnostic assessment of individual reading behavioiur.

Subject population. Children six to 12 years. Younger advanced readers and older children with reading difficulties.

Administration time. Depending on age and reading ability 10 to 20 minutes. Scoring five minutes, but longer for diagnostic assessment.

Materials. One manual. One reader containing three colour-coded sections for parallel forms, and diagnostic tutor. Colour-coded record forms and demonstration cassette.

Structure, administration and scoring. There are two standardized, parallel forms and a parallel diagnostic tutor form each containing six graded passages of prose. Each passage has a limited number of words and a definite storyline accompanied by a picture. Each form is preceded by a practice passage and there are between four and eight comprehension questions at the end. The child reads each passage (starting at a basal level for older children) to his or her ceiling level. Prompts are supplied every four seconds except when using the diagnostic tutor.

For the two parallel forms passages are scored for accuracy (by deducting the number of errors from a maximum for each passage), comprehension (number of questions answered correctly for each passage) and rate of reading (by timing each passage). These are converted to the respective reading ages by use of standardized tables. Additional measures are equivalent age ranges (for the reading age), percentile rank and stanines. Errors can be categorized as mispronunciations, refusals, additions, omissions and reversals.

The diagnostic tutor is not supplied with norms but can be used for miscue analysis, criterion referenced assessment, cloze procedures and so on. It also contains an extension passage for older readers. Four supplementary diagnostic tests are provided, but are not supplied with norms.

Technical details

Standardization. The original revision was standardized on a sample of 1100 Australian children between 1981 and 1984. The British standardization (1988) was based on a sample of 1760 children from 203 representative schools in England and Wales. Children were randomly selected to include 400 pupils from each of the six age bands.

Reliabilities. Reliabilities for the parallel forms range from 0.72 to 0.98 (Accuracy), 0.67 to 0.95 (Rate) and 0.85 to 0.96 (Comprehension). Lower levels of reliability are obtained for the younger children (aged six years to seven years 11 months). Internal consistency measured by Cronbach's alpha coefficient ranges from 0.81 to 0.87 (Accurancy) and 0.90 to 0.93 (Comprehension).

Validity. As a test of passage reading, validity is high. It is not a test of word recognition or silent reading although it does relate to other reading measures.

The *Neale* has high construct validity as it is more like 'real reading' than many other reading tests. In its construction, passages from the original (1958) version were reviewed, adapted and some new passages were inserted in line with the experiences of modern children and their language use. Ceiling is reached at about 12 years of age for the passages, which limits its usefulness in the 11 to 12 age band.

Concurrent and predictive validity have not yet been established for the revised British version. The 1958 version had high correlation with other reading tests and has high correlation with the new *Neale* (0.97 for Accuracy).

Evaluation. This is one of the best tests of its kind (the *New Macmillan Reading Analysis* running a close second). As a test of reading, it is enjoyable to children and has high validity. The instructions are clear and the manual is easy to follow and includes all the relevent information. The additon of the diagnostic tutor is most welcome. The supplementary tests have limited usefulness and there are better and more detailed diagnostic assessment procedures available (e.g. the *Macmillan Diagnostic Reading Test*, the *Domain Phonics Test*). The original *Neale* has proved invaluable as an educational, clinical and research tool.

Country of origin. UK.

Publisher. NFER-NELSON.

References
Ames, T. (1980). *Macmillan Diagnostic Reading Pack.* Basingstoke: Macmillan.
McLeod, J. & Atkinson, J. (1972) *Domain Phonics Test.* Edinburgh: Oliver and Boyd.
Vincent, D. & de la Mare, M. (1985) *New Macmillan Reading Analysis.* Basingstoke: Macmillan.

Leonora Harding
Royal Aberdeen Children's Hospital

New Macmillan Reading Analysis (NMRA)

Test authors. D. Vincent and M. de la Mare.

Purpose. The NMRA is on individually administered test of oral reading ability and comprehension.

Subject population. Children of average reading ability in the seven to nine year age range and for older readers reading at the level of the average seven year old or above.

Administration time. 15 minutes; scoring time 3 minutes, plus extra for qualitative analysis.

Materials. The test is offered in three parallel forms with associated passages and pictures attractively printed in a reading booklet. There is a detailed and extensive manual and well-structured record form is used for each child.

Structure and administration. The child reads aloud up to six prose passages of increasing length and difficulty in terms of words used, language and meaning. Each passage is followed by three to eight comprehension questions. 'Words in context' of increasing difficulty are identified to the tester by bold print on the record form, within most passages.

Scoring and interpretation. Age equivalent age ranges for accuracy and comprehension (of 12–13 months) are calculated. These represent the chronological age range for which the reader's performance on the test is typical. A single reading age is not given which makes the test cumbersome from a practical point of view.

It is also possible to calculate a Scale Score for 'Words in Context' and for comprehension using three passages of reading.

The manual describes qualitative analysis of errors and a miscue analysis.

Technical details

Standardization. The tests were given to 600-plus London children aged seven years five months to 12 years seven months who were average on the *Primary Reading Test.* This limited sample is insufficient for within group comparisons such as standardized scores.

Validity. Results are not compared with other tests, teacher ratings or subsequent progress in reading. The nature of what is being tested and its links with other materials is consequently unclear.

Reliability. Reliability was measured between different forms of test (correlations 0.76–0.94) and between the possible scales scores (coefficients 0.58–0.87). Measures were low and raise concerns particularly regarding the considerable variations between different testers and in comprehension items.

Evaluation. *NMRA* is a well-prescribed test that will be useful in the further analysis and monitoring of children who have already been screened for reading difficulties. The qualitative opportunities for analysis are similar to other such tests (e.g. *Neale*). The major measures for users seem likely to be age equivalents for accuracy and comprehension but these would be more popular if they offered a single reading age and, a centile level. *NMRA* shows limited application as a screening instrument or in monitoring reading progress. It has a limited average age span, is expensive of time and record forms, and has considerable technical limitations in such a setting.

Country of origin. UK.

Publisher. Macmillan Education.

Date of publication. 1985.

Margaret J. Snowling
The National Hospitals College of Speech Sciences

Peter Brooks
Educational Psychologist

Pre-school Behaviour Checklist (PBCL)

Test authors. Jacqueline McGuire and Naomi Richman.

Purpose. This is a quick screening device for use in preschool settings to identify children with emotional and/or behaviour problems and it may form the basis of an intervention programme by focusing the attention of staff and helping them articulate their views of children and problem behaviour.

Subject population. Children aged two to five years about whom staff are concerned.

Administration time. Up to ten minutes per child.

Materials. Handbook, check-lists and scoring overlay. The handbook is needed as the basis for staff discussions, since it contains both explanations of the use of the check-list and case studies to illustrate its application. For the observations of children, check-lists and scoring overlay are needed.

Scoring and interpretation. Staff complete the record by ticking the appropriate box on the check-list, having decided which of a set of descriptions most accurately describes a child's observed behaviour. The clear plastic overlay is then used to calculate the child's score. The maximum possible score is 44 for the 22 items. Children who are not yet talking, or who do not speak English are exempted from two items, and their scores adjusted to take this into account. The cut-off point is a score of 12. Children with a score of less than 12 will not, in general, give cause for concern, whereas children with higher scores will need to be monitored more closely and positive intervention plans should be developed in collaboration with parents. The check-list has a final secton in which staff are invited to add comments which are not covered by the check-list and which may be deemed important, including any changes in behaviour over the intervening period since the first use of the PBCL.

Technical details

Standardization, reliability and validity. Approximately 650 children were assessed to standardize the PBCL in a variety of settings. Boys and children attending day nurseries tended to be overrepresented in the higher-scoring groups, as would be expected. Reliability was checked from the point of view of: (a) Inter-observer reliability, which was tested by having staff teams in different groups rate their charges. It was generally good, except where items referred to behaviour likely to be staff-specific, such as whining or withdrawing from staff. (b) Retest reliability relating to whether or not a child's score was above or below the cut-off point, gave a correlation of 0.88. (c) Internal consistency as measured by the split-half method yielded reliability coefficient of 0.83. The validity of the PBCL was also tested and the results obtained demonstrate that the PBCL is a useful tool, usable by all staff irrespective of training, to focus attention on those children most needing support.

Evaluation. McGuire and Richman's research has indicated the long-term nature of some children's emotional difficulties and to this end, the *PBCL* has much to contribute. There is the danger, however, that staff predjudices may simply be confirmed by such diagnoses and it is therefore essential that the check-lists are not used in isolation, without discussing the issues raised in the handbook, most particularly the importance of positive intervention. A high score for a number of children in a preschool group may indeed be an indication that certain children are experiencing emotional difficulties, but it may also be an indication that the group's organization and ethos need some examination.

Country of origin. UK.

Publisher. NFER-NELSON.

Date of publication. 1988.

**Tricia David and
Ann Lewis**
University of Warick

The Primary Reading Test (PRT)

Test author. Norman France.

Purpose. This is a multiple choice group reading test in which items become progressively more difficult so as to discriminate the full range of difficulty in primary school children. One suggested use for the test is that teachers could give it early in the school year to aid the structuring of reading groups. Then the alternative form might be given at the end of the school year to provide information for the new teacher and to give feedback on reading progress.

Subject population. Children six to 11 years.

Materials. There is a teacher's guide providing psychometric information and test booklets at two levels, with an alternative version at each level.

Administration time. Thirty minutes for a group. Scoring time less than a minute.

Structure and administration. The Level 1 test is administered to children aged approximately between six years and eight years nine months, and Level 2 to children aged between eight years four months and eleven years, nine months. For the first item for Level 1 there is a picture of a bed and the child circles the correct word from a set of five. The difficulty increases, and from the seventeenth item onwards a sentence is given and the child selects the correct word to go within a gap in the sentence. In Level 2 there are pictures for the first eight items only. The final item tests the reading and comprehension of the word 'synchronized'. According to the manual the sentences can be read aloud to form a 'word recognition test' for the younger children. But strictly speaking it is still a comprehension test as the child needs to understand the meaning of the word within the context of the spoken sentence in order to identify it correctly.

Scoring and interpretation. There are 48 words tested and the maximum score is 48. The raw scores can be converted to reading ages, standard age scores, stanines or percentiles. There are separate tables for Scotland.

Technical details

Standardization. The test has excellent credentials. Initial construction was based on testing a representative sample of 12,000 children in the UK on 224 items, to produce Levels 1 and 2 with 48 items each. Testing for standardization was based on testing a further 8000 children distributed throughout regions of the UK. Variations in samples were adjusted by appropriate weightings. Most of these children were selected from second-year infants to third-year juniors. A much smaller selected sample in the middle range of reading ability was also tested on both levels from the third-year juniors to second-year seniors. The alternative forms for Levels 1 and 2 were standardized later on 2000 children.

Reliability. Test–retest reliabilities, with an intervening week between Levels 1 and 2, produced reliabilities of 0.85 for the first- and second-year juniors. Order of presentation was immaterial.

Validity. At the standardization stage teachers were asked to assess their children independently on a nine-point scale for reading skill and comprehension. Correlation with the *PRT* ranged between 0.73 to 0.89. During the stage of item selection for the final forms of Levels 1 and 2, an effort was made to minimize sex differences. The difference that remains is fairly typical, girls are slightly better at the median in each year group and get progressively superior in the lower ability range.

Evaluation. Many reading tests involve the child reading aloud words which get progessively more difficult. But the child may be able to decode and pronounce a word without understanding it. While children are likely to understand words they read which are also in their spoken vocabulary, as they progress in reading they may encounter words for which they can produce a correct pronunciation but not have an understanding. The *PRT* is consistently based on assessing understanding while reading silently which is a more natural setting for reading assessment. It is very easy and quick for the classroom teacher to administer and the accuracy of its assessment is very good because it has been so thoroughly and carefully prepared.

It is difficult to criticize this test for its intended purpose. It is a quick test for assessing reading level. However, if the teacher wants to make a diagnosis of particular weaknesses in reading, other tests would have to be used in conjunction with it.

Country of origin. UK.

Publisher. NFER-NELSON.

Date of publication. 1979; revised edition 1981.

John R. Beech
University of Leicester

Profile of Mathematical Skills

Test author. Norman France.

Purpose. This test sets out criteria against which pupil attainment can be assessed. It aims to have a diagnostic function in a number of areas of mathematical understanding which can form the basis for remedial action by the teacher.

Subject population. Children aged eight to 15 years.

Administration time. Guidence on testing time would be misleading; each subtest can be given within a single lesson. Scoring time ten minutes.

Materials. A Teacher's Book gives direction on the use of consumable pupil booklets and the pupil profile chart.

Structure and administration. The *Profile* is focused on two levels: Level 1 relates directly to third-year junior school pupils; Level 2 relates directly to second-year secondary school pupils. Each level has also been standardized on three consecutive year groups to ensure continuity. Level 1 assesses addition, subtraction, multiplication, division, choice of operation, measurement and money; Level 2 assesses each of these, and also fractions, decimal fractions and percentages, and diagrams.

Details of test administration take the form of suggestions rather than instructions. Testing is to take place in an informal atmosphere, and the purpose of testing is to be explained to pupils. No more than one subtest should be given in the same lesson.

Scoring and interpretation. Scoring is achieved with the use of a scoring key but a good deal of cross checking is required. Interpretation is direct. Special attention should be paid to pupils whose profiles show marked differences in attainment on different subtests. The Teacher's Book explains the use of standard scores, percentiles and stanines, and discusses errors of measurement. It warns against the dangers of over-interpreting small differences in subtest scores (less than 15 points). Teachers are advised to prepare a profile of the whole class performance in order to identify areas of skill deficit. This activity should be followed by a detailed analysis of subtest items (using the item content descriptions provided) to identify those skills which should be the focus of further attention.

Technical details

Standardization. After large-scale initial trialling of items, standardization took place in 1978 and involved between 1300 and 1400 children in each of the six year groups, selected so as to be representative of the UK school population. A supplementary group in middle schools were tested using both levels, to enable standard scores derived from Levels 1 and 2 on the larger samples to be verified.

Reliability. Scores from one-sixth of the pupils were chosen at random. Median reliability was 0.87; the lowest value found was 0.68. Considering the *Profile* as a whole, reliabilities were found to be 0.98 for Level 1, and 0.99 for Level 2. These are remarkably high.

Validity. The manual provides an item-by-item description of the content of each subtest, so that surface validity can be inspected directly. To explore concurrent validity, teachers were asked to rate pupils' mathematical ability and mathematical skill. The two teacher estimates were highly correlated (0.95) but were rather weakly correlated with pupil performance on the whole collection of subtests (values 0.63 to 0.73 in junior school; 0.29 to 0.51 in secondary school). A factor analysis which used each subtest score at each level produced five factors which accounted for about 90 per cent of the total variance. These factors were interpreted to be: mathematical and spatial reasoning; addition; multiplication; division (at Level 1) or operational (at Level 2); and teacher–pupil interaction. These data offer some evidence about construct validity but do not really support the choice of seven subtests in the profile.

Evaluation. Test development was conducted carefully. Scoring and recording schemes are easy to use. Reliability is high. The manual provides detailed descriptions of items, and sets out to educate (or remind) the user about errors of measurement and the dangers of over interpreting scores.

The author states clearly that testing is meant to support and not replace professional judgement, and that it is an aid to the education process rather than an end in itself. The *Profile* is designed to diagnose pupil strengths and weaknesses in particular mathematical skills; to pinpoint problems quite exactly; to monitor pupil progress; identify areas where the whole class can benefit from improvement; and to act as a focus for discussion with pupils, parents, colleagues and teachers in other schools. On the range of skills chosen (in 1977) it seems capable of being used for all these functions. The test focuses heavily on technical skills, with approximately half of the items on Level 1 and about one-third of the items on Level 2 being devoted to technical skills on the four basic operations. These skills are undoubtedly important, but are perhaps overemphasized at the expense of a wider range of mathematical topics. Nevertheless, the *Profile* can be recommended to users who are satisified with the range and balance of mathematical skills assessed.

Country of origin. UK.

Publisher. NFER-NELSON.

Date of publication. 1979.

Jim Ridgway
University of Lancaster

Raven's Progressive Matrices

Test authors. J.C. Raven, J.H. Court and J. Raven.

Purpose. The *Progressive Matrices* test a subject's ability to observe and think out relationships between abstract figures. The problems are ordered so that picking up the underlying logic will lead to easier solution of the later items (that is, there is a learning process involved). The *Matrices* are often used in conjunction with a test of vocabulary. Together, these tests assess the abilities to think out abstract relations and to reproduce learned verbal knowledge.

Subjects. The *Matrices* can be used with subjects from the age of five upwards.

Administration time. Thirty to 40 minutes should be allowed for administration.

Materials. The problem items are printed in a booklet and the subject's answers are written on a record form. The subjects normally write their own answers, but in the case of handicapped people or young children they can simply point to their answer.

Structure and administration. There are three sets of *Matrices*, Coloured, Standard and Advanced, and they have overlapping difficulty levels allowing flexibility in use. The *Matrices* can be administered to a group of subjects or to an individual subject. Each problem consists of a pattern with one segment missing. The subject has to choose from six alternative segments of pattern, the one which will complete the pattern satisfactorily.

Scoring and interpretation. Scoring is straightforward using the key given in the manual. Tables of norms are provided for numbers of items correct. At an individual observational level the *Matrices* can supply some basis for insight into trial and error behaviour, perseverance, impulsiveness, etc.

Technical details. *Raven's Matrices* is a very widely researched set of tests.

Standardization. Because of their longevity (50 years) and their worldwide application, there are extensive norms available for the *Matrices*. These cover various countries, include norms for deaf people and for a variety of other social and occupational groups.

Reliability. The reliability is high at between 0.8 and 0.9 depending on subjects, form and method of administration.

Validity. High correlations have been found between the *Matrices* and tests of general intelligence with spatial ability being of some significance also. Though the *Matrices* are predictive of school attainment and correlate with it, they do not predict school outcome with a high degree of accuracy, due to the many other social and intellectual influences involved in school attainment.

Evaluation. The *Matrices* are easy to administer and enjoyable to do. They are extremely flexible in operation, and can be usefully applied across a wide range of subjects, including deaf and handicapped individuals who might find some tests rather awkward to do. They give a good estimate of general intelligence level in a non-verbal test, reducing to some extent problems of educational or cultural bias found in other tests. They are extensively normed and fully researched. A large research bibliography is available from the publishers and the Manual and its various supplements contain all the information and references required for the user to become fully acquainted with the test and its many applications.

Country of origin. UK.

Publisher. H.K. Lewis.

Date of publication. 1985 (2nd revision).

Murray Porteous
University College Cork

Schonell Graded Word Spelling Tests A and B

Test author. Fred Schonell.

Purpose. These two parallel tests examine the accuracy of children in spelling individual words. Test B is also included in the Aston Index.

Subject population. Children five to 15 years.

Administration time. The test is untimed but is likely to take about 15 minutes to administer and three minutes to score.

Materials. There is a handbook for the *Schonell Reading and Spelling Tests* which includes instructions for administering and scoring the test. The child writes responses on ordinary paper and there are no usable materials.

Structure and administration. Each test contains 100 words grouped according to word length and apparent difficulty. The words are not organized according to any description of phonemic or rule content. The test can be offered individually or to groups and the aim is to find the total number of words the child can spell correctly. Each word is read aloud and then inserted into a tester-generated sentence which clarifies its meaning. The child writes down the word.

Scoring and interpretation. Every word spelled correctly adds 1/10 month to five years to give a spelling age. A formula is offered for calculating a spelling quotient.

Technical Details. No data are offered as standardization or in support of reliability and validity.

Evaluation. The most surprising feature of these tests is their initial and continuing popularity in teaching and research settings, given their inadequacy as psychometric instruments. They may offer a measure of progress in a child's remedial programme. The *Vernon Graded Word Spelling Test* offers a similiar word list with a reasonable recent standardization in the UK and Canada, and extension to ages 17½ years and over. This test can offer just as good as comparison of individuals and groups, data for screening children with difficulties and for reviewing the progress of such children under remedial assistance. There seems a major need for a current standardized spelling test extending to further education age range. It should be well structured, paying due attention to developmental features, phonemic and rule frameworks (for example, immediate whole word recognition, major visual segments, C-VC to multi-syllabic phonemic skills and basic rules).

Country of origin. UK.

Publisher. Oliver and Boyd.

Date of publication. 1955.

Margaret J. Snowling
The National Hospitals College of Speech Sciences

Peter Brooks
Hampshire Country Council

Social Skills Training with Children and Adolescents

Test author. Sue Spence.

Purpose. This manual aims at providing basic background information for the assessment and training of social skills. It is *not* a handbook but looks at the function of social skills in interpersonal relationships and explores the various techniques which are effective in teaching social behaviour to children and adolescents. The programme aims to break sophisticated social skills into simple component parts and to teach these in a structured way.

Subject Population. Strict age boundaries are not delineated for this programme but it is perhaps slightly more suitable for older children and adolescents than it is for children under ten years of age.

Administration time. The example of a complete programme includes 12 sessions. The length of each session is undetermined and the leader can tailor them to suit the group.

Materials. The materials needed for each group session vary according to the stated needs of the group but it is useful to have a video recorder in order to give the group members instant feedback about their performance.

Structure. The manual first explores the basic skills components of non-verbal skills, verbal skills, conversational skills and perception of emotion. It then examines the various methods of assessment available to the group leader.

Method 1. The first method looked at is a staff questionnaire on social behaviour which consists of a five-point rating scale on 24 items looking at the child's relationship with peers, with staff and his or her general social behaviour. Examples of rating scales are given for adolescents and for younger children.

Method 2. This method addresses self-report questionnaires for older children who have more self-awareness. The scales consists of a list of 60 problem situations to which the respondent has to answer yes or no. There are no norms available and the manual suggests that the group leaders develop their own tests relevant to the client group. It is therefore a highly valid scale but not a sensitive measure of change.

Method 3. The third method examined is that of direct behavioural observation and the various pitfalls and advantages of doing this are explored by using the methods of sampling behaviour in the natural environment and by using video taped interactions.

Method 4. The author gives an example of a basic social skills assessment chart and rating scale which is designed to highlight specific areas of basic social skills deficits for individual clients. This is a most useful measure of change and understandable at a glance. Again there is no normative data given. The chart assesses the client's performance on 32 specific basic social skills. Each of the eight segments looks at a different group of social skills and each group concerns four individual skills. The eight segments deal with non-verbal responses, verbal responses, basic non-verbal skills, perception of emotions, basic conversation skills, listening skills, content of speech, quality of speech and voice quality.

Method 5. Finally the author provides examples of how to assess emotional perception from facial expression, posture cues, gesture cues, voice cues and situational components. The assessment procedures can be used to identify problem areas which then provide a framework for the design of a therapeutic programme.

The manual then discusses the various processes involved in teaching and the methods used, that is roleplay, modelling, using video equipment, and explores the various ethical considerations in planning a social skills group. Finally the manual gives an example of a social skills training programme for adolescents setting out a 12-week structured programme.

Evaluation. The manual provides a readable and practical guide to social skills assessment and training. It should stimulate group leaders to develop their own assessments and tailor their own programmes to the needs of their particular group. It is perhaps more applicable to the older age range and does not deal in depth with the problems of running a group for younger children.

Country of origin. UK.

Date of publication. 1980.

Publisher. NFER-NELSON.

Royal Aberdeen Children's Hospital

Test for Reception of Grammar (TROG)

Test author. Dorothy Bishop.

Purpose. *TROG* is an individually administered test of language comprehension tapping the understanding of grammatical contrasts in English. It is especially suitable for testing children with specific language deficits. Its construction allows the nature of a comprehension deficit to be pinpointed which has direct remedial implications.

Subject population. Children from four to 12 years. It can also be used diagnostically with older children and adults.

Administration time. The test is untimed but is likely to take 15–20 minutes to administer and score. Qualitative error analysis can take a further ten minutes.

Materials. There is a test booklet containing pictures to which the subject points. A manual describes standardized administration and scoring details. Testers work from a scoring sheet.

Structure and administration. The test consists of 80 forced choice items arranged in blocks of four. Children are required to indicate from a choice of four pictures the one which matches a phrase or sentence. Usually the sentence is spoken, but it can be presented in printed form (for example, for testing deaf subjects). Comprehension of 20 grammatical contrasts of increasing difficulty is tested, the test being discontinued in the event of five consecutive blocks being failed. The first five blocks assess whether the subject has the prerequisite skills to cope with grammatical structures. The remaining blocks tap a range of constructions, for example singular/plural personal pronouns (the cow is looking at *them*), comparative/absolute terms (the box is *bigger* than the cup), post-modified subjects (the cow chasing the cat *is brown*). The range of constructions sampled is necessarily limited to those which are pictureable, for instance, it is difficult to assess the child's understanding of tense (past/present) in this way. However, it is more comprehensive than other similar instruments and especially useful for examiners whose understanding of linguistics may be limited but who wish to gain insight into language problems.

Scoring and interpretation. A child is considered to have failed a block if one out of four items is completed incorrectly. This can sometimes be frustrating, especially in the case of an inattentive child whose poor concentration rather than language deficit may lead to a poor score. The number of blocks passed can be translated into a centile or an age equivalent score.

The test data can also be analysed qualitatively. This gives an indication of whether a child's language comprehension is normal but delayed, or deviant. Guidelines are given in the manual for interpreting patterns of deviance viz., limited span of processing or memory, understanding of sentence elements not structures, use of order of mention strategy to decode word order and so forth.

Technical details. The standardization sample for *TROG* was reasonably balanced and of an acceptable size. A noteable advantage is that the present form of the test grew out of theoretical work and since then, it has proven to be a valid and extremely useful instrument. Reliability data are not, however, reported.

Evaluation. The main disadvantage is that it can be too time consuming to include *TROG* as one of a battery of tests. A second disadvantage is that a child's failure on a specific block may not be a reliable indicator that the child does not understand that particular contrast. Further testing could, however, substantiate this. Generally though, what *TROG* lacks in detail, is well compensated for in terms of comprehensiveness.

Country of origin. UK.

Publisher. The author: Dorothy Bishop; Department of Psychology, University of Manchester, Manchester M13 9PL.

Date of publication. 1983.

Margaret J. Snowling
The National Hospitals College of Speech Sciences

Peter Brooks
Hampshire County Council

Sandwell Bilingual Screening Assessment

Test authors. D. Duncan, D. Gibbs, N. S. Noor and H. M. Whittaker.

Purpose. This screening test was devised to assess the expressive language skills of children learning English whose mother tongue is Punjabi in both Punjabi (L1) and English (L2).

Subject population. Children, whose mother tongue is Punjabi, aged six to nine years who have been learning English for up to eleven school terms. The test may be used cautiously, outside of these limits.

Administration time. The test is untimed and administration time depends upon the linguistic competence of individual children. Two testers are required – one to test in English (L2) the other, a native Punjabi speaker, to test in Punjabi (L1), and for error analysis in both languages. It is therefore costly to administer in terms of professional time.

Materials. There is a clear picture book, an attractive puppet for the presentation of test items and well-designed individual record forms. The manual is clearly written and concise.

Structure and administration. Stimuli for the items are provided by 38 pictures for the English scale and 44 for the Punjabi scale.

The pictures elicit selected grammatical features which can be efficiently recorded on the record form. Where testees give no response, standard prompts are given in the case of certain items. On both scales, some complex structures, for instance coordination and subordination have been included. For the last section, Interrogative Clauses, a conversation is simulated with a monkey puppet.

Scoring and interpretation. Scoring is by error analysis. The features which appear on the check-list are scored for errors. Norms are provided so that a pupil's scores in both L1 Punjabi and L2 English may be compared with those of other children who have attended English schooling for a similar length of time. Norms also indicate whether there is a mild or serious deviation from the mean. If the child's behaviour varies seriously in both languages, there is the suggestion of language handicap. If the deviation is only with respect to English (L2) scores, then specialist ESL advice should be sought.

Technical details

Standardization. Initially 135 subjects were selected for the standardization sample according to the length of time they had been exposed to an English-speaking environment. Subsequently, the sample was extended to 300 by including children from different geographical areas. The sample is thus small, but given the specialized nature of this test, might be considered adequate. It is particularly valid as a screening instrument and for criterion-referenced testing. Inter–tester and test–retest reliability are high.

Evaluation. The test is comprehensive and easy to administer making it ideal for the use of teachers and other professionals who are not skilled in linguistics. It will be especially relevant to the work of speech therapists for routine clinical use and diagnostic purposes.

Country of origin. UK.

Publisher. NFER-NELSON.

Date of publication. 1988.

Margaret J. Snowling
The National Hospitals College of Speech Sciences

Peter Brooks
Hampshire County Council

The Staffordshire Mathematics Test

Test authors. C.W. Barcham, R.S. Bushell, K. Lawson and C.M. McDonnell.

Purpose. This test attempts to serve many purposes, beginning with the provision of information for local and central government policy. Pupils and parents need to know about mathematical progress; teachers need to know that pupils are learning effectively and that teaching methods and materials are appropriate. The test sets out to identify pupils with particular learning difficulties, and to define specific areas of weakness so that appropriate remedial action can be taken, rather than to provide a bland overall statement. It claims to be 'criterion referenced' to allow the analysis of individual and class needs. Analysis of the weaknesses of the whole class can be used to direct classroom work.

Subject population. Children aged between seven years and eight years seven months.

Administration time. About 60 minutes; scoring time about ten minutes.

Materials. The test comprises a manual, disposable pupil booklets, pupil profile sheets, a class profile sheet, a class sub-test proficiency profile, and a 'low proficiency analysis' sheet which is simply a form for recording comments about pupil performance on different subtests.

Structure and administration. There are 64 questions arranged into 16 sections, namely, the basic operations, sets, place value, fractions, time, area, length, angles, pictorial representation, sequences, shape matching and money. The test is administered orally in two parts, perhaps either side of the morning break to either groups or individuals; no additional materials are to be used by pupils. Administration details are clear and sensible.

Scoring and interpretation. No scoring key is provided. Raw scores are first converted to standardized scores in order to find 'the correct mathematical gradient'. Score bands, which should be used to indicate the inherent error of measurement, are not used. Users are told that a child's 'true score' may be two points either way of their test score, and are warned against over-interpreting small differences. A crude idea of each child's relative progress can be obtained by finding the age for which their raw score corresponds to a standard score of 100, then comparing this with the child's chronological age. The manual also provides a table showing 'mathematics ages' – this is a dubious concept, at best (see Ridgway, 1987) and users are warned about the problems of interpretation. Pupil profiles can be constructed based on scores in each of the 16 sections. An item-by-item class proficiency profile can also be constructed, as can a class subtest proficiency profile to identify overall strength and weaknesses.

Technical details

Standardization. Preliminary trials were based on three samples (1000, 2400 and 13,000 children) in Staffordshire. Some formal changes were made before the test was given to children in Lincoln, Cheshire, Wirral and Hampshire attending 47 different schools. Somehow, these scores were combined with those of some of the Staffordshire children, and pruned to a sample size of 5222 children between the ages of seven years and eight years seven months. Although large samples have been used, we cannot be sure that they represent the natural school population.

Reliability. The standard error of measurement of children in one month age bands is reported, and ranged from 0.62 to 0.98 (mean value 0.79). This is acceptably high.

Validity. No validity data are provided. Surface validity can be judged from the assembly of test items, which the authors believe cover 'all the main mathematical skills'. A case study is briefly reported for a single class in which subskills in need of remediation were identified, a remedial plan worked out and 'successfully operated'.

Evaluation. The test is well presented. Test content focuses heavily on fact and technique, and several of the items seem to require knowledge of particular schemes of work (for example, set diagrams, number sentences). It is *not* criterion referenced, as the authors claim, for the obvious reason that no criteria are given. The idea of supporting a diagnostic test with a set of remedial activities (*Mastering Maths Skills* – not reviewed here) is a good one; a better example of such use would have improved the manual. It is unfortunate that the general example contains arithmetic errors in some of the column totals. Users should satisfy themselves about the content of this test before they use it, and should heed warnings given here about the standardization sample and the problems of errors of measurement.

Country of origin. UK.

Publisher. Macmillan Education.

Date of publication. 1986.

References.
Barcham, C., Bushell, R., Lawson, K. & McDonnell, C. (1987). *Mastering Maths Skills Books 1–3.* Basingstoke: Macmillan Education.
Ridgway, J. (1987). *A Review of Mathematics Tests.* Windsor: NFER-NELSON.

Jim Ridgway
University of Lancaster

Stanford-Binet IV

Test authors. R.L. Thorndike, E.P. Hagen and J.M. Sattler.

Purpose. This is described as a measure of general reasoning ability (g) and of four specific areas: verbal reasoning, abstract/visual reasoning, quantitative reasoning and short-term memory.

Subject population. Two years to adult. A few of the tests are not appropriate at all age levels.

Administration time. Varies according to age level of testee and to the number of tests given. Between 60 and 90 minutes for a comprehensive assessment and 30–40 minutes for screening battery.

Materials. Two manuals, four item books, four sets of blocks/beads and formboards, and pictures/paper/record form etc., all contained neatly in a small case.

Structure and administration. The *Stanford–Binet IV* has a good theoretical background based on a hierarchical model of intelligence and uses an extension of items used in the *Stanford–Binet* Form L–M presented in an adaptable testing format. The 15 tests are administered in a multi-stage procedure commencing with the vocabulary test. In common with previous versions of the test the examiner has to establish the examinee's basal and ceiling level for this (and other) tests. The result of the vocabulary test together with chronological age is used to determine the examinee's level (from A to Q). This level is then used to determine the starting point for each test. The testing procedures are clearly described in the four item books. Instructions are usually given on one face of a flip book as the examinee is looking at an item on the other face. Scoring procedures and criteria are clear. Many items will be familiar to L–M users in the brief outline of the tests which follows.

Verbal Reasoning

Vocabulary. Test 1. All age levels. Coloured pictures and oral items. Examinee gives verbal response. Some problem items, for example, baseball bat, American flag.

Comprehension. Test 6. All age levels. Six items pointing to body parts. Items seven to 42 verbal (and some written) questions requiring a verbal response. Some problem items, for example, question about the American Bill of Rights.

Absurdities. Test 7. Ages two to 14 years with estimates for ages 15 to 17. The examinee must say what is silly or wrong about a picture or certain parts of a picture. Items one to four require pointing, items five to 32 a verbal response.

Verbal Relations. Test 14. Ages 12 to 18 years with estimates for ages ten to 11. The examinee has to say what is similar about three things and not similar about the fourth thing.

Quantitative Reasoning

Quantitative. Test 3. All age levels. Various exercises involving blocks, dice, counting and other responses to pictures, and verbal problems. Several items involve American currency.

Number Series. Test 12. Ages seven to 18 years with estimates for ages five and six. The examinee has to work out the two numbers which fit next in a series.

Equation Building. Test 15. Ages 12 to 18 years with estimates for ages ten and 11. Examinee has to make a logical equation from a series of numbers and signs, for example, 1 3 4 + = .

Abstract/Visual Reasoning

Pattern/Analysis. Test 5. All age levels. Items one to six form boards, items 7–24 duplication of a black and white cube pattern, items 25–42 duplication of picture of a cube pattern.

Copying. Test 9. Ages two to 13 with estimates for ages 14 to 17. Levels A–F duplication of a block design, levels G–N pencil and paper copying of design (strict scoring criteria given).

Matrices. Test 11. Ages seven to 18+ years with estimates for ages five and six. Examinee has to 'figure out the rule' and point to a pattern which fits into a given pattern or series of pictures.

Paper folding and cutting. Test 13. Ages 12 to 18+ years with estimates for ages ten and 11. Two examples of folding and cutting given. Examinee has to indicate which of a series of pictures corresponds to given diagram of folded and cut paper.

Short-term Memory

Bead Memory. Test 2. All age levels. Beads varying in colour (three) and shape (four) are used to reproduce a bead pattern (picture exposed for five seconds).

Memory for Sentences. Test 4. All age levels. Examinee has to repeat sentences varying in length from two words to 22 words.

Memory for Digits. Test 8. Ages seven to 18+ with estimates for ages five and six. Repetition of numbers given at the rate of one per second (three to nine forwards and two to seven backwards).

Memory for Objects. Test 10. Ages seven to 18+ years with estimates for ages five and six. Coloured pictures of objects exposed for one second each. Examinee has to identify the pictures from an array in the order presented (two to eight objects presented).

Scores for individual tests within the four areas are converted to Standard Age Scores (SAS) with a mean of 50 and standard deviation of eight. SAS (mean 100, standard deviation 16) can be computed for any of the four areas, for any combination of them and for the composite test. Difference scores (between areas) required for statistical significance at 5 per cent and

15 per cent confidence levels are also given. In general these range from eight or nine (5 per cent level at age 18 to 23) to 13 to 18 (5 per cent level at age two). Profiling is possible, but there are few instructions on the interpretation of scores, as the test authors assume a highly qualified examiner. However, an expanded guide is available from the publishers.

Technical details

Standardization. After two extensive field trials item analysis and Rasch scaling were used to identify items for the final form. The final standardization of 5000 subjects was undertaken in 160 testing centres from 47 states of the USA. Sampling design was based on five variables: geographical region, community size, ethnic group, age and gender. Data from the 1980 US census was used to establish numbers. Socio-economic status was also monitored and reported. Standardization data for the 24–32 age group was rejected as unrepresentative of the population and it was necessary to employ a weighting procedure to adjust for SES in many groups (as much as 45 per cent managerial/professional). The SES categorization is not sufficiently explicit.

Reliability. Subtest correlations within areas are reported as between 0.80 and 0.99, depending on the number of tests given. In general there are lower reliabilities at lower age levels. Internal consistencies for individual tests are given as between 0.78 and 0.96 and are 'inflated by an unknown amount', because the tests assume all items below the basal level are passed and all items above ceiling level are failed. Median reliability coefficients across ages two to 17 are reported at between 0.83 and 0.94 except for Memory of Objects (14 items), which has a low reliability at 0.73. Test–retest reliabilities (with intervals of 2–8 months) are lower at ranges from 0.51 (quantitative reasoning age eight) to 0.87 (verbal reasoning age eight). Composite reliabilities (KR–20) are also given for the abbreviated batteries and are generally lower the fewer the number of tests used (average reliabilities across ages range from 0.87 to 0.99).

Validity. *Stanford–Binet IV* is based on the hierarchical model of intelligence and as such has high construct validity. It incorporates the concept of general intelligence (g) with crystallized abilities (subsuming verbal and quantitative reasoning), fluid ability (subsuming abstract/visual reasoning) and short-term memory as second order factors (see below).

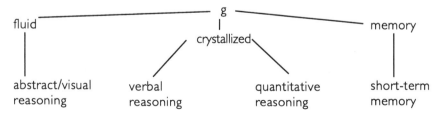

Although there is no evidence presented for the fluid/crystallized categorization there is strong evidence for the other four areas. All tests had substantial loadings on g ranging from 0.51 (Memory for Objects) to 0.79

(Number Series). Test intercorrelations ranged from 0.32 (Verbal Relations/Memory for Objects) to 0.73 (Vocabulary/Comprehension). Factor analytic studies for three age groups established the validity of the four areas though some tests loaded substantially on more than one area, notably Memory for Sentences (verbal and memory factors) and Bead Memory (memory and abstract/visual factors).

The test has good content validity in the types of items already used in the L–M version and use of item analysis in the formulation of final test.

Concurrent validity is established by the tests' intercorrelations with other tests of g. Generally these are in the region of 0.50 to 0.70 between the areas and various subtest scores. Some of the higher correlations are set out below.

Stanford–Binet IV	Composite/*Stanford-Binet* L–M Total	0.81
Stanford–Binet IV	Verbal Reasoning/*WISC-R* Verbal IQ	0.72
Stanford–Binet IV	Composite/*WISC-R* Full Scale IQ	0.83
Stanford–Binet IV	Abstract-Visual/*WAIS-R* PIQ	0.81
Stanford–Binet IV	Verbal Reasoning/*WAIS-R* VIQ	0.86
Stanford–Binet IV	Composite/*WAIS-R* Full Scale IQ	0.91

A limited study of the validity of the abbreviated forms of the test has been carried out (Carvajal & Gerber, 1987).

Unfortunately there is no British standardization at the present time and no British validation studies are reported.

Evaluation. The new *Stanford–Binet* is an interesting and well constructed test if used with US populations. It is easy to follow and provides a comprehensive and managable test for all ages. It incorporates other useful areas besides the familiar verbal/performance categories, namely quantitative reasoning and short-term memory. Particularly useful tests are: Number Series, Paper Folding and Cutting, Bead Memory and Memory for Sentences as they tap hitherto untested abilities. Care has to be taken in the interpretation of differences between areas (some areas not really independent). The lack of British data is a major drawback. There are many items which would not easily find a British equivalent and the lack of validation data on a UK sample renders the test unusable at present despite its obvious advantages as a test package which covers a wide range of ability areas and ages.

Country of origin. USA.

Publisher. The Riverside Publishing Company, and the test is available from the Psychological Corporation.

Date of publication. 1986.

References

Thorndike, R.L., Hagen, E.P., & Sattler, E.P. (1986). *Technical Manual, Stanford–Binet Intelligence Scale.* Chicago, IL: Riverside.

Carvajal, H. & Gerber, J. (1987). 1986 Stanford–Binet abbreviated forms. *Psychological Reports, 61*, 285–6.

Leonora Harding
Royal Aberdeen Children's Hospital

Wechsler Intelligence Scale for Children – revised (WISC–R)

Test author. David Wechsler

Purpose. The WISC–R is as a general purpose test of intellectual development in children. It was conceived as a test of intelligence though currently its use is as a general assessment instrument, enabling the psychologist to study a child's approach to problems, as well as specific levels of ability and skill in a variety of verbal and practical tasks.

Subjects. The test is appropriate for children aged six to 16 years. Part of the WISC–R is suited to the assessment of children with hearing loss, for which special norms are available (Anderson and Sisco, 1978).

Administration time. This usually takes about 40 minutes.

Materials. An extensive administration and scoring manual includes some minor adaptations for British use. A record form is required for each child. The test materials include coloured blocks, cardboard jigsaws and pictures.

Structure and administration. There are ten separate self-contained subtests, and a further two optional subtests. The subtests are grouped into two sets, Verbal and Performance, and separate composite scores called IQs are given for these. The ten subtests are administered alternating verbal with performance in the following order.

Information. Asks basic general knowledge questions in order to test the immediate retrieval of learned material.

Picture completion. This tests speed of perceptual closure by using pictures in which a missing part has to be identified.

Similarities. This subtest examines the ability to infer and compare verbal meanings by asking how two things are alike.

Picture Arrangements. The subject is asked to arrange four or five related pictures on cards into a meaningful sequence, thus testing the ability to derive meaning from pictures and seriate appropriately.

Arithmetic. This is a short test of verbally presented numerical problems whose solution depends both on being able to understand the requirements of the problems as well as doing the arithmetic.

Block design. The child has to copy designs using coloured cubes. Reasoning and spatial orientation skills are tested.

Vocabulary. The subject is asked for the meaning of words presented in increasing order of difficulty.

Object assembly. This subtest requires the child to assemble plain cardboard jigsaws of common objects (such as a horse) thus testing spatial constructive abilities.

Comprehension. Sometimes referred to as social reasoning, this subtest requires the subject to give a reasoned response to a social situation.

Coding. This subtest consists of an inspection and copying task in which the child has to write in the appropriate symbols demonstrating concentration and eye–hand coordination.

Digit Span and Mazes are optional subtests.

Some subtests are timed and credit subtests are grouped into Verbal and Performance sets and composite IQs are given for these. Three factors underly the subtests at most age levels; verbal comprehension, perceptual organization and freedom from distractibility (Kaufman, 1979).

Some subtests are timed and credit is given for fast accurate performance.

In the case of deaf children the Performance subtests provide a useful indication of ability.

Technical details

Standardization. The test has been competently standardized on 2200 American children. British studies indicate a slightly higher mean IQ score but overall the subtest conversions are accurate.

Reliability. Test–retest coefficients are high at over 0.9. Split half correlations are at a satisfactory level. The standard measurement errors of the Full Scale Deviation IQ figures are around three, giving a confidence interval of plus or minus six for quoted figures of IQ.

Validity. The test has high construct validity and correlates with other tests of intelligence; 0.82 with *WPPSI*, 0.95 with *WAIS*, 0.60 to 0.73 with *Stanford–Binet* (1972 norms), 0.25 to 0.65 with *BAS* (depending on scale).

Evaluation. The *WISC–R* has a high degree of popularity among psychologists owing to the simple format and straightforward administration and scoring. The user has few choices to make, the subtests are compact, scoring guidelines are mainly unequivocal. Children are usually interested in doing the test and are easily engaged on the tasks which change frequently enough for them not to get bored or feel defeated. The conversion of raw scores into profiles and overall IQ figures are simple tasks once learned. The interpretation of the results of the *WISC–R* is more problematic, calling for a high degree of training in developmental and educational psychology.

The *WISC–R* is undoubtedly a reliable and valid test. Research has demonstrated high correlations with other ability measures, and good prediction of future educational attainment. It has been shown to discriminate fairly well between various clinical groups, such as people with learning disability or brain damage (Kaufman, 1981). A number of studies have demonstrated characteristic subtest patterns associated with levels of reading attainment. At the individual level, as opposed to group discriminant work, it provides no cut and dried answers without involving considerable clinical judgement and other data.

Other advantages of the *WISC–R* are its suitability for assessing children with hearing difficulties and also the fact that there are several fairly reliable short forms of the test which can be useful in research contexts (Phillips, 1984). An extensive literature is available on the *WISC–R* and practitioners can become very skilled in its use.

Country of origin. USA.

Publisher. Psychological Corporation.

Date of publication. 1974.

References
Anderson, R.J. & Sisco, F.H. (1978). *A Standardization of the WISC–R Performance Scale.* New York: The Psychological Corporation.

Kaufman, A.S. (1979). *Intelligent Testing with the WISC–R.* New York: Wiley.

Kaufman, A.S. (1981). The WISC–R and learning disabilities assessment: State of the Art. *Journal of Learning Disabilities, 14, 9,* 520–6.

Phillips, C.J. (1984). Use of abbreviated cognitive tests in the assessment of children's special educational needs. *British Journal of Educational Psychology, 54,* 168–76.

Murray Porteous
University College Cork

Glossary

Alexia
Loss of or impaired ability to read due to brain damage.

Aphasia
Loss of or impaired ability to speak, write or to understand the meaning of words due to brain damage.

Auditory discrimination
The ability to detect a difference between sounds (usually speech sounds) when presented orally.

Basal level
The point at which it is assumed that a subject would have received credit for earlier and easier items in the test.

Ceiling
The point at which it is assumed that a subject would not be able to get credit by further testing.

Centile
A score indicating the percentage of persons scoring at or below a specified level (also known as percentile).

Cloze procedure
A cloze passage is a prose passage from which certain words have been deleted and replaced with gaps. The pupil's task is to supply words for these gaps.

Cognitive
Referring to a mental process of reasoning, memory, judgement and comprehension as contrasted with emotional and volitional processes.

Concurrent validity
The extent to which a test correlates with other measures or tests which are said to measure the same thing.

Content validity
The extent to which a test contains items which are representative of the domain to be measured.

Consistency
See *internal consistency*.

Construct validity
The extent to which a test may be said to measure what it has been designed to measure or a theoretical construct.

Correlation Coefficient
A measure of the association between two sets of scores. Values lie between +1.00 (perfect association). through 0.00 (no association) to -1.00 (perfect disassociation).

Criterion referenced assessment
An assessment based on whether an individual can pass (at a specified level) certain specified items of the curriculum (in contrast to norm referenced assessment).

Diagnostic assessment
Assessment based on diagnosis or specification of an individual's underlying strengths and weaknesses (abilities and difficulties) in the particular area.

Dyscalculia
Inability to make calculations.

Dyslexia
Literally, bad ability with reading words. Originally thought to be due to brain disfunction the term is now often used synonymously with specific reading difficulty.

Factor analysis
A statistical technique aimed at uncovering the structure of a set of variables (the factors). It is based on correlation coefficients between variables or scores.

Grapheme–phoneme correspondence
The orthographic or alphabetic correspondence of phonemes.

Hyperactive
Excessively active.

Internal consistency
A measure of reliability. The extent to which different parts of a test measure similar skills. For example, split-half reliability is based on the correlation between the first half of a test and the second half of a test and odd–even reliability is based on the correlation between odd items and even items on a test.

IQ or intelligence quotient
The ratio of an individual's intelligence (determined by mental tests) to the average intelligence for his or her age. The average IQ on the *WISC–R* is 100. (Formerly measured by the ratio of mental age to chronological age and multiplied by 100.)

KR-20
Kunder and Richardson's equation 20 which is a measure of internal inconsistency.

Mean
Arithmetical average.

Median
The middle number in a series of numbers arranged in order of magnitude.

Mental age
The age corresponding to the chronological age of individuals who score at the mean for a specified test. Through standardization it is possible to calculate the mental age for a child who is much older but scores below the mean, or for a child who is much younger and scores above the mean.

Miscue analysis
An analysis based on the types of mistakes or miscues children make in reading.

Norms
Tables of standardized scores based on the assessment of many individuals.

Norm referenced assessment
Assessment based on the comparison between an individual's scores and those of others who have taken the test (the standardization sample) (compared with criterion referenced assessment).

Parallel forms
Parallel forms of tests are designed to be equivalent in terms of what they measure and the scores they produce. They aim to have identical statistical characteristics.

Percentile
See *centile*.

Phonemes
Speech sounds.

Phonics
Used as a term to cover the knowledge and teaching of grapheme–phoneme correspondences.

Phonological
Of speech sounds.

Predictive validity
The extent to which a test predicts ability in the same or similar areas in the future. For example, a test might be correlated with GCSE examination success (usually expressed in terms of a correlation coefficient).

Psycholinguistic
Literally mind and language. The study of mental processes that underlie the acquisition and use of language.

Reliability
A measure of the degree to which a individual will obtain similar scores on retesting or on various parts of the test. Reliability refers to the consistency of a measure, usually divided into internal consistency and test–retest reliability.

Sensori-neural hearing loss
Loss of hearing due to damage or dysfunction in the neural pathways or cerebral cortex, rather than by damage to the inner ear.

Special educational needs
A child is said to have special educational needs if he or she has a learning difficulty which calls for special educational provision to be made.

Special learning difficulty
A child of average or above average intelligence who has difficulty in a specific area is said to have a specific difficulty in that area (such as specific reading difficulty, see below).

Specific reading difficulty
Reading ability which is significantly below the level of abilities in other areas.

Split half reliability
See *internal consistency*.

Standard deviation
A measure of variability. The square root of the variance (see below).

Standard error of measurement
A measure derived from reliability which tells us how close a person's obtained score is likely to be to his/her true score.

Standardized score
A scoring system where the mean score is set at a particular value (usually 100) and the standard deviation is set at a particular value (usually 15 for IQ tests).

Standardized test
A test that has been administered to large samples of individuals and for which norms have been established.

Stanine
Literally, standard nine score. A standardized score with a mean of five and range from one to nine.

Test–retest reliability
The correlation between scores obtained on the first occasion of testing and a second occasion of testing, using exactly the same test.

T score
A standardized score with a mean of 50 and a standard deviation of ten points (on the *British Ability Scales*).

Validity
The extent to which a test measures what it is set out to measure. Types include content, concurrent, construct and predictive (see above).

Variability
The dispersion of values from the average. Standard deviation and variance are measures of variability.

Variance
A statistical term. The product of the sum of deviations of actual scores from the mean and divided by the number of actual scores.

Subject Index

Author Index